AF608261

MAVIS GALLANT

The Eye and the Ear

Mavis Gallant.
Upon accepting the Blue Metropolis International Literary Grand Prix (2002).
Courtesy of the Thomas Fisher Rare Book Library, University
of Toronto, Mavis Gallant papers.

Mavis Gallant

The Eye and the Ear

MARTA DVOŘÁK

UNIVERSITY OF TORONTO PRESS
Toronto Buffalo London

Toronto Buffalo London
utorontopress.com

ISBN 978-1-4875-0530-1

Library and Archives Canada Cataloguing in Publication

Title: Mavis Gallant: the eye and the ear / Marta Dvořák.
Names: Dvorak, Marta, author.
Description: Includes bibliographical references and index.
Identifiers: Canadiana 20190127139 | ISBN 9781487505301 (hardcover)
Subjects: LCSH: Gallant, Mavis – Criticism and interpretation. |
LCSH: Gallant, Mavis – Aesthetics.
Classification: LCC PS8513.A593 Z588 2019 | DDC C813/.54–dc23

This book has been published with the help of a grant from the Federation for the Humanities and Social Sciences, through the Awards to Scholarly Publications Program, using funds provided by the Social Sciences and Humanities Research Council of Canada.

University of Toronto Press acknowledges the financial assistance to its publishing program of the Canada Council for the Arts and the Ontario Arts Council, an agency of the Government of Ontario.

Canada Council for the Arts Conseil des Arts du Canada

Funded by the Government of Canada Financé par le gouvernement du Canada

Canada

To Mavis, the truest of friends. And to Patrick, who honed *my* eye and ear.

Contents

Acknowledgments

I wish to express my appreciation to Siobhan McMenemy and Mark Thompson, acquisition editors at the University of Toronto Press, for their valuable guidance – the former in the early inchoate stages of my manuscript and the latter when it was bursting at the seams. Mark's advice to privilege the specific focus which led to my title helped me overcome the challenge of juggling clarity and breadth of scope.

My thanks to Shelley MacDonald Beaulieu for the skill and care with which she prepared the manuscript for submission to the press. I also wish to thank Frances Mundy, production editor at the Press, and Anne Laughlin, copyeditor, for their efficiency throughout a publishing process all the more complex as the press has so many works going through "the pipeline" at the same time. I am equally grateful to the two anonymous reviewers whose generous comments led to the ASPP funding that made publication possible. One in particular gave me the enchanting feeling that I'd met The Ideal Reader. Thanks as well to Mary K. MacLeod, literary executor for Mavis Gallant's estate, for her encouragement, and to John Thleme and W.H. New for their support (at the inchoate and production stages respectively).

I want to extend my appreciation to Jennifer Toews, in charge of the Mavis Gallant papers at the Thomas Fisher Rare Book Library, for a dedication and helpfulness clearly rooted in a heartfelt esteem for the writer and her work. Finally, my fervent thanks to my husband Patrick Chézaud, my first reader and critic. His expert comments at each stage of my work are unfailingly illuminating, and his rigour can always be counted on to spot the slightest fuzziness in word or concept.

MAVIS GALLANT

The Eye and the Ear

1
"ACQUISITIONS": MAPPING WORLD & WORK

The beginning writer has to choose, tear to pieces, spit out, chew up and assimilate as naturally as a young animal — as naturally and as ruthlessly.

Mavis Gallant, "What Is Style?" (37)

... the concept of art has no content beyond what art *has been.*

Jerrold Levinson, *Music, Art, & Metaphysics: Essays in Philosophical Aesthetics* (7, emphasis in original)

an acrostic for Mavis

When the PEN/Nabokov Literary Award was attributed to Mavis Gallant in 2004, but poor health would not allow her to attend the award presentation ceremony in New York City's Lincoln Center, a special tribute was organized for her in Paris in December at the Maison des Écrivains. Alberto Manguel, who was to introduce her, found himself on an operating table and had to cancel, so Mavis requested that I stand in for him. I chose to introduce her through the qualities called up by the letters of her last name — an embryonic acrostic which I redeploy here to provide the point of entry into this book:

G for Gifted/Gallantry, Gumption, Grit
A for A/mazing
L for Learned & anything but Lazy
L for Language
A for Acute
N for Notable
T for True

I shall dwell somewhat on the opening term "Gifted." As applied to a writer who has dazzled readers, especially other writers, to the point of being called "the God of the Short Story" (Adderson 78), the term can seem tame and self-evident, but its two acceptations underpin the overarching argument of this book. Michael Ondaatje insists that "Gallant seems beholden to no one" (xi); Neel Mukherjee compares Gallant to the goddess Athena springing fully formed and armed from the head of Zeus (11); and Carol Shields in private referred to "the divine Mavis, the divine Alice."[1] How indeed then, wonders Caroline Adderson, can she presume to review Gallant:

> How does one review God? She is great. She is good. The end. (Adderson 79)

In this sense, "gifted" obviously involves exceptional talent or natural ability. Yet Ondaatje adds that "Gallant's *craft* and empathy, with that *skill* in evoking subtle and obsessive voices, is always ahead of us" (xii).[2] In essence, he appends a second meaning. Gallant's extraordinary creative power — posited to be *connate* – takes on the added contours of an acquired accomplishment or mastery involving work or construction, related to the Greek *techne*: skill or industry. When we wonder if Gallant, like Athena, emerged as a writer "fully formed with all her gifts resplendent" (Adderson 79), the age-old nature/nurture debate unfurls.[3] It will nourish this book's central thesis arguing a modernist osmosis between the literary text and both visual culture and music, through the twin "gifts" (alternately seen as channels of craftsmanship) announced in my title. The double focus on the eye and the ear – either innately acute or honed, or both – involves an emphasis on the art, film, and music Gallant was immersed in, and it connects with the visual studies

1 The conversation in which Shields confided such esteem for the two great short story writers took place over lunch with Carol (already very ill) and her husband Don when she came to Paris for the premiere of her play *Thirteen Hands/Treize Mains* (adapted and directed by Rachel Salik). Shields reiterated the comment made the day of the first performance at Théâtre 13 (20 Nov. 2001) in a personal email in which she thanked me for having put her in touch with the Gallant she hugely admired. Shields explained, "When my daughters and I talk about Canadian writers we always talk about the divine Alice, and then, immediately, the divine Mavis (that's the extent of our divinity division, just two members)" (Shields, email to Dvořák).

2 Italicized emphases in quotes are my stresses unless otherwise stipulated.

3 Hemingway observed that a great writer "seems to be born with knowledge" but really is not. He suggests that such a writer has only been "born with the ability to learn in a quicker ratio to the passage of time" than others, and, to boot, "without conscious application" (*Death* 168) – which sounds suspiciously like a gift to me!

and sound studies currently on the rise. It plugs into an era's logic of the heterogeneous and the heteroclite, inherent to the *bricoleur* who – like me with respect to my original acrostic – adopts, adapts, and recombines the tools and materials at hand, even when these result from anterior constructions and destructions and are not originally designed for the operation at hand (Lévi-Strauss 31; Derrida 409–28). James Joyce's seminal *Ulysses* (1922), published the year Mavis was born, and Pierre Henry's equally seminal electroacoustic nod to Bach's *The Well-Tempered Clavier*, namely *Le Microphone bien tempéré* [*The Well-Tempered Microphone*] (1951), created when Mavis[4] was reborn in Paris, deliberately adopt such bricolage as method.[5] These artworks can exemplify artistic practice subsequently appropriated by postmodernists. Such practice innovates by situating itself within (and manipulating) sets of pre-existing recombinable elements making up our cultural heritage – sets which can offer over fifty thousand combinations (P. Schaeffer 218),[6] but which are ultimately *closed*.

This book raises epistemological and ontological questions on invention, origins, and creativity, as I examine Gallant's intercultural, intermedial, but distinctive modus operandi. I shall argue that unlike, say, Joyce's general strategy consisting of transmutations of pre-existing structures – a strategy which is also the bedrock of jazz (Berendt) – Gallant's art-making leans rather towards that of Lévi-Strauss's "engineer," the one who begets rather than (re)assembles. Gallant's disclosures that the first flash of a story takes the form of a film still (Dvořák, "When Language";

4 As a rule I use the familiar term of address, "'Mavis," to provide insights on the woman in her life and in a French habitat we shared, and the formal "Gallant" for the more scholarly analysis, namely everything involving what happens on her pages and how. Still, questions of inclination, taste, talent, perception, influences, and experience are all vital to the vocation and craft of writing, and make it hard to compartmentalize the human being, Mavis, from the writer, Gallant. Given the difficulty of ontologically separating the two, the switches in terms of address may at times be quite fluid.

5 In a 1958 public debate taped by the University of Virginia when he was Writer-in-Residence there, William Faulkner made a similar analogy between a writer and a carpenter, affirming that the wordsmith too has "a grab bag, a barrel full of odds and ends, of boards and nails, and – and the sort of things he might possibly some day need." When he does need something in the heat of writing the story, he "scrabbles around in his barrel until he finds something that fits" ("Faulkner at Virginia").

6 Henry's mentor, sound pioneer Pierre Schaeffer, whose journals on concrete music have recently been made available in English translation, is referring to the numerical combinations of the sets in his sound classification system, in analogy with mathematical language. The discussion which follows will reveal the multiple analogies with literary language (beyond the issue of methodology), notably the fact that sound characterology is physiologically "accessible to the direct experience of the musical ear" (199).

Gallant, Interview with Daphne Kalotay) gesture to how the writer *opens* up and positions herself outside and *beyond* (Lévi-Strauss 31). In her introduction to Gallant's recently reissued *Collected Stories* (2016), Francine Prose, too, claims the writer's work is "unlike anyone else's" ("Introduction" xii), meaning unlike any other writer's. She does see an analogy outside the literary system, notably likening Gallant's "technical daring and innovative freedom" to a painting by Velásquez, hidden unless you pay close attention and also accept that the art cannot be reduced or summarized (xii). Gallant seen as "engineer," coming from *ingenium*, points us once more to the concept of (the equally Latinate) *genius*, i.e., an innate disposition, a transcendent intelligence naturally inclined towards invention. In the polyvocal critical reality which has surrounded Gallant's work,[7] I address from different angles this generative power of her unique *eye*, her gaze on being human in a world of upheavals and quiet sea changes. "Look for the source of light in her work as you would in a painting," advises the book critic Susan Salter Reynolds. Mavis's vision of life not only bathes but emanates from her pages and spills onto the world, as does the light in chiaroscuro canvases. The vision is both connate and experiential, palpable from the dark first novel *Green Water, Green Sky* (1959/2016),[8] to the wild, quirky novel *A Fairly Good Time* (1970/2016), which Peter Orner describes as "a new wave *Sun Also Rises* written by a woman with a better sense of humour" ("Introduction" vii).

My G for Gifted also points to Gallantry, Gumption, and Grit. The young Mavis started out with *less* than nothing: she borrowed $200 for a typing course because at every job interview she heard: you're a girl, can you type. Then, when she had established a career as a feature journalist at the *Montreal Standard*, she threw it up and headed for Europe with just a typewriter and a suitcase – what Jhumpa Lahiri has called "a revolutionary act" by a woman who both "in life and on the page, blazed a trail no one since has dared follow" ("Mavis Gallant's Choice").

The A for Amazing is as multi-tiered as the woman who wrote, "Here one was handed a folded thought like a shapeless school uniform, and told, 'There, wear that.' Everyone had it on, regardless of fit" (Gallant, *Home Truths* 296; *Varieties of Exile* 145).[9] The folded thought, a startling

7 It is naturally not possible to acknowledge all the valuable works which constitute international Gallant scholarship.

8 Readers will find the recent publication date after the date of original publication.

9 Regarding quotations, these much-quoted story collections will henceforth be designated as *HT* and *VE* respectively; the name Gallant will be understood.

conceit compressing the abstract and the concrete, triggers a clothing simile which in turn modulates into an extended metaphor. All show a craftsmanship that is "amazing" in the sense of "admirable," overset by another acceptation: "astounding," notably regarding the writer's hallmark analogies and challenges to ready-made beliefs. In addition, Gallant a/mazes in the sense of deciphering or disentangling a complicated world and the jumbled human mind. She illuminates the minute intricacies of our social interactions, from the smallest familial unit to the macro geopolitical sphere of imperial and postwar cultures.

The first L in my Gallant stands for Learned. Like earlier modernists such as T.S. Eliot, Joyce, and Vladimir Nabokov (who had a career in Russian before being born again into English), Mavis read voraciously and extensively, as testify the books in her personal library touching on multiple fields[10] and authored in multiple languages. Analogous to a Cubist collage of pre-existing material, the intertextual web of displaced or cunningly disguised cultural references underpinning the cultured Gallant's work bifurcates and refracts. This same L also indirectly nods to the *energeia* of a writer who produced 116 short stories in *The New Yorker* alone (Rothman; Orner, "Introduction" xi) as well as novels, essays, and drama, many of them recently reissued. She is a powerhouse of a writer whose recently reissued volume of *Collected Stories* makes up less than half of her output but still crushes you if you read it in bed.

The second L for Language calls up Gallant's "dazzlingly precise, virtuosic writing" (Prose, "Introduction" xii), and will provide the focal point of my analysis – both the point *at* which identified perspectives meet and the point *from* which diverging lines proceed. Famously coming from a split linguistic, cultural, and thus axiological environment, Mavis stood up for the integrity of language when she was only four years old, and was punished for it. The child objected when the French-speaking nun teaching the convent school's little French-Canadian boarders told the pupils that Mavis's book brought from home, Lindsay's *The Joyous Travellers* (which she told me was actually a children's version of *The Canterbury*

10 Her personal library testifies to Gallant's intellectual curiosity and wide range of interests. In the sphere of classical music alone, the concert-goer (and adept of the Bayreuth Festival) owned, to mention at random, the complete (trilingual) program of the now mythical Pierre Boulez/Patrice Chéreau 1979 Wagner Ring Cycle; the bilingual *Fischer-Dieskau Book of Lieder* (bookmarked at the Schubert/Goethe lied *An Schwager Kronos*); *Der Rosenkavalier von Richard Strauss* (the complete text in German); Cosima Wagner's *Journals* (translated from German into French); *Mozart's Letters* (in Emily Anderson's original 1938 English translation); musicologist Alan Walker's biography *Franz Liszt;* and Robert Craft's *Stravinsky: Chronicle of a Friendship*.

Tales), meant *Les Joyeux Travailleurs*. Little Mavis was deprived of food until she admitted that travellers somehow meant the same thing as workers. The writer's preoccupation with the relations between language and perception, imagination and memory, may well have originated in this violation. This discussion will investigate the superb stylist, the haunting Imagist, and the master of irony, stressing an expert use of language based on *the eye and the ear*. Gallant's vision and voice, like Chaucer's, come "from a high altitude" (Kakutani). They leave no community or mindset unscathed, but – like those of the Samuel Beckett she frequented — never miss the absurd even in the grave and grim. The ironist's stratospheric viewpoint, something she has in common with visual satirists and caricaturists, vectors both laughter and interrogation. Irony's pragmatic function consists of signalling evaluation (Hutcheon, *A Theory of Parody* 53), but when the laughter remains undetected, Gallant's irony can be taken for cold judgment. Her quiet but sustained humour rests in fact on the *reader's ear* and recognition of tone, as Mavis herself confessed in a letter: "I have often been told, at readings, that this or that reader did not realise such-and-such a thing was meant to be funny until it was read aloud, by me" (Gallant, Letter to Dvořák, 11 October 1994).

Mavis has famously identified the beginning of writing as "a jolt that unbolts the door between perception and imagination" (Gallant, "Preface," *Collected Stories* 10).[11] My second A for Acute encapsulates her perspicacity and wit, the sharpness of both eye and tongue required for great essayists and aphorists. "There are two races, those who tread on people's lives, and the others" (*HT* 280), remarks the writer's canny alter ego, Linnet Muir, in the Montreal of the 1940s. But Gallant unsettles readers who too quickly equate the binary with Montreal's "two tribes" (281), or with a gender binary, the male office workers "rotting quietly until pension time" (280) and the "girls ... parked like third-class immigrants at the far end of the room" (293). For a hastily concluded gender binary explodes when we readers learn that the one "up on the life raft, stepping on girls' fingers" (293) is a female superior who conceals a Polish name which would have relegated her application "to a bottom drawer" (296). Similarly, Gallant does elsewhere skewer the binary tribal politics of Montreal's "Anglostocracy" (Weintraub 149), who believed there was "a difference in physical substance between people who spoke English exactly as [they] did, and the rest of mankind" (Gallant, *My Heart Is Broken* 59). But in the story under scrutiny above, "Between Zero and One," she also depicts Montreal's French-Canadian population before

11 All my paginations refer to the 2016 edition of *The Collected Stories*.

the Quiet Revolution in an equally caustic manner which some contemporary readers might find disturbing or politically incorrect. Cohabiting with the Anglos who refused to hire people with "funny names" (*HT* 283), the French were trained to venerate only "the dead and defeated, ranging from General Montcalm expiring at his last battle to a large galaxy of maimed and crippled saints" (281).

With respect to my N for Notable, Gallant occupies the puzzlingly paradoxical position of both centre and margin. She was the recipient of too many international awards and honours to list here, both for individual works and for her life's work.[12] With one exception (Morley Callaghan), she was the first Canadian to penetrate *The New Yorker*, that literary citadel which, she confided to me privately, as late as the 1950s saw Canadians in general as "hicks eating ice-cream in the street," and saw Mavis herself as "a sort of Eskimo with talent."

The short story genre in the second half of the twentieth-century on the North American and international scenes was dominated by the figures of Gallant and Alice Munro, as Munro's biographer Robert Thacker points out. Gallant began publishing in *The New Yorker* in 1951, and "had published over seventy stories there before Munro's first appearance in its pages in 1977" (Thacker 188; 208, 2nd ed.). Likewise, Gallant had published three books in the United States and the United Kingdom before Munro published her first in Canada in 1968. When Adderson compares Gallant to "that other God" (79), Munro, she declares, "Munro started out good and became great. Gallant was always great" (79). Thacker asserts Munro's status as "*the* significant presence in the landscape of the Canadian short story" (189),[13] while Gallant's *A Fairly Good Time*, "one of the most neglected masterworks of the last century" (Orner, "Introduction" vii), along with her first novel, remained out of print for decades.

Reputed to be a writers' writer – even "a lodestar for writers from Michael Ondaatje to Russell Banks" (Cole 19), Gallant has dazzled[14] but also baffled critics. Unlike Munro, she has not enjoyed the loyal following of a wide mainstream audience for a variety of reasons, which Barbara Godard and Winfried Siemerling have touched on (in "Modalities of the Edge" and "Perception, Memory, Irony" respectively), and which

12 See Dvořák, "Like A Spoonful of Water in a River: An Appreciation of Mavis Gallant" (33).

13 Attenuated to "her leading presence" in the second edition (209).

14 When Random House published *In Transit* in 1989, one unnamed reviewer affirmed that "Gallant is a quietly dazzling writer, and it is tempting to pronounce this volume perfect" ("In Transit"). The choice of the term "quietly dazzling" is astute, for Gallant is never ostentatious in her virtuosity.

Janice Kulyk Keefer has thoroughly explored (in "Strange Fashions of Forsaking").[15] As an expatriate addressing a global audience and engaged with disquieting cityscapes in flux, Gallant was long marginalized on a Canadian literary/media scene "obsessed with national textures" (Boyagoda), even caught "in the crossfire of the Tarzanist/cosmopolitan debate in Canadian culture" (Godard 75). In one of her letters Mavis confided:

> *For many years I avoided most visitors + did not keep track of Canadian writers (...) Don't forget that I had thirty years of career in New York + London before Canada took an interest (sort of) in my work.*[16] *So, I wasn't really interested in the oatcakes of culture* in the town of Snoodle-Boodle (Alberta.)*
>
> *Since then Canada has truly made up for it, but I have an elephant's memory. Memory doesn't stop me from standing up for Canada, when decency requires it, but that is just like sticking up for my ex-husband even after we divorced.* (Gallant, Letter to Dvořák, 3 May 2008, original asterisk)

The asterisk in red ink which follows "oatcakes of culture" was apparently inserted when Mavis reread her letter (handwritten in blue ink). It directed me to an eloquently revealing post-script passage also added in red ink regarding a hurtful "incident in Edmonton, where (she'd) been invited to a short story conference (in the mid-seventies) + where the other writers made a point of showing disdain to the Person from Paris" (Gallant, Letter to Dvořák, 3 May 2008). We can see that for having "laid claim to two continents," Gallant was "for a time unclaimed by either, viewed from both perspectives to be allied with foreigners" (Helm). Her stories have been in demand by foreign audiences: new selections of her work were published in seven countries in 2009 alone. But despite glowing reviews in France of her translated works,[17] Gallant remained on the

15 George Woodcock and David O'Rourke also raised the issue in the 1970s and 1980s, and more recently Randy Boyagoda, Stephen Henighan, Michael Helm, Russell Banks, Peter Orner ("The Way Vivid"), and Francine Prose, among others.

16 Although Robert Weaver compiled and published her first Canadian story selection, *The End of the World and Other Stories* in 1974, Mavis had 1979 in mind, when Macmillan finally bought the rights to publish her work (*From the Fifteenth District*) alongside the New York and London publishers which alone had been distributing her until then.

17 The 1970 novel, *A Fairly Good Time,* for instance came out in translation only in 2009, but to superlative reviews, and was placed by France Culture radio and the magazine *Télérama* among the top ten foreign novels of the year.

edge of the French arts scene (Savigneau, "Nouvelliste Mavis Gallant" 14), unlike the highly mediatized, young and stunningly beautiful Nancy Huston, writing in French. In addition to issues of marketing and public relations, French readers dislike squirming under a satirical lens sharpened by an outsider's gaze on insider experience.[18] Others simply suffer from what Gallant diagnosed in a satirical essay as a "well-known distaste for short stories" – a "dying art in France" (Gallant, "A Prix-view" 46).[19]

Critics have been divided, and readers enthused or uncomfortable, about a number of the features of Gallant's writing which make her texts an adventure in reading. These include her free-floating vantage points – which British writer and critic Adam Mars Jones claims "unmoor the reader," a "Cubist" manner of unsettling realist space-time (Ondaatje vii), and the trademark ironic vision and voice which sees and says two things at once – an increasingly sustained comic vision which performs pain through farce.[20] Gallant "places a huge amount of faith in her reader's intelligence, a faith which demands and rewards careful reading" (Prose, "Introduction" xii),[21] precisely because an ironic text by definition dissimulates its encoded directions and requires the reader to recognize and decode the unsaid[22] – and this in "a world that seems to be growing deaf to the unsaid, if not to its power" (Hutcheon, *Irony's Edge* 8). As

18 "Nothing could be more Canadian," Godard has pointed out, than "her acerbic, detached outsider's unveiling of the narrowness and arbitrariness of French society" (75).

19 Gallant commented on the French aversion to the short story genre to the editor of *Le Monde*'s book section (Savigneau, "Nouvelliste Mavis Gallant" 14) as well as in this satire on literary prizes for *The New York Times*. In it, she hands out a Prix des Petits Monstres for the best children's book, a Prix Chauvin for "the finest novel written by a French-speaking foreigner," and a short story prize meant to "encourage a dying art in France." Her parody of the winning book also skewers French readers' taste, notably their penchant for beginnings such as "The butcher of my little southern village is a true sage" ("A Prix-view" 46).

20 When it first came out, Elizabeth Janeway described Gallant's novel *A Fairly Good Time* as "very funny and very frightening," and identified the share of pain and pleasure allotted to the reader, who cannot help "wincing with helpless laughter and horrified recognition" (5).

21 Hermione Lee in 2004 calls Gallant "a paragon and a delight, a writer of the utmost *subtlety,*" and remarks at the same time that Gallant is "seriously underrated" or even little known by "moderately knowledgeable British readers" (Lee). One can put two and two together.

22 Frank Davey remarks as late as 2006 a continued resistance to the adventure of poetics, which he defines as the theory of how things "signify, or can be imagined to signify, or can be made to signify unanticipated meanings," a resistance which he surmises rests on "a stubborn fondness of simpler understandings of signification – that poets write what they mean" (174).

Michael Helm has confessed, Gallant "produced notes of irony outside [his – and often our] hearing range." On a higher general level, Gallant's stories "require constant adaptation" because of what Tamas Dobozy has astutely termed Gallant's "designed anarchy" (86, 85):[23] stories which "very much require an altering of 'cognition,' of the way in which we process the text" (86).

"The resemblance of Miss Gallant's characters to most of humanity, living or dead, is far from coincidental," notes Janeway (5). One Gallant character tears up his novel because he fails to make life "sound *true*" (*Overhead in a Balloon* 174). As does Janeway, this character in "The Colonel's Child" gestures to the final letter T in my limping acrostic. Rivers of ink have remarked on Gallant's scrupulously accurate representations of a historically and geographically verifiable world, her eye for the telling detail which conjures up a whole life, and her depictions of the objects making up a cultural milieu, "maintained with fine and fierce exactitude" (Dorris). Yet beyond these notions of factual exactness and textured reality effect, "true" also signifies "right" (as in the right word and tone), and "genuine," with never a false inflection – precisely what Mavis valued in Colette when she maintained the writer "was not false, not even when she lied" ("The Pursuit of Pleasure"). Getting it right involves Gallant's remarkable gift for capturing a voice – a true voice for each dissimilar character – but also points to her ability to sustain an overarching monophony (her own recognizable voice) in the polyphonic ensemble.[24]

In the vein of this left-field introduction, my book blends essay with fragments of not-quite biography and memoir which disclose illuminating connections, the driving principle being that "the art of a given moment must *involve*, as opposed to merely *follow*, that which has preceded it" (J. Levinson, *Music, Art, & Metaphysics* 4, original stresses). Well before Levinson, Hemingway had observed that a writer needs to understand and assimilate "what is available as his birth-right" and what he or she in turn must "take his departure from" (*Death* 169). Mavis, for instance, found Joyce's *Ulysses* original and new. She inscribed Thursday 16 June 1904 (Bloomsday) on the title page of her well-thumbed copy alongside Joyce's birth and death dates, and every year on 16 June she

23 I shall come back to Dobozy's interesting analogy between Gallant's "chaotic patterning of language" and the musical form of "the fugue" (79) – which is actually anything but chaotic.

24 In this my position differs from that of the French critic Michel Fabre, who sees the authorial voice disappearing under "a polyphonic voice, a collective voice born from the overlapping of points of view" (156).

would telephone her old friend and fellow Joyce admirer in Montreal, Barbara Kilvert, to read aloud favourite passages from the novel to each other. Even after Kilvert's death, Mavis went on reading portions of the novel on her own on Bloomsday, "usually at breakfast," as she specified in one of our formal interviews (Gallant in Dvořák, "When Language" 17). Yet while her art-making dovetails with a number of Joycean predilections, it also differs profoundly, regarding the nature and limits of language itself, both as *langue* (pre-existing semantico-cultural system or code) and *parole* (the creative individual utterance or act of language) – the one constituting the ground for the other (Saussure). I put Gallant's work in dialogue, then, with other international modernists (with Joyce notably serving as a foil),[25] and also with those they (and she) were reading, watching, and listening to – from the French realists to the Russians. In a piece from the restored version of Ernest Hemingway's memoir, which I read to Mavis (affected by macular degeneration) on Christmas Eve, 2012, Hemingway confided, "at first there were the Russians; then there were all the others. But for a long time there were the Russians." He also confided that Ezra Pound advised him to "Keep to the French" (*A Moveable Feast* 102). Flaubert did clearly teach Hemingway to excise superfluous words, and show him that rhythm was the ground of the sentence. Like Hemingway and Nabokov, the young Mavis read in waves. "There was a long wave of Russian writers, in English translation of course. Chekhov, Gogol, Turgenev, Dostoevsky. That was followed by a wave of French – Stendhal, Flaubert, Proust" (Gallant in Hancock 21). The wave naturally also includes Balzac, as we see below when Mavis equates his protagonist Rastignac (from *La Comédie humaine*, notably *Le Père Goriot*) with Aravind Adiga's Balram (from *The White Tiger)*. Winfried Siemerling was the first to my knowledge to discuss at length the place of French literature in Gallant's bicultural heritage as well as her play of referentiality with French texts in general and with Proust's and Flaubert's in particular.[26]

This book addresses the important questions of audience and cultural DNA all the while tackling challenging formal speculations in a new way. I engage with the question, How does Gallant's work *work*? My method

25 In addition to formal considerations comprising significant convergences and divergences between Gallant and Joyce, the two writers share a strong French connection. Of all his years as an expatriate, Joyce lived longest in Paris, where *Ulysses* was first published in book form and where he wrote *Finnegans Wake*.

26 See Siemerling, "Perception, Memory, Irony: Mavis Gallant Greets Proust and Flaubert."

offers adventures in hands-on microanalyses: close readings paying careful attention to the writer's shining language and to what I identify as her poetics of rhythm. Drawing on the philosophy of aesthetics, it simultaneously discloses the congruences of her *techne* with film, painting, and music, also something which to my knowledge has never been done before. Literary analysis cohabits with forms of "témoignage" or witnessing, providing readers with Mavis's backstage views on art and life, imparted throughout a twenty-year-long friendship in a shared Paris/French habitat. Offering privileged insights into Mavis's creative life, my discussion will naturally draw on our private conversations, telephone calls, and correspondence. Interspersed throughout the unfolding argument are excerpts from her letters or cards – spoken-tongue texts which move off into light, often parodic, anecdotes.

Mavis, osmosis, & the Artful Dodger

Hailed as "a supranational phenomenon" (Grant 31) resisting "any sort of border – political, sociological, or even spiritual" (Moore), Mavis jettisoned a safe journalistic career in Montreal in 1950[27] to live and write (and perhaps starve) in the Paris she knew only through art. The modernists continued to occupy the cultural spaces, some – like Marcel Proust, Albert Camus, and Louis Ferdinand Céline – publishing even from the grave. But Mavis's Paris was still at the heart of the genuinely new. One can call up the "gangling, spider-limbed" (Romney) French counterpart to Charlie Chaplin, Jacques Tati, (also compared to Buster Keaton and Stan Laurel), whose brilliantly original films (which I shall allude to) range from *Jour de fête* (1947) and *Les Vacances de M. Hulot* (1953) to *Playtime* (1967), *Trafic* (1971), and *Parade* (1973). One can also evoke the painter whose unfolding international career corresponded to and benefited by the development of the mass media. Pablo Picasso, who

27 Readers may wonder how "safe" Gallant was with McCarthyism rearing its head in Canada. She was indeed left-leaning in her sympathies, but did not cover politically sensitive topics. In her feature articles in the *Montreal Standard* in the last half of the 1940s, she covered a broad range of societal and cultural issues ranging from war brides and libraries to progressive schools and even the question "Why Are Canadians So Dull?" She also had a weekly column about radio (entitled "On the Air"), and she reviewed books, films, and theatre. One can even say Mavis had too safe a job for her own comfort. She once told me that one of the reasons for which she decided to throw it all up was that she and the other regular journalists with bylines were going to be invited to sign up for pension plans. She felt it was time to kick up her heels or she would tie herself down into a secure bourgeois path, all traced out.

arguably first made the space-time continuum theory visible and inspired Gertrude Stein's literary Cubism (and more generally, (post)modernist multiview and multivocality), may partly explain why Michael Ondaatje should observe that Gallant's stories "feel cubist" (vii). When Stein asked Picasso to explain his Cubist art, he famously told her, "You paint not what you see but what you know is there" (Flanner, *Paris Journal* 3, 146). Actually, Picasso was not painting the invisible; he was painting what was concealed from his located and temporal vantage point, challenging the limits of our space-time by showing two irreconcilably disjunctive spaces synchronically. Yet rather than evoking Picasso's earlier analytic Cubism stressing the deconstruction and fragmentation of forms (which influenced Stein), Gallant's technique, as we shall see, is more analogous with synthetic Cubism, whose formal arrangement of lines suggests forms or even re-embraces figuration. In this permanent revolution in the arts, Picasso then would be an "acquisition" for Gallant, in the sense she explains in her well-known essay on style:

> For "influences" I would be inclined to substitute "acquisitions." What they consist of, and amount to, are affected by taste and environment, preferences and upbringing (even, and sometimes particularly, when the latter has been rejected), instinctive selection. The beginning writer has to choose, tear to pieces, spit out, chew up and assimilate as naturally as a young animal – as naturally and as ruthlessly. ("Style?" 37)[28]

The concurrent retrospectives of Picasso's work Mavis would have seen and chewed up at the Louvre and the Bibliothèque Nationale in 1955 and then again at the Grand Palais in 1966 comprised many paintings never seen before. Some, like *Les Demoiselles au bord de la Seine, d'après Courbet* (1950), and Picasso's series of variations on Eugène Delacroix's *Les Femmes d'Alger* [*Women of Algiers*] (1834), illustrate my thesis that the modernists (and postmodernists) delight in intertextual and intermedial borrowings and dialogical responses. An omnivorous reader as well as an art-lover, Mavis confessed in a *Le Monde* interview to having, when young, chewed up and assimilated the French writer Anatole France (who was a model for both Apollinaire[29] and the young Proust (Karpeles; Muhlstein,

28 Gallant's chewing up or spitting out bring Hemingway once more to mind, namely when the early modernist asserts that great writers are born "with an intelligence to accept or reject what is already presented as knowledge" (*Death* 168).

29 "Apollinaire set out to duplicate Anatole France, his model, and failed magnificently," declared Cocteau to William Fifield (Cocteau).

The Pen and the Brush).[30] She recognized the imprint, astonished, when one of her stories was translated into French and the original Anatole France phrase (in French) lay there unfolded and complete (Savigneau, "Mavis Gallant, nouvelles intimes" 3). In an interesting analogy, Proust knowingly or unknowingly "went so far as to plant real France sentences in passages of [his invented writer] Bergotte's prose" (Tadié qtd in Tahourdin).

Mavis and I often talked about such osmosis, which we detected stretching out to contemporary writing in India. When I gave her Anita Desai's *In Custody* (1984), she found it Chekhovian. When I gave her Aravind Adiga's 2008 Man Booker Prize–winning *The White Tiger*, she enthusiastically collocated it with Balzac and Dickens, astutely decrypting authorial intent.

Paris, 9 May 2009

Dear Marta,

... The White Tiger is so gripping that I wanted it never to end and when it did I hoped the Indian Artful Dodger would never be caught (how would[31] *Dickens have handled it, by the way?) + the Indian Rastignac would marry well + get away with murder. And that he will not just simply turn into the Indian Al Capone ...*

With love,
M. xx

Mavis wrote again a week later, sending along with her note an article on Adiga in French from *Le Monde* magazine, which she had clipped out and annotated.

Paris Tuesday 19 May (2009)

Dear Marta,

I'm sending this on because you may not have seen it. And because of a rare sort of coincidence: I wrote to you mentioning Balzac + Dickens, "Rastignac"

30 Mavis stayed on top of contemporary publications, too. On arriving in Paris, she read Marguerite Yourcenar's *Mémoires d'Hadrien* (1951), just out, with three years to go before the English translation [*Memoirs of Hadrian*]. When in London in 1956 she bought Thomas Mann's freshly translated *Confessions of Felix Krull, Confidence Man* (1955), which appeared only a year after the original novel was published in German.

31 Underlined by Gallant.

+ "the Artful Dodger." At the end of this interview (p. 46) Adiga says, "... j'ai l'impression que le Paris de Balzac comme le Londres de Dickens ressemblent au Bombay d'aujourd'hui ..."[32]

William Maxwell – my New Yorker editor[33] *– believed that literary coincidences floated in the air + were picked up by unwitting writers.*

xx M.

The Paris Mavis crossed an ocean for certainly captured what was "floating in the air." It was where the Hungarian and Russian composers Béla Bartók and Igor Stravinsky met the year Gallant was born, and also where and when Vladimir Mayakovsky attended Marcel Proust's funeral. When Mavis moved there, the city was still the site of a transnational interaction among the visual arts, music, the performing arts, and literature – fields all preoccupied by subjectivity and perception. Composers set texts to music, poets wrote on painting, painters absorbed cinematic techniques or turned to fiction, dance and literature deserted story for abstract sound, and all vibrated to the sound of jazz. Verbal practices have often influenced the non-verbal media of painting, music, and dance, but the influence has also been reciprocal or even the other way round. The spiralling *Finnegans Wake*, which Umberto Eco saw as an Einsteinian universe bending back on itself (*Role of the Reader* 54), drew fiction towards the pure sound of musical composition. Yet Joyce's earlier multiple viewpoints and abrogation of temporal linearity can be traced to the Cubist rupture with traditional figuration and spatial perspective, and it is tempting to argue that the medium calling the tune may well have been the visual arts.

the medium calling the tune?

Russell Banks has remarked that Gallant's oeuvre gives readers the same shock of self-recognition that we feel before "the atmosphere of

32 In this interview with Frédéric Joignot, Adiga confessed to admiring the great French realists Balzac, Maupassant, Flaubert, and Zola, and declared (quoted by Mavis) that Balzac's Paris, like Dickens's London, resembled today's Bombay (Adiga, "L'Inde démocratique 46). Interestingly, in his introduction to the 2006 edition of *Midnight's Children*, Salman Rushdie, too, acknowledges his debt to Dickens for "his great rotting Bombay-like city, and his ability to root his larger-than-life characters and surrealist imagery in a sharply observed, almost hyper-realist background, out of which the comic and the fantastic elements of his work seemed to grow organically, becoming intensifications of, and not escapes from, the real world" (Rushdie, "Introduction" xii).

33 With *The New Yorker* then at the epicentre of American literature, Maxwell was also the editor of writers such as J.D. Salinger, Eudora Welty, Vladimir Nabokov, Frank O'Connor, and John Cheever.

a painting by Edward Hopper or a Duke Ellington orchestral suite" (x). Mavis had never known a world without books and paintings and music. She grew up with painters and pictures, including moving pictures. Mavis's Christmas and birthday gifts when she was small would be books from her mother and a new box of paints from her father, who – like Cocteau's – painted and frequented painters. Looking back, she confided that her father's style (in the 1920s) was Impressionist, rather like Armand Guillaumin's. She often alluded to how her father would hold her up before pictures to point out the multiple tints making up a colour. She would also evoke the sensual pleasures of mixing her paints for her own watercolours. Never happier than in an artist's studio, Gallant can be said to exemplify the osmosis between literature and visual culture. Hemingway claimed to have learned things from Paul Cézanne. I infer that these were the reduction of form and the unsettling of traditional perspective – effectively connecting painting with notions of literary vantage point (Hemingway, *A Moveable Feast* 23, 71). In a similar instance of osmosis from the pictorial to the verbal medium, Picasso, who alongside others like Marcel Duchamp exploded the spatial perspective which Cézanne had unsettled,[34] can partly account for the floating, multiple perspectives of Gallant's stories, realist in a fraught way but "cubist in their angles and qualifications" (Ondaatje vii).

My approach to Gallant transcends the classic focus pairing literature with the arts,[35] and it plugs into the recent rise in visual studies

34 Duchamp's Cubist-Futurist *Nu descendant l'escalier* [*Nude Descending a Staircase, No. 2*] caused shock waves at New York's Armory Show in 1913. But Cézanne had already isolated left-eye and right-eye views and showed both at the same time. His deconstruction of binocular vision defied traditional linear perspective grounded in the simultaneous processing carried out by the visual cortex of the brain.

35 Brad Bucknell's *Literary Modernism and Musical Aesthetics: Pater, Pound, Joyce, and Stein* (2001), among the twenty-first century's first inter-art, mixed media forays, knowledgeably investigates verbal-music interchange (such as Ezra Pound's opera score on François Villon, and Stéphane Mallarmé's endeavour to collapse into music's unmeaning). Michael Fried's *Flaubert's "Gueuloir." On "Madame Bovary" and "Salammbô"* (2012) puts forward analogies between Flaubert and Courbet, arguing that the writer's description of Emma's funeral cortège in *Madame Bovary* (1856) was inspired by, and was intended to surpass, Courbet's shockingly realistic monumental picture *Un Enterrement à Ornan* [*A Burial at Ornans*] (1850), twice exhibited in Paris (1851 and 1855). Anka Muhlstein's *The Pen and the Brush: How Passion for Art Shaped Nineteenth-Century French Novels* (2017) culturally explores the relations of five major nineteenth-century novelists (including Flaubert and Maupassant but also a chronological exception: Proust) with the works of fine art displayed at the Louvre as well as with the contemporary painters they frequented.

and sound studies. Identifying Gallant as a late modernist figure at the juncture of multiple, interacting fields also connects with the thrust of twenty-first century modernist studies – an international movement of scholars rethinking spatial and temporal circulation and the transnational, cross-disciplinary flow of ideas. My central thesis breaks with the nationalist and geographical restraints which have until recently marked the field, and provides a departure-point for researchers new to the split with a traditional cartography which excludes from the modernist canon works which occurred "too early or too late" (Ross and Lindgren 19).[36] This book is the logical outcome of my intellectual as well as personal relation with Mavis, and of long reflection, sustained throughout my (often collaborative) research and writing. *Tropes and Territories* (2007, edited with W.H. New) engages with the short story genre across cultural divides, while *Crosstalk: Canadian and Global Imaginaries in Dialogue* (2012, with Diana Brydon), uses the device of crosstalk as a metaphor "for the ways in which *audial and visual imaginaries* interact to create complex forms of interference" (Brydon and Dvořák 1). *Translocated Modernisms: Paris and Other Lost Generations* (2016, with Emily Ballantyne and Dean Irvine) approaches a number of late modernist Canadian visual artists and writers through the network of transnational exchanges they experienced in Paris. Its opening chapter, my personal appreciation of Gallant and her oeuvre, opened up the spaces of investigation for this book.

Mavis loved pictures, films, and music, high and low. She shared Proust's fascination with the visual arts and music and their relationship with literature. She liked the way the painter and writer Eric Karpeles turned John Ruskin's comment about the Venetians inside out to fit Proust, the writer she reread most, who told Cocteau in a letter, "My book is a painting" (Karpeles 10). If, according to Proust's idol Ruskin, painting was the way the Venetians wrote, then "writing was the way Proust painted" (20). Karpeles's *Paintings in Proust: A Visual Companion to "In Search*

36 The following examples can be invoked. Richard J. Lane and Miguel Mota's collection of essays, *Malcolm Lowry's Poetics of Space* (2016), addresses Lowry's relations with photography, film, and jazz. In *Disciplining Modernism* (2010), Pamela Caughie's authors engage with disciplines ranging from architecture, design, and technology to fashion and film. The contributors of Stephen Ross and A.C. Lindgren's *The Modernist World* (2015) map global modernisms according to their geopolitical locations (and their place on the axis of postcoloniality) as well as their disciplinary parameters. Charles A. Riley's *Free as Gods: How the Jazz Age Reinvented Modernism* (2017) engages with the interconnections among the artists, writers, and musicians who converged in Paris during the Jazz Age.

of Lost Time" (2008), which Mavis was so delighted with that she gave me a copy for my birthday,[37] engages referentially with the collaborative visual substructure of Proust's verbal art. The author has tracked down and reproduced for those with less of a mind's eye (or visual culture) than Proust the pictures to which he makes profuse allusions. In the same vein, Lesley Clement's *Learning to Look: A Visual Response to Mavis Gallant's Fiction* (2000) was the first to relate Gallant's literary texts to visual art.

why Degas?

Breaking free of Riley's early modernist time frame and Ross and Lingren's sweeping geopolitical approach, this book also goes beyond Karpeles's pairing of word with image and Muhlstein's thematic crossover, which privileges the role of painters as characters in the plots under scrutiny, as well as the novelists' painterly erudition and love of ekphrasis. Similarly, this discussion goes beyond Clement's Gallant-based comparative approach with painting, which, like Karpeles's, concerns itself not so much with a dialogical relation, but rather with learnedly identifying the pictures Gallant may hypothetically have had in mind when making her painterly allusions.[38] These are legion. Barbara, all white and gold and pink, is told in "The Remission" that she is "like a Fragonard" or "a Boucher" (*Paris Stories* 221): pictures which point me not to the writer's evident knowledge of visual culture, but to her method of signifying obliquely. They notably overlay peep show voluptuousness onto the role of an English wife and mother not as devastated by her husband's fatal illness as she could be.[39] Sylvie in "The Cost of Living" ought to be

---

37 Karpeles in turn greatly admired Gallant's work. After meeting her in 2010, he sent her a grateful letter along with a book (*Japanese Portraits*) by Donald Richie, in which Karpeles found a fellow sensibility (wry, acerbic, and compassionate) as well as a somewhat parallel path in life, Richie's Japan to Gallant's France.

38 Clement for instance comments on the opening sentence of Gallant's short novel, *Its Image on the Mirror*, notably its reference to "gesticulating people" in "those crowded religious paintings that tell a story" (*My Heart Is Broken* 57). According to Clement, the painterly allusions "*could* have in mind the pointing John the Baptist and other demonstrative gestures of the Crucifixion panels of the Isenheim altarpiece in its closed state" (266).

39 Mavis confided that this story (published in 1979) was haunted by her own mother. In the earlier, more openly autobiographical story, "In Youth Is Pleasure" (1975), the narrator deploys a dense chiasmus to configure her young, dying father and equally young, unfaithful mother: "*he* was ill and he couldn't hide it; *she* had a lover and didn't try" (*HT* 265, original italics).

drawn, no, has been drawn, we are told: she is "the coarse and grubby Degas dancer, the girl with the shoulder thrown back and the insolent chin" who for two pins "would stick out her tongue or spit in your face;" Sylvie, to boot, has "the voice you imagine belonging to the picture" (*Going Ashore* 177; *Cost of Living* 207).[40] Where others might provide an inventory of the Degas dancer pictures, I ask, *why* Degas?

With his decentred figures, oblique, high-angle or low-angle vantage points influenced by Japanese art, Degas had destroyed traditional Western perspective. As the philosopher Nelson Goodman points out, "When Degas painted a woman seated near the edge of the picture, and looking out of it, he defied traditional standards of composition but offered by example a new way of seeing, of organizing experience" (*Worldmaking* 137). Gertrude Stein was clearly intent on achieving an analogous effect. She destabilized traditional modes of identification in a work whose title alone announces a collision of hybrid sidestepping of voice, *The Autobiography of Alice B. Toklas* (1933), and in which she attributed her literary formation to her links with the pre–First World War painters' milieu. Mavis, too, enjoyed the company of painters over that of writers, and I want to investigate her formal "fit" as a writer with Degas's painterly practice. I can also offer a parallel musical analogy, notably the common overtones in design, representation, and structuring of experience produced through the materiality of line, diction, rhythm, and harmonics. "The Doctor" begins with a biting satirical commentary on Luke Fildes's social moralist genre painting, *The Doctor*, and other edifying "Victorian miseries" (*VE* 69) in which sign-laden composition and message-loaded detail rest on the standard judgment and habit which have naturalized them, and serve only to preach and persuade predictably. This is at opposite poles from the poetics which inform Gallant's writing, which seeks the unusual frame of reference that reveals fresh aspects of reality. The protagonists of "In the Tunnel" visit an abandoned, out-of-the-way chapel in the mountains near Nice, which contains frescoes of what they take to be the Last Judgment, the life of Jesus, and "Judas after he hung himself" (*HT* 106). I can factually point out that this is the medieval chapel of Notre-Dame-des-Fontaines, a pilgrimage sanctuary in a borderland long disputed between Italy and France, which is covered by Giovanni Canavesio's fifteenth-century fresco cycle of the Passion, which includes a Judas Iscariot. Facts aside, Gallant's characters are embarrassed by Christ, but enthused by the hanged Judas with, to

40 Regarding quotations, this much-quoted story collection will henceforth be designated as *GA*; the name Gallant will be understood.

boot, his guts spilling out.[41] I, too, am more interested in the grotesque realism presented pictorially by Canavesio and verbally by Gallant, in a graphic ekphrastic echo that gives voice to a mute art object, then spins off on a life of its own. I find it valuable to call attention to important parallels, and interlock my analysis with discussions of Gallant's special brand of realism as well as her rhetorical mastery, notably her art of sinking and rising again.

I have given random examples pointing to the vast extent of Mavis's visual culture, which it is not my purpose to prove. Yet again, but in a wider sense, *why* Degas? When I make parallels between pictorial representation and Gallant's verbal denotation, it is for their efficacy in clarifying certain obscurities or lighting up certain subtleties in meaning-making which do not correlate with a more accustomed system of representation. My book is grounded in how modernity's linguistic and non-linguistic aesthetic systems meet head-on and commingle, and it engages with the new literary techniques resulting from the reciprocal dynamics, of which ekphrasis is but one component. I home in by identifying the painterly eye and formal *painterly dynamics* which are the cornerstones for certain writing practices, notably the ground of verbal as well as visual irony and caricature. But I also radiate out by discussing the intermedial dynamics and creative collaborations of the transcontinental cultural context which nourished Gallant. The cross-pollination or osmosis is visible in Samuel Beckett's now iconic play *En Attendant Godot*. First staged in Paris in 1953 shortly after Mavis's arrival, it felt "Russian, though done in the Irish manner and spoken in French" (Flanner 1: 198). The period's taste for mixing is literally embodied in French filmmaker Robert Bresson's practice of privileging the soundtrack even more than the image track (*Interviews* 240), and of identifying the final process of editing or mixing as "the truly creative act" – "the moment when all of a film's elements, sound and visual, are put in contact with one another, are acting upon one another, and become transformed" (199). My method will thus involve confronting Gallant's writings with a variety of other international productions which are not necessarily direct influences, but which participate in what she identified as "the distillation of a lifetime of reading and listening, of selection and rejection" ("Style" 37), and which can serve a valuable exegetical function. I notably engage with the

41 The focalizer, Sarah, goes so far as to filch a postcard reproduction of the hanged figure. I have the same Judas postcard in a drawer from when I passed through following a conference in Nice, as did Mavis when she spent time in her well-loved Menton region. See *The Hanged Judas* image on page 61.

confluences of writing – her writing – with the musical developments and the moving pictures that shaped her and her generation.

Mavis, the (moving) pictures, & music

Mavis and F.W. Murnau's masterpiece of German expressionism, *Nosferatu,* were born the same year (1922), and she and the cinema grew up together. Even more intensely than *Nosferatu,*[42] Murnau's painterly *Faust* (1926)[43] deploys jaw-dropping chiaroscuro images animated by dynamic framing which operate in the double registers of splendour and horror, realism and the fantastic, the grotesque and the abstract. Along with Wallace Worsley's gothic *The Hunchback of Notre Dame* (1923) and Henri Fescourt's poignant *Les Misérables* (1925), they were among the earliest silent motion pictures the small Mavis had been taken to see. She confided how the immediacy of their huge images on the big screen, shot in darkness and light, made her reel with pleasurable shock. The image would become the catalyst of her creative imagination.[44]

Yet the cinema, plastic art in motion, involved the collaboration of radically different fields, from music and architecture to the decorative arts and costume design. It is valuable to remember that while silent films had no soundtrack, they were rarely projected in silence. *Nosferatu* and *Faust* for instance came with scores authorized by Murnau, meant to be performed by an orchestra (or piano) during the screening. Gustav Hinrichs, for instance, composed the accompanying musical score to Rupert Julian's *Phantom of the Opera* (1925). In 2015, the composer and pianist Jean-François Zygel improvised live during the first screening of the digitally restored version of Fescourt's *Les Misérables* at Paris's Théâtre du Châtelet. In 2019 Zygel composed and performed (with a small ensemble back-up) an instrumental piece with choral fragments to accompany a screening of Murnau's *Nosferatu* at Paris's Philharmonie. As Zygel was aware, all this programmatic music was designed from the

---

42 *Nosferatu* was released in the United States in 1929, encountering immediate critical and box office success.

43 *Faust* has been likened to a walking Albrecht Dürer or a Pieter Brueghel (the Elder), but is arguably more in congruence with the work of Hieronymus Bosch.

44 As a young journalist working for the *Montreal Standard*, Mavis began to run photo-stories of books she read, such as Gabrielle Roy's *Bonheur d'occasion* (1945), yet to be translated as *The Tin Flute* (1947) and still unknown to her Anglo readers. She thought of those pictures as "stills from a film" (Gallant, "Afterword," *Paris Stories* 372), and the fiction which she had already begun to write was always triggered by a fixed image she famously likened to a "freeze frame" (375).

start to buttress the visual symphony of images, intensify the atmosphere and emotion, and nudge viewers towards a desired, denoted interpretation in a way the intertitles never could.[45] So the cultural matrix which nourished Mavis also comprised music, an art which holds salient differences with respect to the other aesthetic systems, but which is equally concerned with perceptual and conceptual underpinnings.[46] My zooming out also involves this ubiquitous non-linguistic aesthetic system which can stand alone completely outside denotation, but which finds itself at the core of the performing arts[47] and even of literary composition. My pairing of literature with music is in fact natural in that music, as Proust points out, is also "*sine materia*" (*Du côté de chez Swann* [*The Way by Swann's*] 250).[48] Unlike the visual arts, in other words, literature and music are "*nonphysical* arts" in which there is "no physical 'thing' that one can plausibly take to be the artwork itself" (J. Levinson, *Music, Art, & Metaphysics* 63).

A dynamics of breakage gained momentum, part of a generalized modernist *air du temps*. From Duchamp's *Nu descendant un escalier*[49] [*Nude Descending a Staircase, No. 2*] T.S. Eliot's *The Waste Land*, and John Dos Passos's *Manhattan Transfer*, poets were shattering traditional metrical patterns, novelists exploding the conventions of literary realism, and visual artists accelerating the atomization of the Impressionists via analytic and synthetic Cubism and their derivatives, such as machine-age-mad Futurism and Constructivism.[50] Since the premiere

45 It was actually the advent of the soundtrack that invented silence, as Bresson points out (*Notes on the Cinematograph*). With the rise of audiovisual cinema, Bresson was one of the few filmmakers to use music (as opposed to sonic objects) sparingly (rather than as constant accompaniment), to "add a value and a significance to the images that they do not have on their own" (*Interviews* 201).

46 Pierre Boulez has noted that Wagner's music – post-romantic and arguably proto-modernist – is the first to stress indeterminacy; the philosopher Theodor Adorno claimed the composer elevated ambiguity to a principle of style, while Linda and Michael Hutcheon perceive "an ordering impulse" both articulated and undermined (*Opera: Desire, Disease, Death* 92–3).

47 While Mavis loved pure, abstract music, she also enjoyed opera, which as Linda and Michael Hutcheon note, is a "most impure" art form, owing its power to "its combining the musical and the dramatic, the *aural and the visual*, the emotional and the intellectual" (*Opera* 1)

48 Formerly translated as *Swann's Way*, this is the first volume of Proust's *À la recherche du temps perdu* [*In Search of Lost Time*], formerly translated as *Remembrance of Things Past*.

49 The French is the original title.

50 Being machine-mad was actually not new, as demonstrates Henry Purcell's "Wondrous Machine!" movement in *Ode to St Cecilia* (1692).

of Stravinsky's seismically dissonant, percussive *Le Sacre du printemps* [*The Rite of Spring*] (1913), which Cocteau identified as the detonator of the art revolution,[51] composers, too, were breaking down classical harmony and fracturing the melodic line in sundry ways: disjunctive leaps (rather than the proximal ordering of scales and arpeggios), dissonant augmented and diminished intervals (rather than consonant major thirds and perfect fifths of tonic-median-dominant combinations), syncopation destabilizing the rhythmic or metrical beat, serialism, aleatory or chance music, and the atonal and twelve-tone systems. All rebelled against a perceived tyranny of conventional timbres, rhythms, and tuning systems. *The Well-Tempered Microphone* showed technology could even replace the musical instruments it had been invented to enhance. With *La Bien-Aimée* [*The Beloved*] (1928), a rearrangement of piano pieces by Schubert and Liszt, Darius Milhaud had already composed for orchestra and player piano – a piano giving the performer multiple hands, capable of playing eighty-eight notes at once.[52]

Mavis's painter father had taught her how to *see*, and her painter's eye is manifest in the slightest tossed-off essay. It radiates from a parenthetical remark distinguishing Pissarro's kind of white from Utrillo's: "The most truthful painter of the Paris winter is Pissarro. Not Utrillo; you will never see his particular kind of white, not even after a snowfall" (Gallant, "Paris When It Shimmers"). It also glows in her descriptions. Paris in November is "an opaque gray" calling up "old spider webs, or the floor covering at Beaubourg, or the outer walls of the Swedish Embassy on Rue Barbet de Jouy." The Tuileries are "gray-white with a wash of pink," and at night the reddish light on clouds and snow is "like a decanter of wine with a light behind it" ("Paris When It Shimmers").[53] In addition, Mavis's pictorial experience is such that she often sees people and surroundings through the filter of art. In *A Fairly Good Time* we are told that behind

51 Although Bartók actually beat Stravinsky to it (having composed his radically percussive and dissonant tritone-based *Allegro barbaro* in 1911), it took time for the West to discover his work. Cocteau declared in his interview with Fifield that the Russian composer was the "chief architect" of the art revolution, notably that "Everything began, finally, you see, with Stravinsky's *Sacre*. The *Sacre du printemps* reversed everything" (Cocteau).

52 I attended the first contemporary revival of the original concert version of Milhaud's ballet score at the Paris Philharmonie in 2016. Like the modernists before me, I found the piano roll technology's magnitude of sound electrifying.

53 George Woodcock was among the first to identify in Gallant's work "the marvellous painterly surface of the scene imagined through the translucent veil of words," deriving from "a close and highly visual sense of the interrelationship of sharply observed detail" (74) – in other words, a sense of composition.

the protagonist Shirley there are "plane trees and a Sisley sky" (25). The omniscient narrator also remarks that Shirley sits "like a widow by Vuillard," explaining the pictorial simile with another drawn from the everyday world of money and underwear: "like someone with her life's savings sewn up in her corsets" (224). Shirley herself sees her world through the same filter of art, remarking when she first meets her fiancé's mother and sister that these are "Goya people" (27).[54]

On the other hand, it was Mavis's musician husband who taught her how to *listen.*[55] She learned to listen so well that she soon admired composers like Bartók, Stravinsky, Shostakovich, and Hindemith, who developed new ways of listening to the world and relating to it sensually and cognitively. Contemporary music's privileging of atonality, serialism, dissonance, and disjunctive sound sequences took part in modernity's aesthetics of decentring and dislocation. Actually, jazz and its ground, the blues form – which fascinated composers from Erik Satie and Maurice Ravel to Stravinsky and Arthur Honegger – had done much of the dislocating in an analogous fashion to the Cubist rupture with traditional figuration and spatial perspective. By the time Mavis settled in Paris, concert tours by Dizzy Gillespie and Count Basie had whipped the French passion for jazz white-hot. As Janet Flanner remarked to her *New Yorker* readership, "French *jazz-hot* fans are as intellectual in talking of *swingue* as if they were discussing Schoenberg" (Flanner 1: 215, original stresses).

borderblur

Halfway through the twentieth century, when Mavis was beginning to write and publish,[56] the Ballets Russes's Leonid Massine had further

54 When living in Madrid, the young Mavis spent much time in the Prado, notably going "Back to Goya." She relates in an extract from her *Journals*, "I go back and back, and still he is haunting and terrifying" ("The Hunger Diaries" 50).

55 Nineteen-year-old Mavis met the young pianist John Gallant at the apartment of mutual friends who had recordings and piano reductions of Shostakovich's work. Johnny sat down and played the Shostakovich Fifth. Asked if she liked it, she answered, "there's no melody," but "Johnny said, it's full of melody. It's you who doesn't know how to listen" (Gallant in Dvořák, "When Language" 13).

56 "Thank You for the Lovely Tea," published in *The New Yorker* in 1956, was actually written in 1940 when Mavis was only eighteen. Other stories such as "Jorinda and Jorindel" and "Up North" were also written in the 1940s and were re-excavated from the family picnic hamper containing her material a decade later, to be published in *The New Yorker* between 1954 and 1959. Like "Saturday," set in early 1960s Montreal, and the other stories collected in *Home Truths*, as the author points out in her introduction to the original edition (unfortunately not reproduced in the 2001 edition), each of them "needs to be read against its own time" ("An Introduction" *HT* xiii).

transformed the performing arts by creating borderblur symphonic ballets. These moved away from mimed narrative to abstract movement visualizing pure (unprogrammatic) music. Converging with the anti-mimetic agenda of the Cubists, dance putting music into visible form found its literary counterparts in the experimental modernism of writers like Stein and Joyce. As she related in *The Autobiography of Alice B. Toklas,* Stein had posed ninety times for her portrait only to have the young Picasso paint her head out. He did finish it later without her – brushing off complaints that Stein didn't look like that by saying, she will – but Stein responded with a *verbal* portrait of Picasso entitled "If I Told Him, A *Completed* Portrait of Picasso" (1924).[57] Her anti-mimetic poem translates the Cubist phenomenological and aesthetic agenda into abstract language. It volatilizes the rational premises of the classic art of portraiture based on resemblance and, – just as the symphonic ballet eschews gestural meaning – empties the composition of discursive meaning in favour of pure sound.

Luigi Russolo's Futurist manifesto *The Art of Noise* (1913) broke down the boundaries between denotational and non-denotational aesthetic fields and was arguably at the bottom of Stein's linguistic liberation from signifying. The Futurist ambition to unite music, language, and noise promoted the inclusion of urban and industrial noise in musical compositions,[58] and would provide the backdrop to French filmmaker Jacques Tati's use of speech as mere sound. Tati would mix the voices down and meld the dialogue – both fragmented and multilingual[59] so as to signify nothing (see *Trafic* [1971]) – with the concrete music of his post-synched sound and the plonks and buzzes of our sonic machine environment. I sense a close intermedial analogy between Gallant's oeuvre and the "unsettling detached oddness" (Romney) of Tati. The analogy may seem paradoxical considering the deliberate wordlessness of Tati's aesthetic agenda, or rather his choice to use speech as just another element of

57 See Stein's own reading of "If I Told Him, A Completed Portrait of Picasso" (1924), available online.

58 One can evoke Cocteau, Picasso, and Satie's Cubist ballet *Parade* (1917) and its noise-making instruments (typewriter, milk bottles, and foghorn), George Antheil's *Mechanical Ballet for Pianos, Percussion, and Airplane Engine* (1924), composed to accompany Fernand Léger's experimental film on mechanical technology, *Ballet mécanique* [*The Mechanical Ballet*] (1924). Also notable is Edgard Varèse's *Ionisation* (1931) for a percussion ensemble including sirens (see May), which a critic covering the premiere in Carnegie Hall called "a sock in the jaw" (Staff).

59 Art Buchwald notably provided the fragments of English dialogue for *Playtime.*

modern urban space's white noise, but the filmmaker, who in *Mon Oncle* (1958) makes a gimmicky automatic garage door look like a Venus fly-trap snapping shut, provides a visual key to the narrative sleights-of-hand and tonal shifts with which Gallant destabilizes. The Futurist manifesto also probably triggered Joyce's use of onomatopoeic compressions ("Are you off? Yrfmstbyes. Blmstup") and even noises instead of signifiers: "Will lift your tschink with tschunk. Fff! Oo! ... Rrrpr. Kraa. Kraandl. ... My eppripfftaph. Be pfrwritt" (*Ulysses* 285, 256). I have already evoked how Mavis enjoyed giving voice to Joyce's game-playing, but we shall see further on whether Mavis would find lines which dispense with meaning "a sock in the jaw" or rather "linguistic taradiddles" ("An Introduction" *HT*, xviii).

The border-blurring of musical theatre shows like *Guys and Dolls* (which Mavis saw in London shortly after it premiered in the West End), *Singin' in the Rain*, and *West Side Story* – which built on Massine's way of stylizing movement – was what ballet-lover Mavis found "a sock in the jaw." She found them "new"[60] precisely because they merged drama and music just as they melded song and speech, natural movement and dance. In choreographer Jerome Robbins's cross-cultural but also culture-specific *West Side Story*, his expropriated Capulets and Montagues run, snap their fingers, play ball, fight, and die in back-alleys and vacant lots. While watching the DVDs, Mavis and I would marvel at how one can never isolate the precise moment when the ordinary movements, stretched and amplified, become dance, or when – calling up Louis Armstrong's scat singing – the ordinary speech in the untrained mouths of dancers[61] becomes song.

60 Mavis and I would watch the DVDs of these musicals when diabetes-induced ailments stopped her from leaving her apartment. *Singin' in the Rain*'s double time slot spoke to her. Released in 1952 when the freshly expatriate Gallant was publishing her first stories in *The New Yorker*, it is set in 1927 during the dawn of the sound revolution she had experienced first-hand. The parodic depiction of the birth pains of synchronized sound (which she broached in her fiction, as I shall show), complete with the technological glitches of out-of-sync lines and over-magnified or extraneous noise, always provoked her delight.

61 Those who could both sing and dance often could not act, and vice versa. Natalie Wood playing the role of Maria in Jerome Robbins's film version of *West Side Story* managed to sing only a part of Leonard Bernstein's challenging contrapuntal Alban Berg–like duo with Anita from the Broadway version, "A Boy Like That"/"I Have a Love." Mavis wanted to hear all about the stage revival I attended at the Paris Théâtre du Châtelet in 2012 (choreographed by Joey McKneely, former assistant to Jerome Robbins), and was delighted to learn the whole song had been restored.

beyond our current way of seeing

I have evoked the multiple border-crossings of this book, namely geographical/transnational and interdisciplinary/intermedial. Intermedial dialogues and analogies illuminated by real-life considerations have begun to thread their way through this book and will continue to irrigate this discussion, which dares to question some currently fashionable positions. Touched on in this introductory chapter, the questions which can go against the grain range from an artwork's intrinsic features and its *essence* (whether nebulous, flexible, or less so), to its relations with the general climate, notably the "repository of art" existing at the time of creation or earlier, since art "has no content beyond what art *has been*" (J. Levinson, *Music, Art, & Metaphysics* 7). As Julia Kristeva, too, reminds us, any text – in the broad sense of cultural product – is "the absorption and transformation of another" (*Desire in Language* 66). Seen in this way, the word on Gallant's page is also oriented towards, nourished by, and inseparable from her whole habitat. I investigate how Mavis positions herself with respect to the temperature of life, to intermedial modernist currents which stress process (over product),[62] privilege sound (over sense), foreground craft, and identify writing, like the other arts, as *performance*. I shall show how her art-making is intercultural, transnational, and multifarious, but also profoundly individual and distinctive.

"Is it dead or alive?" This is the question that Gallant used as a yardstick to measure a work of art. What makes her own prose so alive?[63] Can one circumscribe "the inborn vitality and tension of living prose" ("Style" 6) such as hers the way one identifies style in non-verbal fields such as painting and music? Or such as film, which Bresson defines as "a *writing* with images in movement and with sounds" (*Notes* 7)? Is it harder to displace a word to restore its freshness than to displace an eye to "make a portrait jump into life," as Cocteau claims?[64] How does

62 Umberto Eco even designates Joyce's *Finnegans Wake* as one giant metaphor "for the process of unlimited semiosis" (*Role* 70).

63 "It grows like a living thing," Mavis remarked in her 1952 diary about the novel she was working on, which she also referred to as "this bird in my mind" (and which later died on her) ("Hunger Diaries" 51).

64 Interestingly, when Bresson affirms that an "image is comparable to a word in a sentence," he joins Cocteau by observing that "the most commonly employed word, the most worn, when used in the right place, will suddenly take on an extraordinary brilliance" (Bresson xii). The Bressonian principle of non-performance with its hallmark deadpan deliveries ensures that no appended expression should divert us from the word stripped to the bone.

Gallant create this "freshness" and this "extraordinary brilliance"? What are her writerly equivalents of the painterly collision which, in Cocteau's words, "gives the sense of multiview"?

With the issue of "acquisitions" now solidly underpinning my investigation, these are the issues of style which my second chapter tackles and the third develops. I address how Gallant's expert use of language – like that of the Imagists and Vorticists – springs from spoken-tongue yet poetic prose grounded in precision and clarity and *resting on both the eye and the ear.*[65] I argue that Gallant's prose, scannable like verse, is meant for oral delivery, designed to move the audience the better to persuade them. Unusual as it may seem to perform a poetic analysis of prose, I shall analyse how the melodic and rhythmic curves of Gallant's balanced sentences control our reading, organizing the groups of signifying discursive cells in the manner of a musical score. Advancing into critically unexplored territory, I argue that syntax is sense, and that we need to pay attention to *how* we read, not what we read. If we, the audience, operate as interpretive performers lifting the living voice off the page, we gain access to the text's structures of thought and modes of persuasion. I shall also explore Gallant's use of the image – notably the metaphor, agent of both compression and expansion – as the vortex from and through which ideas rush, and through which she moves our gazes beyond our current way of seeing. Image and rhythm were plainly at the heart of both poetic and film theory and practice, as was the perception of the fourth dimension, time. Though he was also a painter who exhibited and a friend of Max Ernst, Bresson declared, "Aim for the audience's ear more than for its eye," and added: "The ear is far more creative than the eye" (*Interviews* 201).

Likewise, Gallant thinks by and through metric organizational principles which I investigate, when focusing on rhetorical figures which generate rhythm and the broader functions these perform. What I identify as Gallant's Cubist Realism and techniques of dissonance and syncopation will be investigated in depth. These rest on a central organizing principle of her vision, irony, which I examine in the process.[66] Convinced that

65 Interestingly, in the controversial (see Hotchner) restored edition of *A Moveable Feast*, we learn from Hemingway's grandson, Sean, that the writer had given his Paris memoirs the tentative title, *The Early Eye and the Ear* (S. Hemingway, "Introduction" 11).

66 W.H. New noted Gallant's "sardonic asperity" as far back as 1980 ("The Art of Haunting Ghosts" 154), but in 1990 Siemerling observed in the Special Gallant issue of *Essays on Canadian Writing* that the writer's irony was still "rarely considered as a central organising principle in her fiction" (135). Almost two decades later, Neil Besner lamented that irony was "a major element that still remains mostly unaddressed in Gallant's work" ("Reading Muir, Asher, and Frazier" 158).

"the function of the ironic trope is to lead to truth through reflection" (Godard 97), I argue that Mavis's vision of the human comedy, often misunderstood, is on the whole simultaneously elevated and comic.[67] Informed by theories of philosophical aesthetics (notably by Nelson Goodman, Arthur Danto, and Jerrold Levinson), my discussion identifies the perceptual substructure which makes Gallant such a remarkable ironist – a substructure I show to be analogous to that of visual artists. My rhetorical microanalyses will draw from a wide array of Gallant's writings, including the critically neglected, recently reissued novels and the earlier stories, many of which were collected for the first time in 2009, about which the two of us had many conversations. The genuinely new attention paid to the formalistic features of Gallant's epistemological and compositional processes will illuminate their common parameters with both visual and sound culture. It will expand the existing critical reality surrounding her oeuvre by lighting up its common parameters with the arts she loved, and by addressing the rhetorical devices she deploys to engineer a fictional world as multidimensional as a Cubist picture, or as a symphony – depending on whether we lean towards the eye or the ear.

67 I situate my standpoint among those (Fürst; Wilde; Hutcheon) who have moved away from seeing irony "as a limited classical rhetorical trope" and treat it as "a vision of life" (Hutcheon, *Irony's Edge* 2).

2
"Is it dead or alive?"

La vraie vie, la vie enfin découverte et éclaircie, la seule vie par conséquent réellement vécue, c'est la littérature.[1]

Marcel Proust, *Le Temps retrouvé* [*Time Regained*] (895)

When all of the elements – images, voices, sounds, silence – find their exact place within the whole, links are revealed between them. It's these links that can make life suddenly irrupt.

Robert Bresson, "The Grail: The Story's Hidden Engine," *Bresson on Bresson* (247)

Like every other form of art, literature is no more and no less than a matter of life and death. The only question worth asking about a story – or a poem, or a piece of sculpture, or a new concert hall – is, "Is it dead or alive"?

Mavis Gallant, "What Is Style?"

Colette glows. Willy is like doused ashes.

Mavis Gallant, "The Pursuit of Pleasure"

In the above epigraph taken from her review of Judith Thurman's biography of Colette,[2] Mavis takes the measure of Colette's style with a yardstick she shares with Proust, as we can also see above, and also with Flaubert before him.[3] Colette's prose is alive; Willy's is dead.

---

1 "Real life, life at long last unveiled and illuminated, thus the only life truly lived, is literature" (my translation).

2 Mavis declared Judith Thurman's 1999 book "a fine and intelligent" biography "in spite of its title": *Secrets of the Flesh* ("Pursuit").

3 Idolized by writers ranging from Willa Cather to Ezra Pound, Nabokov, and Beckett, Flaubert remarked when he praised Jules Michelet for his gift of making things come

The immediate issue at hand is that Colette's first husband, "a literary charlatan known as Willy, took credit for six of her early books" (Gallant, "Pursuit"). Mavis took the trouble to consult a polemical pamphlet in Paris's Bibliothèque Nationale in which Willy attempted to prove he wrote most of Colette's first work. Mavis's judgment, or rather flair, is categorical:

> The examples he gives, comparing their work and style, denounce him on every page. Colette glows. Willy is like doused ashes. ("Pursuit")

The broader issue, then, is that Mavis was able to encompass Colette's thumbprint, in spite of her review's concluding claim that facts "never reveal the source of the river we call genius." Can we in turn encompass what makes up Gallant's thumbprint?

Gallant's shining language: wholeness, harmony, and radiance

Eco's essay, *The Aesthetics of Chaosmos,*[4] has famously addressed Joyce's opus via the dialectic between two world views: medieval and Renaissance thought (and its preoccupation with order and moderation) and the modernist avant-garde (and its fascination with disorder and excess).[5] Joyce spearheaded the international resurgence of interest in Aristotelianism, and, like the two-headed Janus, looked both forward and back. Gallant's oeuvre, too, discloses a mix of opposite poetics, a dialectic of contraries. But unlike Joyce's, the tension is not a question of rules to be followed or broken, for many of Gallant's admirers who are writers themselves have claimed that her stories "follow no formula and obey no laws" (Banks viii). The issue is rather one of inclination and taste. Gallant's poetics or personal artistic program, to borrow Eco's definition,

---

alive, that this was the mark of the chosen few with regard to style. Flaubert's terms were: "ce don de faire *vivre* enfin, qui est la marque des élus en fait de style" (*Oeuvres complètes*). Interestingly, Faulkner, too, addressed the issue of style in such terms, namely that "like anything else to be alive it must be in motion too. If it becomes fixed, then it's dead. ("Faulkner at Virginia").

4 The essay *The Aesthetics of Chaosmos* was first published as the last chapter in Eco's *Opera Aperto* (1962), then dropped from later editions, and published on its own in 1966.

5 Joyce also engages a dialectic between theoretical poetics and creative practice, his work being essentially a discussion of the artistic procedure subtending it – the poetics of itself, as it were. Not so Gallant, whose work is often parodic but so transparent that it never dips into the self-consciousness, even narcissism, of metatextuality (Hutcheon, *Narcissistic Narrative*).

is notably rooted in the *classical* conception of form which Joyce's mouthpiece, Stephen Dedalus – an eponymous avatar of the mythical master craftsman – evokes in *A Portrait of the Artist as a Young Man* (1916). The author's alter ego expounds on the scholastic aesthetic philosophy listing the three qualities or requirements pertaining to the artistic apprehension of universal beauty: *integritas*, *consonantia*, and *claritas*, which Stephen translates as wholeness, harmony, and radiance (Joyce, *Portrait* 192). This clear radiance is consubstantial with the concept of essence, "the scholastic *quidditas*, the *whatness* of a thing" (193).[6] Just so does Gallant's craft serve the exactness of apprehension and representation of humans in their habitat, in all their excesses and folly. It is dedicated to the structural proportion and balance which generate harmony.[7] In turn, the resulting shining language illuminates and outshines reality in alignment with her well-loved Proust's artistic manifesto in *Le Temps retrouvé* [*Time Regained*]. Proust's mouthpiece argues that art allows us to see anew a world which convention and habit have masked. A writer's style – not a technique but a vision – carries a qualitatively different world from the one that shows itself to you or me. Gallant's program – like Proust's – interestingly dovetails with the formalist Viktor Shklovsky's theory of *ostranenie* or defamiliarization, which already concerned itself with a habituation of perception resulting in our seeing an ordinary object "as though it were enveloped in a sack" (Shklovsky 15). Gallant induces a heightened state of perception by transmuting average language into language that is both poetic and transparent.

Unlike Gallant's general approach, the early modernists' appropriation of the estrangement-effect they found and admired in Tolstoy and Chekhov tended to impede clarity. To borrow Bakhtin's term, Joyce's "other-languagedness" (Bakhtin 294), his deformed/reformed language in *Ulysses* and *Finnegans Wake,* makes language *opaque* so as to draw attention away from the story to the language itself. *Ulysses* arrives at cognitive-estrangement by addressing both the acoustic and visual elements composing language, even playing the eye *against* the ear. This is done via graphological torsions which disrupt the smoothly acquired process through which we move from arbitrary (but recognizable) signifiers

6 The Romantics, moreover, had rediscovered Plato – Shelley notably having translated *Symposium* – and transmitted to the early modernists their fascination with the concept of *eidos*, which for the ancient Greeks signified both form and essence.

7 Gallant, wary of excess, is always in absolute control of her language, governed by restraint and homology between form and content. On the occasions when the language or style is at odds with the subject, action, and character, it is, as I shall show, for burlesque ends.

to the signified. While Gallant herself never dislocated standard usage, preferring as we shall see to *wrench through her trademark metaphors* rather than through play with sound and form, she did enjoy Joyce's *metaplasms*, metagrams, and anagrams – all altered configurations that achieve with sound and sight *the torsion that metaphor achieves with imagery*.[8] Rhythm and sonority were so vital to Gallant that one's inner ear can actually hear her voice telling or performing, but she never adhered to strategies drawing readers' attention away from the sense to the sound. She did admire the inventiveness of such tactics in *Ulysses*, from atomization[9] and the notorious seriations[10] to alliterative overkill paired with sense-wrenching rhyme, scrambling, and homophonic (sometimes bilingual) puns. All tend to obey the dynamics of *musication* or imitative harmony, the privileging of the sound patterns of a text over its meaning.[11] Joyce's use of such strategies can be linked to chant, nonsense verse and Dadaism, but also to the Imagist program of treating a signifier as a numinous object in itself (Barbour), and it largely helped to trigger certain transatlantic movements.[12] Many of Gallant's more crafted musical devices dovetail with those of Joyce, whose sound harmonies drew fiction away from narrative towards the pure sound of abstract musical

8 When I first identify the use of a rhetorical device such as the metaplasm (a figure which involves altering a word by adding, deleting, or inverting sounds or letters), I italicize and gloss the term. Further references to the device receive no mark of emphasis.

9 Atomization can involve chopping up a sentence into a series of one-word sentences (*Our. Little. Beggar. Baby.* [*Ulysses* 97]) or even chopping up a word into syllables. It can also involve (rather like a stutter) reduplicating a word's central syllable to foreground its phonemic components (*lugugugubrious* [282]), which amounts to drawing attention away from the sense to the sound.

10 See for instance Bloom's chaotic list of entropic femininity: "She is a hoary pandemonium of ills, enlarged glands, mumps, quinsy, bunions, hay fever, bedsores, ringworm, floating kidney, Derbyshire neck, warts, bilious attacks, gallstones, cold feet, varicose veins" (420).

11 Joyce's heteroglossic transcription of diverse sociolects (heard while moving through a crowd) culminates for instance in a list that seems chaotic and nonsensical: "Beer, beef, business, bibles, bulldogs, battleships, buggery and bishops" (*Ulysses* 421). But the proximal arrangement of lexemes obeys a particular logic – all begin with a B – which invites readerly glee at the resulting levelling equivalences.

12 France in the 1940s and 1950s housed lettrism, an art and literature movement which granted absolute priority to sound. Canada was home to Black Mountain and L=A=N=G=U=A=G=E poets like Bob Perelman, Charles Bernstein, and Susan Howe (who emphasized the arbitrariness of sound, alphabet, syntax, and typographical forms), and then to the performances of sliding syllables and pure utterance of bill bisett, bpNichol, Raoul Duguay, and Penn Kemp.

composition. But as my close readings will show, in spite of gleeful forays into sound-propelled language such as "a kneeling gnat" (*A Fairly Good Time* 196), Gallant radically diverges from Joyce's Dada-rooted aesthetic agenda, which like Stein's privileges sound over sense and engineers textual opacity. Gallant's prosody is a *vehicle* for thought rather than the *object* of thought.

Unlike that of many modernists and postmodernists – from Faulkner, Dos Passos, and Beckett to Derek Walcott and Salman Rushdie – Gallant's style is not at all derivative of Joyce's pyrotechnical language-bending. The articulate Gallant enjoyed the way Joyce invited the text to open its mouth and put its foot in it.[13] But she did not practise Joyce's noises, neologisms, and homophonic wordplay. The bilingual Gallant enjoyed but did not practise Joyce's bilingual puns and other conscious, intentional language hybrids (which Nabokov, too, practised quite outrageously in his first English-language novel, *The Real Life of Sebastian Knight*, and in *Pnin* [1957], and which Beckett also took up and honed), namely the perception of one language by another language, its "illumination by another linguistic consciousness" (Bakhtin 359).[14] What Gallant did practise herself were the unfinished sentence, the unfinished quote, onomastics, parody and pastiche (also Nabokov's ballpark), and playfully concealed intertextuality – all of which will come under scrutiny.

But rather than drawing attention to itself, her prose, as Jack Hodgins remarks, "tends to be transparent" (51). Gallant's translucency may explain a greater affinity with Nabokov than with Joyce, manifest in her review of *Transparent Things*. She notably pays homage to the Russian writer's clarity, equating it with a true love of the English language:

> Love and death, past and present, are one on the other like panes of glass – transparent things. (Is there need to say that every sentence of Mr. Nabokov's is also crystal clear? That if anything is loved in this loveless story it is the English language?) (*Paris Notebooks* 202)

Gallant's own pellucidity actually comprises both acceptations of the term transparent: that of admitting maximum passage of light without

---

13 "Text: open thy mouth and put thy foot in it" is an authorial invocation which follows a syntactical violation in which Joyce has scrambled direct speech (italicized here for clarity) and narration: "*Is that first epistle to the Hebrews*, he asked, as soon as his bottom jaw would let him, *in*?" (*Ulysses* 568, emphasis added).

14 Joyce's "muttoning clouds" (*Ulysses* 223) are derived for instance from the French image "moutonner," which sets up an analogy between drifting white fluffy clouds and a moving herd of sheep.

diffusion or distortion, and that of reflecting light evenly from all surfaces. In his review of *The Cost of Living*, a recent collection of Gallant's stories from the 1950s, the writer Neel Mukherjee called attention to the radiance of her writing, comparing her stories to "little gems, perfectly cut and glittering, whichever way you turn them" (11). He also detected something crucial and radical happening to her writing of the 1960s:

> Gallant's style, always lapidary and luminous, becomes elliptical [...] and she begins to leave out more and more information, concentrating on interiority and the movements of thoughts [...] The sentences pack in more while remaining pellucid but, at the same time, tight with a dozen emotional possibilities. (11)

"the rest is just rice pudding": compression & expansion

Now alongside highly compressed satirical pieces, many of which can be found in *Going Ashore*, Gallant did author a number of stories which are actually novellas and short novels,[15] as well as the two novels I shall discuss, overlooked for half a century. Although it was published a decade later than the "radically compressed" *Green Water, Green Sky* (1959/2016) (Orner, "Introduction" xii), *A Fairly Good Time* (1970/2016) is an exuberantly baroque romp which shows Gallant "at her most experimental and spontaneous" (xi). As Orner goes on to observe in his introduction to the double reprint, *Green Water* is "as desolate as *A Fairly Good Time* is crowded" (xii).[16] While the former is "a spare and undiluted nightmare," the latter is "a messy, anarchic daydream"(xii). It is arguably the only work which "refuses restraint," and in which the writer "almost gleefully luxuriates in digressive opportunities" (xi).[17] "If I can't

15 In *The Cambridge Companion to the Short Story*, Martin Scofield situates the novella form as being between 50 and 150 (4). Gallant's story collection *My Heart Is Broken* contains a hundred-page-long short novel, *Its Image on the Mirror* – the same length as Nabokov's penultimate novel, *Transparent Things*. In his study of Gallant's "three novels," Robertson Davies examines the eighty-five-page-long novella, *The Pegnitz Junction* (1973) alongside *Green Sky* and *Fairly Good Time*. In *From the Fifteenth District* (originally subtitled *A Novella and Eight Short Stories*), the nine-page-long eponymous story cohabits with four roomy ones five times as long. "Virus X" originally stood at sixty-five pages, and as Mavis told Hancock, "Potter" was originally almost of novel length (Gallant in Hancock 49).

16 When quoting from the novel *A Fairly Good Time*, I shall henceforth designate it as *FGT*.

17 Interestingly, Robertson Davies judged all three of her novels to be "classically spare" (69).

laugh, I don't want it," says Shirley, the Mavis-look-alike protagonist for whom – with the exception of love, which needed to be secret, violent, and dark – "everything had to be in primary colors, clear, and on the verge of burlesque" (*FGT* 115). I shall discuss the use of caricature and the burlesque in this byzantine novel, but want to insist on the presence of Gallant's comic vision throughout. Hers is a deadpan, absurdist, rarefied kind of comedy close to Jacques Tati's, based on the acute, detached observation of a cultural hybrid.[18] *A Fairly Good Time*'s spontaneous romp is an exception in scope, however, for as Besner was the first to point out,[19] Gallant cut ruthlessly. She dismissed what she saw as the novel's superfluous stuffing,[20] and she preferred to focus exclusively on numinous moments. More than once in private and then again at a joint reading and discussion with Jhumpa Lahiri in Paris, which I attended, Mavis pointed out that there are only a few turning points in life, and that "the rest is just rice pudding."[21] There certainly was no rice pudding in her stark *Green Water, Green Sky*. When it was first published, *The Saturday Review* marvelled at the "exactness" of her imagery, and at her "astonishing talent for evoking a time and a place by the use of a single, sharp detail" (qtd in Weintraub, *Getting Started* 244).

"No one writes more compactly, more densely, with more compression," affirms Francine Prose in her introduction to Gallant's reissued *Collected Stories* (xiv). Lahiri marvels at Gallant's "uncanny ability to distill" ("Introduction" x), and Manguel calls her stories "masterpieces of rhetorical stinginess" in which "nothing goes to waste in the telling" (xii).

18 Tati (born Tatischeff), like Mavis, who was constantly transplanted, brought an outsider's gaze to his art, with his French mother, Russian father, Italo-Dutch stepmother, and early childhood years in Russia. I surmise that one source of Tati's stylized comic manner may derive from a possible encounter there with the famous Russian clown team Bim and Bom, to whom Beckett gestures in *More Pricks Than Kicks* (1934) and *How It Is* (1962) (notably with his characters Pim and Bom), and to whom Didi and Gogo compare Pozzo and Lucky in an early draft of *Waiting for Godot* (McManus 76).

19 In his pioneering work, *The Light of Imagination* (1988), the first book-length study devoted to Gallant's fiction, Besner imputes the intensity of the writer's prose to "compression and restraint" (5), and compares her "taut sentences" to "Hemingway's terse prose style" (43).

20 Such stuffing arguably went against the grain of *integritas* and *claritas*. Gallant's stance coheres with Edgar Allan Poe's. The first theorist of short story aesthetics observed that the novel deprives itself of "the immense force derivable from *totality*" (qtd in Scofield 32) – arguably another term for wholeness or *integritas*.

21 The issue came up on 19 February 2009 at Odile Hellier's now regrettably closed Village Voice Bookshop, when Lahiri had flown to Paris to interview Mavis for *Granta* (Lahiri, "Useless Chaos").

Robertson Davies, even before Besner, had identified Gallant's signature as "control and economy of means" and an unerring eye for the telling detail (72, 69) – precisely what Ondaatje stresses when he calls attention to how the writer "will have circled a person, captured a voice, revealed a whole manner of life in the way a character avoids an issue or discusses a dress" (x). We are in the presence of a symptom or manifestation of good art, which the philosopher of aesthetics Nelson Goodman identifies as *density*: *syntactic density*, which symbolizes the finest differences, and *semantic density*, which provides symbols for things distinguished by the finest differences (*Worldmaking* 67–8).

To illustrate these notions of density, I can take an example from "The Remission" (1979) in which a dying Englishman, Alec, whose wife, Barbara, has taken a lover, is admitted to a private room in a French Riviera hospital as a concession to his status as owner of a large villa. The "private" room reveals itself to be the place where the staff goes to unwind. "They cleared away the plates and empty wine bottles and swept up most of the crumbs and wheeled a bed in" (*Paris Stories* 218). Gallant's stroke of genius lies in "*most of* the crumbs." It is precisely what the staff does not bother sweeping up which eloquently signifies the general climate of disillusionment generated by a gap between legend and reality. The cook at the villa has departed, taking everything she could lay her hands on; French social security has fined Barbara for not declaring the people she hired. The gardener has also been receiving unemployment benefits, which makes the fine stiffer.

> Rivabella turned out to be just as grim and bossy as England – worse, even, for it kept up a camouflage of wine and sunshine and olive trees and of amiable southern idiots who, if sacked, thought nothing of informing on one. (217)

The sentence above, refracted through Barbara's consciousness, configures the differences between romantic appearance and sordid reality – the "broken blinds and chimney pots" and "dingy shades/In a thousand furnished rooms" which T.S. Eliot evokes in *Preludes* (*Collected Poems* 23). Gallant's sentence also distinguishes the fine line between cheating and being cheated, exploiting and being exploited, depending on whether one's vantage point is English or that of a "southern idiot." Staying with Gallant's humble crumbs, I can also hold up to the light another simple sentence which resonates beyond what is explicitly stated, driven by a rhythm that concludes on a strong masculine ending. In "Forain," Gallant describes the recently deceased writer Adam Tremski, who had owned only one suit and "had shambled around Paris looking as though he slept under restaurant tables, on a bed of cigarette ashes and crumbs" (*Paris Stories* 258). In the ashes and crumbs we find the compression and essence of a human life – redolent of *quidditas*, the substance behind word and thing, with the shadows of Plato and Aristotle on the doorstep.

We also find that uncanny ability to decant at the root of Gallant's gift for metaphor, which will be examined thoroughly as a site of double vision. For our purposes here, I shall merely point readers through two eloquent examples to her numinous metonyms and extended metaphors morphing into unusual conceits. In "Baum, Gabriel, 1935–( )" pure despair is the essence of "empty rooms, letters left behind, cold railway stations washed down with disinfectant, dark glaciers of time" (*Paris Stories* 191).[22] In "Between Zero and One" the narrator on the contrary concretizes one of the periods of "inexplicable grace" when every day "is a new parcel one unwraps, layer on layer of tissue paper covering bits of crystal, scraps of words in a foreign language, pure white stones" (*HT* 285). The ability to distill is also the ground of satire and caricature, both verbal and visual, which involve, as we shall see, paradoxically combining *reduction* on the one hand with *emphasis* on the other.

We encounter yet another apparent paradox in the rhetorical figures above. Gallant condenses, but also expands. Discursive *amplification* is considered the opposite of *condensation* (Greimas 74). But we can actually equate the mounting intensity it engineers – albeit inversely – with the intensity produced by compression. Like condensation, amplification is a valuable tool of *caricature*: both distort the given so as to create an effect. Apart from the extended metaphor alluded to above, the augmentation can be generated through diverse rhetorical devices. Gallant often resorts to *concretization* (often achieved through exemplar and apologue), whose distortions can create comical effects. She also favours *enumeration*, which linguists see as the exposure of the paradigm, outside the function of communication, noteworthy of its capacity to display in a small space. In an early story satirizing a community of British expatriates in the south of Spain, "By the Sea" (1954), Mrs. Parsters has appropriated what she sees as an "English beachhead," for here she has "survived a husband, two dogs, and a war" (*Collected Stories* 203). The middle item of the list trivializes both the first and the last, and discloses the shallowness of the focalizer who grants equal importance to the three. Also set in Spain and published the same year, "Señor Pinedo" depicts a

22 The story was initially part of the collection *From the Fifteenth District* (1979), since reissued (2001), but for readers' convenience I shall avoid dispersing my references whenever possible.

pension in Madrid where the young Mavis stayed, taking the pulse of life under Franco, writing, and pawning her things to buy food. The extract below shows how the chaotic enumeration of belongings engineers a slippage from the concrete to the abstract, producing a faithful portrait of the owners:

> Like many *pensions* in Madrid, the flat had once housed a rich middle-class family. The remnants of the family, Señorita Elvira Gomez and her brother, lived in two cramped rooms off the entrance hall. The rest of the house was stuffed with their possessions – cases of tropical birds, fat brocaded footstools, wardrobes with jutting, treacherous feet. Draperies and muslin blinds maintained the regulation *pension* twilight. (*Collected Stories* 188)

The twilight can be taken metaphorically as well as literally, for the inherited stuffed exotic birds and footstools upholstered with opulent gold and silver-threaded fabric are relics of a vanished colonial way of life, swept away by modernity. In the Pinedos' own room, the more recent accumulation of odds and ends ("trinkets and paperweights shaped like charging bulls or Walt Disney gnomes" [188]) evokes a souvenir stand and bears witness to an Americanized homogenization of culture whose spin-off merchandising equates the traditional rendezvous with death, the bullfight, with the kitsch of cartoon fantasy. Political deflation occurs as well when we are told that a rusty camp stove, a "relic of Señora Pinedo's hearty, marching youth" (188) – ironically equating the ideals of zealous young Fascists with those of folksy Girl Guides – is now used for heating the baby's bottles.

The relation to things is eloquent as well in Gallant's short novel, *Its Image on the Mirror* (1964), whose first-person narrator, Jean, declares she and her younger sister, Isobel (the family favourite), are alike – "our sameness was stamped on our faces and spoke in our breath: Eastern Canadian, Protestant, Anglo-Scot" (*My Heart Is Broken* 88). Imported from another continent, the seed of their characters is marked by the bloom of the Old Country: "the mistrust of pity, the contempt for weakness, the fear of the open heart" (89). Yet the neat, orthogonal Jean warms her regulated life at Isobel's bohemian existence, lived extemporaneously. She comes to Isobel's makeshift apartment to stare at the Matisse drawing torn carelessly from a magazine and pinned to the wall, the ends of cigarettes smoked with strangers, the tulips drooping in a milk bottle. Isobel's careless relation to things, which she accumulates, uses, and discards, is at the opposite pole of Jean's, and the respective enumerations draw up two antithetical portraits. Jean gives an exhaustive enumeration of the things Isobel leaves behind when she changes apartments. Gallant then practises an original form of *preterition*[23] by having Jean draw up a *negative* list which tells us as much, or more, about herself as it does about Isobel:

> She did not keep or collect the odds and ends that seem to me, now, the symbol of women: I mean the chocolate box containing lipstick brushes, hair curlers, imitation pearls, lighters without wicks, a glove, a stamp from Finland. She did not keep buttons, or match folders with something scribbled inside. (93)

Outside the function of plain communication, Isobel's lightness of being floats in the anaphora (the echoed "She did not keep"). So does the narrator's leaden attachment to life's jetsam: the single earring and the left-hand blue suede glove with no mate which Jean cannot throw away. The author reveals even more in the small space of the list. We sense that it is not so much the object of the match folder which counts for Jean as the sentiment which it houses and the connection it provides with a time, a place, a person: the "something scribbled inside."

Isobel's easy-going relation to things is a mirror image of her relation to people. Before she drops family and friends and vanishes to Venezuela, she collects what for 1940s Montreal was an odd, exotic assortment of people: "She knew Greeks, Italians, refugees, Jews; people from the north end of the city who could not pronounce '*th*' and never would" (94), as well as "French Canadians." Jean admits these are not foreign, but qualifies them as "sullen and blasphemous" (94). The enumeration, which the narrator interprets for us (from *could not/never would* to *blasphemous*) exposes the paradigm of Montreal's mid-twentieth-century two solitudes, a pattern which continues to rear its head even in the young.

Thirty years later, "Scarves, Beads, Sandals" (1995), Gallant's last story to be published in *The New Yorker*,[24] depicts Mathilde's new French husband, Alain Poix,[25] working for the Ministry of Culture on the eve of Socialist

---

23 In conventional uses of preterition, something is mentioned via a declaration that it will not be. In the case above, we are equally confronted with a gap between what is revealed and what is omitted.

24 *The New Yorker* did subsequently publish non-fiction pieces of Gallant's. In 2001 Mavis mailed me a copy of the 24/31 December issue in which an extract from her diaries had been published. It engages with "a deep pool of grief" triggered in a Proustian fashion. She sees herself entire at the age of thirteen, still waiting for her absent father to come and claim her, her heart lurching as she hears, "Don't you know he is dead?" (Gallant, "Paris Diary (1992)" 102).

25 Gallant plays with onomastics here, in the best ironic tradition. Alain's surname signifies "pitch" or "tar" and evokes derivatives such as "poisseux" (sticky) and "poisse"

François Mitterrand's victory in the presidential elections of 1981, with its looming turnover in staff. Alain is suspicious of American hegemony (abstract so far) and of how "it encourages well-bred Europeans to eat pizza slices in the street" (now comically concrete) (*Paris Stories* 351). Mathilde boasts to her painter ex-husband, Theo, that Alain has attained an important position "in the cultural apparat" (351), but the narrating instance qualifies this. It concretizes his true status and worth through his office. The room which Mathilde boasts is on the same floor as the minister's and has "part of an eighteenth-century fresco overhead" has actually been divided in two.

> If Alain looks straight up, perhaps to ease a cramp in his neck, he can take in Apollo – just Apollo's head – watching Daphne turn into a laurel tree. Owing to the perspective of the work, Alain has the entire Daphne – roots, bark, and branches, and her small Enlightenment face peering through the leaves. (The person next door has inherited Apollo's torso, dressed in Roman armor, with a short white skirt, and his legs and feet.) (*Paris Stories* 350)[26]

In a hallmark instance of multivocality, Gallant deflates the proud wifely voice by inserting three qualifying parenthetical segments whose situational signs range from the framing commas (the unheroic cramp) and hyphens (Apollo's head only) to the standard graphic brackets (the office mate's torso, ostensibly added as an afterthought). The author also overlays her ironic vision through two enumerations which are actually adjacent assertions highlighting or modifying values. The ekphrastic details of the complete Daphne underline the incompleteness of the decapitated Apollo. They also carry out an amplifying metonymic function serving to connect the concrete (roots, bark, branches) and the abstract underpinning myth (desire, fear, power, magic, metamorphosis). Similarly, the details of the truncated Greek god's accoutrement gleefully reveal a cultural ignorance underlying the intradiegetic viewpoint which could be that of Alain or Mathilde: the "Roman" armour, the "skirt."

"not mad, not drowning, not Ophelia": a poetics of rhythm

I have examined certain figures characterized by accumulation and saturation. But the key device in Gallant's oeuvre which functions within the dynamics of augmentation is rhythm (explored in depth in the

(bad luck). The spurned but still coddled Theo likes to get the name wrong and call Alain by the homonym "Poids" or "Poisse" (349).

26 When quoting from *Paris Stories*, I shall henceforth designate it as *PS*.

following chapter). The writer's hallmark structural rhythm adheres to the symmetrical ternary armature of the universal folk tale foregrounded by Vladimir Propp, which as the poet and cultural theorist Derek Walcott points out, is discernible from the West Indies tales of Br'er Anancy to *King Lear* (24). Gallant's prose keeps the same "digital rhythm" as the tale's satisfying three movements, three acts, three moral revelations, whether it is "the tale of three sons or three bears," and whether it ends tragically or happily ever after (24). In "A Painful Affair" (1981), a satire of both academia and the publishing world, Gallant depicts in 3/4 time, through the viewpoint of a (jealous) French author, Henri Grippes, why Victor Prism, an obscure lecturer from a university in the north of England, has been given preference for a coveted invitation. "Prism's eagerness to get away from England whatever the season [*member-segment one*], his willingness to travel under foul conditions [*member-segment two*], for a trifling sum of money [*interpolated parenthetical phrase in liaison with segment two*], make him a popular feature of subsidized gatherings throughout the Free World [*clausula or final proposition*]" (*Collected Stories* 893). Grippes recalls a previous lecture by Prism which he attended, and the ternary structure conjures up the man entire: "Prism was wearing a green corduroy suit, a canary-yellow V-neck sweater, and a tie that must have been a souvenir of Belfast" (895).

Examples of such deft symmetry abound in Gallant's "Paola and Renata" (1965).[27] Renata, a young Italian woman from a rich family who is about to be engaged, is holidaying with Paola and their two mothers. Renata is urged to swim without a bathing cap so that the sun will lighten her hair: "Renata idly swam on her back with her hair spread and floating, but she was not mad, not drowning, not Ophelia" (*GA* 77). The fast, forward-moving ternary which clinches the balanced binary sentence makes use of the pounding repetition of "not" to both underscore and deflate the young woman's staging of the self. The motif of simulacrum becomes explicit when the girl comes out of the water. We are told that her hairstyle, like the disdainful look on her face, is "copied from a

27 The story, which appeared in *The Southern Review*, was one of the very few *The New Yorker* had declined to publish. Mavis confided to me that the editors had doubted that the textured reality effect coming from "a Canadian of all things" could be based on a genuine knowledge of Italy. But Mavis knew Italy and the Italian mindset intimately. She had travelled there from north to south (and had fallen in love with Florence). In addition, she spent part of each year in the south of France, near the French-Italian border, from where she could hop over to Italy to join friends for lunch or dinner, or to gamble in San Remo.

magazine" (77). But through another ternary clausula[28] whose accentual beats, too, cut to the bone, Gallant reveals that spectacle and representation are the modus operandi of Renata's social habitat. The adolescent has not yet learned "the hard darting glance her mother and Paola's mother could send other women: the measuring regard that ascertained clothes, hands, and weight in carats" (77–8). The ternary rhythms are complete in themselves, but the extract below can initiate reflections on Gallant's Flaubert-like art of grouping them to form harmonious paragraphs in which we *feel* the progression towards the ending. The extract is taken from a story evoked above, "The Remission," in which the young Englishwoman, Barbara, retreats with her three children and dying husband to an out-of-the-way town on the French-Italian border, where the inhabitants speak a Ligurian dialect.

> Barbara expected them to be cunning and droll, which they were, and to steal from her, which they did, and to love her, which they seemed to. Only the children were made uneasy by these strange new adults, so squat and ill-favoured, so quarrelsome and sly, so destructive of nature and pointlessly cruel to animals. But, then, the children had not read much, were unfamiliar with films, and had no legends to guide them. (*PS* 201)

At first glance one notes a series of ternary rhythms – in fact, a ternary series of ternary rhythms. The first sentence actually discloses a duple, intertwined ternary structure in a sort of call-and-response dynamic between Barbara and "they/them." The primary ternary grouping "Barbara expected them: to be/to steal/to love" calls and receives the response "they were/they did/they seemed to." The sentence which follows shifts to a children/adults face-off in which Barbara is replaced by "children" but "they/them" remain. The sentence ends in a mounting progression with a rhythmic group of three linked binaries: "squat/ill-favoured; quarrelsome/sly; destructive/cruel." Rhetoricians identify this climbing figure which our ears perceive as a crescendo as *gradatio,* a system of ordering items that belongs to the figures of replication and augmentation which include metaphor, *metabole*, parenthesis, and enumeration.[29] Clearly one

28 As understood above, a clausula is the final member-segment of a structured sentence (or period).

29 Gallant wields the full range of *gradatio*, namely rhythmic (involving longer and longer clauses), numerical (groups of augmenting syllables or feet), intensive (kin to *metabole*'s group of synonymous terms which escalate in intensity), and referential (also kin to metabole, but resulting in the reader's acceptance of more and more extravagant terms, in the manner of tall-tale humorists).

of Gallant's hallmark features, mounting or descending *gradatio,* generally acts in a snowball manner to engineer a climax. But it can also adopt an *odd man out* approach (with the final term unexpectedly opposing the others in the series) to achieve the punchline of anticlimax or bathos. We can see in the excerpt above how in order to intensify the amplification and mounting intensity, Gallant combines the *gradatio* with a slant metabole. In the first and third groups, she effectively accumulates synonymous terms which attach slightly new content to reinforce the same general notions: "they" are ugly and brutal. The author then follows this second sentence which has opened out onto the local inhabitants with a symmetrically closing ternary rhythm which collapses back onto the children and qualifies their judgment.

3

THE ORATORICAL TRIAD: "LIKE LOOKING INTO THE SUN"[1]

Prose is architecture, not interior decoration.

Ernest Hemingway, *Death in the Afternoon* (168)

The previous chapter has interrogated Gallant's art-making, notably a genius for making people and things "come alive" (Hemingway, *A Moveable Feast* 102). This chapter turns explicitly to her art of rhetoric. It shall engage more closely with the intrinsic features of Gallant's poetics, thrusting towards her personal signature and the complex vision it carries. It turns to the time-honoured triad known to be the basis of fine oratory. I label Gallant's production as oratory in the full, double sense of the term: prose meant for oral delivery, scannable to the ear just like verse, and designed to move the audience the better to persuade. The triad comprises components which I have already associated with Gallant's style, namely *lexicon*, *rhetorical figures*, and *rhythm*. The latter since Plato's *Laws* has been related to dance[2] and of course music – which, founded on a system of mathematical ratios, was closely associated with geometry, proportion, and the spatial sciences. One of the four mathematical arts of the original curriculum at the Academy

1 The quotation is from William Maxwell, Mavis's *New Yorker* fiction editor, namely a tribute to Mavis he inscribed in a copy he sent her of his own story collection *Over the River and Other Stories* (1977). The full dedication reads: "For Mavis, whose stories I think I ought to study in order to learn how it is done, only instead I am just dazzled by them because they are too like looking into the sun."

2 Song and dance were an integral part of the harmony of the cosmos, in which the celestial order was reflected in miniature by the smaller order – arranged into metrical units making up rhythmical patterns. Each of these encapsulated a specific ethos, and served to join together the world-system, analogous to the practice of joinery, which provided the term *armonia* (Michaelides 127ff).

Plato founded, music (and its partner, dance) were seen as the key to understanding the Kosmos. In addition, rhythm, like types of discourse, has been recognized as a strong element of persuasion ever since Socrates asserted in Plato's *Republic* that "rhythm and harmony penetrate deeply into the inmost soul and exercise strongest influence upon it" (Plato, *Republic* III.401a).[3] Prosody is cognition, as Simon Jarvis demonstrated regarding Alexander Pope, that master of homology between ideas and metre. Gallant's metre, too, is not simply a way of thinking about form and balance; it embodies and illuminates the structures of thought. Her metre and thinking coincide.

The oratorical triad, at the heart of the classical precepts on craft handed down by Aristotle, will be addressed fluidly. My discussion of Gallant's lexicon and poetics of rhythm has already quietly begun. Mavis has paid homage to children's books – "picture books, storybooks, then English and American classics" – which were her companions in the strict French-Canadian convent school where she heard no English, and through which she "absorbed once and for all the rhythm of English prose, the order of words in an English sentence" ("Afterword," *PS* 375).[4] The concept of rhythm actually far exceeds common acceptations of an arithmetical organization of beat. As Henri Meschonnic has argued in his seminal but yet untranslated work, rhythm is what lifts the dead word off the page and animates it with *a living voice*. Coupled with ionation, it exposes the discursive subject's body and shifts in gesture, facial expression, attitude, all part of the semantic activity visible in oral delivery. It melds the space-related sense of sight with the time-related sense of hearing to create the full texture of experience (Meschonnic 299). Above all, it creates the multivocal text's *overarching I*, an "I" with a sustained voice, distinctive from the dissimilar voices of the multiple subjects of utterance, which Gallant always gets right. Arguing that the writer thinks by and through metre, this chapter studies the *micro level* of her sentence and sentence groups, as well as her *macro overarching level* of structural and narrative rhythm. My investigation of her metric organizing principles is nourished throughout by analyses of the

3 As translated in Solon Michaelides, *The Music of Ancient Greece*, 110.

4 Mavis and I often evoked together the children's classics we had both loved. Exposing unlimited worlds and narrative tours de force, these ranged from Charles Kingsley's *The Water Babies* (1863), Anna Sewell's *Black Beauty* (1877) – proving that "I" can be a horse – and Louisa May Alcott's *Little Women* (1868) – with its iconoclastic tomboy heroine aspiring to be a writer – to Gene Stratton-Porter's *Freckles* (1904) and *A Girl of the Limberlost* (1909), Frances Hodgson Burnett's *The Secret Garden* and J.M. Barrie's *Peter Pan* (both 1911).

rhetorical figures[5] which generate rhythm and of the broader functions these perform. Close readings of a wide range of Gallant's stories and novels also serve to explore her hallmark tropes or figures of thought, which are principally the metaphor but also its cousins, metonymy, simile, and that favourite device of T.S. Eliot, the conceit. I will follow, in the next chapter, by evoking discursive sleights-of-hand which move in frictional opposition to the poetics of *consonantia* and, like syncopation's change in step, catch the reader off-balance. Such syncopating devices will in turn provide a bridge with the chapter on Gallant's Cubist Realism, which explores their analogies with the Cubist rupture with traditional figuration and spatial perspective.

upstairs & downstairs: the banal & the barbarism

Gallant's style approaches that perfection of diction which Aristotle defined as clarity without banality (*Poetics* 22.1458a 18–31), and which adheres to the aesthetic agendas of fine writers with classical precepts on craft. These are precepts which Flaubert famously practised, advocated in his correspondence,[6] and transmitted to writers from Guy de Maupassant and Anatole France to Hemingway and Nabokov[7] (all of whom Mavis valued). Gallant, too, sets a steady course for clarity, never running aground the double reefs Aristotle apprises of: the banal or pedestrian on the one hand and the barbarism on the other.

Avoiding both the banal and the barbarism[8] entails the "*mot juste*" (Hemingway, *A Moveable Feast* 102, original stress) or right word, the rhythm of natural speech, and an ear for melody. Gallant, whose writing grounded in rhythmically regular and often alliterative metre wants to be read aloud, adheres to the above-mentioned classical features which

5 These include the diverse figures which can be grouped together under the broader rubrics of repetition, parallelism, and counterpoint.

6 Flaubert's voluminous correspondence has been distilled in the recent published collection, *Le gueuloir, perles de correspondances de Gustave Flaubert.*

7 In a 1964 *Life* magazine interview with Jane Howard, Nabokov declared that by the age of fourteen or fifteen he "had read or re-read all Tolstoy in Russian, all Shakespeare in English, and all Flaubert in French" (Nabokov, interview typescript, *Life*). Nabokov, as well as Joyce, undeniably adheres to Flaubert's practice of absolute authorial control of the illocutionary act: both the thought and the phonic/visual phonemic patterns, and, to boot, the caustic irony.

8 Aristotle's ghost would qualify Joyce's program in *Ulysses* and *Finnegans Wake* as a recourse to barbarism, as did Joyce's contemporary, Virginia Woolf, who argued that the writer's business is to see what s/he can do with the English language "as it is" (Woolf, *Collected Essays II*, 249).

correspond to prerequisites advocated by the Imagists and Vorticists – curiously enough, since (post)modernists have been critical of Aristotelian thought based on essential substance. The Imagists' first prerequisite, too, is clarity (via the stripping down of language to its barest essence and the use of the concrete rather than the abstract). Then come rhythm and melody.[9] According to Pound, rhythm is the hardest quality of a writer's style to counterfeit, along with *melopoeia*,[10] which involves factors such as tone, pitch, harmony, and cadence.[11] The final Imagist requisite is the *image as the node from and through which ideas rush*. As my close reading of "The Ice Wagon Going down the Street" will shortly demonstrate, the image as vortex and the direct treatment of the (metaphorical or metonymic) object to suggest an idea or emotion are at the core of Gallant's strategies of distillation – as they are, naturally, at the heart of the cinema which attracted her, and of visual art in general. By wrenching homely objects outside of their ordinary plane – like Tati shooting factory or office workers from above (*Mon Oncle, Playtime*) to produce the effect of an ostrich mating dance – Gallant generates a fraught fusion which modifies how we normally see the world. Her left-field curve of pure compression, the metaphor, moves our minds towards unperceived filiations in a way logical argument never can.

I will come back to the clarity and precision Gallant brought to her writings which set her apart from early modernist writers like Joyce, Faulkner, Stein, and Djuna Barnes, who all practised a pyrotechnical baroquism in their constant search for bizarre words and figures.[12] Now

9 When Proust's young I-Narrator falls under the spell of the fictional writer Bergotte, modelled on Anatole France (Muhlstein) with touches of Pierre Loti and John Ruskin (Tahourdin), he lauds the melodic flow of the prose and the powerful beauty-propelling images (Proust, *Du côté de chez Swann*, 114–15).

10 Gallant's rhythm and melopoeia were infallible for capturing true voices (which she could hear in her head, as we ought), but also for sustaining a *monophonic* presence in the *polyphonic* ensemble.

11 In *The Sacred Wood* T.S. Eliot addresses the issue of acoustic space and the auditory imagination, a feeling for rhythm and syllable which lies below conscious thought and links us to origins. The poet Dennis Lee in a much-cited article defines cadence as a sort of "luminous tumble" that he listens "into" or overhears before any content presents itself: not simply auditory but like "sensing a continuous, changing tremor with one's ear and one's whole body at the same time" as the "press of meaning" teems towards words (34, 48).

12 In Faulkner's previously cited discussion at the University of Virginia, the writer gave his opinion of Joyce as having been "electrocuted by the divine fire." Apparently feeling out-baroqued by the Irish writer, Faulkner qualified his statement, explaining that Joyce "might have been the greatest, but he was electrocuted. He had more talent than he could control" ("Faulkner at Virginia").

without a good share of those curious words and tropes, one can wonder how Gallant achieves Aristotle's clarity without banality. How does she manage to be clear without being commonplace or "mean"[13] (*Poetics* 22.1458a 18–31)? We can look for the answers in the rhythm and rhetorical figures of our triad, which I have already begun to examine.

Gallant's average sentence is sandwiched between one level of increased complexity above it, and two levels of decreasing complexity below. Gallant rarely chooses to go *downstairs to parataxis*, which does away with syntactic relations of subordination and reduces coordination to a minimum – unlike many postmodernists such as Margaret Atwood who adopt it for its truth effect. Gallant never visits the *basement of hyperparataxis*, with its dislocation and dismantled word-sentences so favoured by Joyce for the interior monologues reflecting pre-phasic consciousness. If *our* average sentence inhabits the ground floor, Gallant lives *upstairs*, on the elevated floor or register occupied by hypotaxis. Hypotaxis, widely called the *period*, is structurally more complex, but is not laden with the excessive subordinate clauses which make up *hyper*hypotaxis (at the *top floor*, inhabited by Proust): a register which by definition requires slow, silent reading (and rereading). Gallant is never excessively on either side of common speech. The harmonious, well-articulated periodic discourse she wields is known to be the rhythm of sustained oratory: unlike the highly contrived hyperhypotaxis, it is designed to be *heard*.

Periodic sentences can be ternary like the balanced clauses which connect ideas in "The Remission," examined above. The duple, intertwined ternaries structured in a sort of call-and-response dynamic are deployed with a twist in the story "Baum, Gabriel, 1935–( )." The protagonist, Gabriel, waits for bit parts in a bar alongside a second generation of émigré actors:

> Unlike Gabriel, they had been everywhere – to Brazil, where they could not understand the language, and to New York, where they complained about the climate, and to Israel, where they were disappointed with the food. Now they were in Paris, where they disliked the police. (*From the Fifteenth District* 186; *PS* 179)

Here Gallant intertwines three ternaries. The euphoric set "to Brazil/to New York/to Israel" is paired through the anaphora ("where") with the dysphoric set "could not understand/complained/were disappointed" and

13 I use the term "mean" in its full acceptation. It can occupy a position that is low, i.e., lower than ordinary, or it can point to a median, a middle ground.

the set which simplistically reduces territories to single components (the language, the climate, the food), rejected for their alterity. But the well-rounded period mutates into a square period through the clinching addition of a fourth set ("in Paris"/disliked/police), foregrounding even more the cliché-based point of view adopted by the disgruntled subjects.

My excerpts from "The Remission" and from "Baum, Gabriel" have illustrated Gallant's art of making the parts of a sentence similar in length and form, resulting in a concordant rhythm or balance. They have also shown that periodic sentences often come in groups, and that they are *homologous*: their shape and rhythmic structure highlight their meaning.[14] Periods may also be binary, composed first of a *protasis* or opening topic (the psychological subject of the speech act), which mounts in intonation and unfolding meaning. The protasis is followed by the descending *apodosis*, or psychological predicate, which Gallant likes to use to deflate through a mismatch. In the story "One Morning in June" (1952),[15] a sixteen-year-old American girl, sent to spend a year in Paris, holds the viewpoint. This Barbara makes dutiful notes of monuments such as "the *Gioconda* ('quite small'), and the *Venus de Milo* ('quite big')." She notes "a hotel where Napoleon had stayed as a young man, 'but which we did not really see because it had been pulled down'" (*Cost of Living* 21). Another protasis is followed by a dive into bathos when the teenager explains to a young man who asks her about her father that he was killed when she was seven: "It was right before my birthday, so I couldn't have a party" (31).

In "Baum, Gabriel" the protagonist playing small parts in plays and films can be seen singing the "Internationale" in a checked cap or bringing Seneca the bad news. One summer he acts in Harold Pinter's politically earnest *The Caretaker*, notably in the role of Aston (who, we remember, is brain-damaged and inarticulate), and as the zoo director (who, we remember, appears only in the final scene) in Vladimir Mayakovsky's Futurist anti-bourgeois fantasy, *The Bedbug*. We learn that "these were staged in working-class suburbs the inhabitants of which had left for the Côte d'Azur" (*PS* 184). The mounting protasis and descending apodosis showcase a correspondingly balanced coming and going but do not provide a psychological fit. The homologous overlay of vertical and horizontal

14 Dobozy has identified Gallant's practice of homology in the story "When We Were Nearly Young," namely remarking that the writer's "parsimonious sentences imitate economic poverty" (79).

15 The story, first collected in *The Other Paris*, is then inexplicably titled "One Morning in May" in *The Cost of Living*.

movement – homologous since the stylistic up and down matches the diegetic to-and-fro – pokes gentle fun at the idealistic fad of the 1960s: taking politically engaged plays out of the bourgeois theatres and into the warehouses and factories of the workers. In *The Bedbug*, Mayakovsky playfully posits an equivalence between the *bedbugis normalis* and the *Bourgeoisius vulgaris*.[16] When Gabriel's production is staged in a Paris working-class neighbourhood, then, the irony of the workers' absence during the actors' presence is overset by a second irony: the workers are holidaying in the French Riviera on the same beaches as the *Bourgeoisius vulgaris*. And Gallant does all this in one sentence.

the calf & the ox: comical cleavage

Such balance between expectation and counter-expectation is rife in Gallant's satire of the art world, "Speck's Idea" (1979). The art market has dropped in the economic decline of the late 1970s, art galleries in Paris are folding, and Sandor Speck, an art gallery owner, decides to mop up a few back bills by showing and selling part of his own collection. He stares at a Vlaminck India ink on his desk: "It had been certified genuine by an expert now serving a jail sentence in Zurich" (*PS* 157). The comical cleavage between the opening topic and its predicate engineers a punch line. Although the meaning of the period is complete in itself, Gallant chooses to expand its theme of guile, not to say fraud, in the successive multivocal sentence which ventriloquizes Speck's voice through the jarring verb: "Speck was planning to flog it to one of the ambassadors down the street" (157). One of Gallant's satires of the publishing world, "Forain" (1991), also provides valuable examples of binary periods. Blaise Forain is a publisher struggling to break even through French translations of contemporary East European authors whose names, like those of their characters, "all sounded alike to barbaric Western ears" (*PS* 267). We learn that "At least once a year he committed the near suicide of short stories and poetry" (267). The binary's protasis is followed by a startling apodosis engineered by an incongruous metaphorical substitution. A speech act equating publishing minor genres which do not sell with an act of suicide is, to boot, a self-deprecating in-joke on Gallant's own practice and own risky perspectives.[17] An equally ironic parallelism conveys

16 The argument is that, having gorged on the body of a human, the *bedbugis normalis* falls *under* the bed. Having gorged on all of humanity, the *Bourgeoisius vulgaris* falls *onto* the bed.

17 In the *New York Times* essay mentioned in my introductory chapter, Mavis mockingly points out how the French ignore the short story genre: "In order to encourage a *dying*

Forain's hopes: "Any day now some stumbling tender newborn calf of his could turn into a literary water ox" (267). In such a small space, we encounter a simultaneous repetition and reaction or distance – a Derridean repetition with a difference. The implied authorial voice *differs* from that of her focalizer, and it detaches the signifiers from their signifieds (the calf) and *defers* or reconnects them to others (the ox). Gallant goes on to make another daring political analogy in a binary-crossed period equating the publisher with the Berlin Wall, but countering the equivalence with a pair of antitheses:

> The truth was that the destruction of the Wall – radiant paradigm – had all but demolished Forain. The difference was that Forain could not be hammered to still smaller pieces and sold all over the world. (268)

We can note how extending the metaphor propels the parallelism and antithesis, as does the strong rising metre (two iambs and an anapest) of the clausula: "and SOLD all O-ver the WORLD."

From such a horizontal balance and reversal, it is just a step to the more complex balance of *chiasmus*, that criss-cross order of two pairs of words highlighting a correspondence in meaning. Gallant's chiasma are as tight and compact as those of Pope, who could in one couplet fix more sense than Swift could in six (Swift, "Verses" 382). One can hold up to the light a line already evoked from "In Youth Is Pleasure" regarding the narrator's young, dying father and equally young, unfaithful mother: "*he* was ill and he couldn't hide it; *she* had a lover and didn't try" (*HT* 265, original italics). The author's italicization brings out the criss-crossed pairing of the pronouns he/she and their corresponding verbs (to be/to have) and predicates (couldn't hide/didn't try to hide). The example shows how the rhetorical device shares one feature with parallelism, namely syntactically similar members, and shares another feature with inversion, namely as a figure of *retort*. The structural correspondence foregrounds both equivalence and antithesis, often for ironical purposes, as we can see more plainly in the illustration which follows.

The protagonist of the story "Irina" (1974), who has recently lost her husband, a famous Swiss writer, grants interviews in four languages to literary magazines. Her grown children, who revere their father's work,

---

art in France a short story prize has been established, with hopes of an *oil*-rich cultural exchange. The Prix Transaction will enable its winner to spend a fortnight in Libya, reading aloud from his own works to an audience especially assembled for the purpose" ("A Prix-view").

are proud at the critics' praise of her beauty, but smile condescendingly at their praise of her intelligence, convinced the interviewers had "confused fluency with wit" (*PS* 35). They impute the alleged critical misinterpretation to "her ladylike undereducation, long on languages and bearing, short on history and arithmetic" (35). The syntactic pairing of opposites (long/short) engineers a positive and a negative pole. The positive pole aggregates the fundamentals of knowledge (history/arithmetic) where women are notably absent. The features relegated to the negative pole, which women allegedly inhabit, are superfluities whose mere ornamental nature is underlined by the contiguity suggesting equivalence between languages and good posture. Through a schematic depiction of the young adults' verbal-ideological belief system, a schemata in which meaning is complete in itself, Gallant's free-floating narrator – significantly distanced here – provides a scathing criticism of sexual politics.

Well-rounded periods generally provide Gallant with heightened means of coupling contraries. I have signposted in italics below the layered ternary architecture of such a period so as to highlight its complex choreographed articulations. I have extracted it from the light satire, "A Revised Guide to Paris" (1980), in which the generic tourist in Paris at the end of the day takes the métro back to his hotel:

> With luck, [*1:*] he may be able to see a few rush-hour passengers taken hostage by a gang of *loulous* [*sic*] – sprightly youths from the industrial suburbs – [*supplement belonging to 1*] and [2:] will observe, with unspoken admiration, [*supplement belonging to* 2] the stoic faces of the other voyagers and their entire discretion with regard to their neighbours [*supplement*] as these are knifed or slugged or kicked in the shins, [*supplement*] and [*3:*] the words of Mme. de Sévigné may recur to remind him that "an ounce of minding your own business is worth a ton of mugging any day in the City of Light" [*supplement*]. (*GA* 171)

If we parse and pare away what the tourist-guide narrator passes off as supplementary information, the story segment rests on the three main verbs, to see, to observe, and to recur. But the true essence of meaning is actually displaced to a parallel network *where irony lies*. One sub-network, framed by dashes or by commas, consists of interpolated remarks which insert something of a different nature while pretending it is the same. The second consists of adjunct phrases and clauses intensified by *polysyndeton* (knifed *or* slugged *or* kicked). Both networks dynamite the logic of the main clause they are supposed to reinforce. Above all, for especially relevant to my ongoing argument here, they enter into *ironic dissonance* with the concordant rhythm and jolly tone.

poetic speech & the heard word

Mavis had that sense of sound and ear for words admired by Pound. In addition to the metrical symmetry and syntactical parallelism I have been exploring, we find in her work, as we do in the Imagist and Vorticist poetry which the adolescent Mavis devoured,[18] a lexical precision as sharp as a scalpel – the "*mot juste*" – accompanied by the melodic curve of oral language rising and falling. In his guide to good writing, *A Passion for Narrative*, Jack Hodgins selects a passage from Gallant's autobiographical story "In Youth Is Pleasure" in which the eighteen-year-old narrator, Linnet, leaves New York for her native Montreal with a picnic hamper which is all she has to remember her father by, and in which she stores her scribbled stories, poems, and journals:

> My luggage was a small suitcase and an Edwardian picnic hamper – a preposterous piece of baggage my father had brought from England some twenty years before; it had been with me since childhood, when his death turned my life into a helpless migration. (*HT* 253; *VE* 106)

Hodgins observes how Gallant's judicious choice of the alliterative epithet "preposterous" – instead of a synonym like "silly" – intensifies the cumbersomeness of the thing (52). Since Hodgins has pre-selected a lexical choice from the Linnet Muir story cycle most readers are familiar with,[19] I will pursue the analysis.

My first remark is that Mavis (when talking or writing) tends to use short Anglo-Saxon words rather than long Latinate ones. Her rare choice here of a Latinate four-syllable adjective stands out. It serves to meld form with content, since long words ending in two unstressed syllables contain an inherent comic quality which poets have long harnessed

---

18 Like writers ranging from Nabokov and Teffi (see *Subtly Worded*) to Margaret Atwood and Jane Urquhart, Gallant wrote poetry – but never sent it out for publication – before turning to prose. It remained her habit to read poetry every morning, and she continued to write with a poet's compression and intensity, as well as sensitivity to tone, pitch, and rhythm. The reviewer Nancy Baele confided to close friends of Mavis's, including myself, that when she read Teffi's story "And Time Is No More" she thought of Mavis and would have sent it to her had it been available at the time (email dated 11 August 2017).

19 The six linked stories, which first appeared separately between 1975 and 1978 before being gathered in *Home Truths* in 1981, illustrate how Gallant honed the story cycle the modernists had revived, along with the composite novel (notably with *Green Water, Green Sky*, 1959).

(notably in hudibrastic verse).[20] Gallant furthermore resorts to the artistic indirection which Roland Barthes – actually rehabilitating T.S. Eliot's objective correlative – has identified as the oblique mode of fine writing, which consists of naming *things* so as to suggest *concepts* (*Essais critiques* 232). Like the Katherine Mansfield she admired, and anticipating Margaret Laurence, Alice Munro, Bronwen Wallace, and Carol Shields, who also liked to equate characters with the items to be found in their kitchen drawers, Gallant transforms objects into signs housing an ontological stance.[21] Gallant here has also cunningly deployed melodic factors within the unit "preposterous piece," namely alliteration blended with a multiple consonance which comprises a phonetic web of three plosives (P's) intermeshing with three fricatives (S sounds).[22] The combined harmonics of the oscillating frequencies make the object – linked to memory and its inherent truth ambition (Ricoeur, *Mémoire*) – resonate or tremble more than any concept she could name. The picnic hamper-cum-suitcase brought from England by the young exiled father-to-be and then diverted a second time from its original function is an exemplar of the image as vortex and the direct treatment of the (metonymic) object to suggest an idea or emotion.

Due to the palimpsestic *form* of the story sequence, which superimposes the components of each individual story onto a fuller composite, readers of this passage will transfer the contents of the basket, namely memories of double uprooting, loss, and death onto the other stories of the Linnet Muir cycle, considerably intensified. Just so at our smaller level of form does Gallant's *mot juste* "preposterous" combine its synchronous vibrations with "piece" to charge the image with greater amplitude and higher emotional energy. It oversets onto the mental image of the hamper a trembling image of presence/absence. The image endures because it also resonates acoustically, in both the qualitative and quantitative sense: enriching and intensifying as well as resounding or echoing. The acoustic and the visual work together synergistically, in contrast to

20 An obvious example is T.S. Eliot's "Macavity, Macavity" who "breaks the law of gravity" in his 1939 *Old Possum's Book of Practical Cats* (41), ideal material for Andrew Lloyd Webber's musical comedy *Cats* (1981).

21 See for instance on Shields and Munro my articles "Disappearance and 'the Vision Multiplied': Writing as Performance" and "The Other Side of Dailiness: Alice Munro's Melding of Realism and Romance in *Dance of the Happy Shades*."

22 Alliteration is a strong component of Gallant's musical prose. In "The Ice Wagon Going down the Street," the story on expatriates I examine below, we encounter Agnes's "wet, weeping face" (22); Peter on "the fringe of a fortune," and his children throwing up "the foreign food" (*PS* 28, 26).

Joyce's practice in *Ulysses* and *Finnegans Wake* of playing the eye against the ear.

Gallant's acute lexical precision thus goes beyond the criterion of signifying; it satisfies an authorial demand for melopoeia, via harmony or tune, but also *tempo*. One can remark that the author's words are lifted off the page by a poetic pulse: the rhythmic pattern of two-syllable units or duplets – the ground of our stress-based speech – which cultural conditioning makes us perceive as steady. To avoid a mechanical metronome effect, these are mixed with fast-moving triplets, but both the duplets and the triplets tend to take the strong, end-stopped beat of rising metre – clearly discernible in the phrase I have been focusing on, in which my upper-case signals the strong stresses and my slashes the iambic and anapaestic metric measures:

> a pre-POS/te-rous PIECE/of BAG/gage my FA/ther had BROUGHT/from ENG/land some TWEN/ty YEARS/be-FORE/. (219)

I want to highlight the flexible but conspicuous pattern of stresses and unstresses which can be schematized for clarity as {xxSxxS xSxxS xxSxS xxSxSxS} – in which S represents a stressed syllable and x an unstressed syllable. Gallant's crafted pulsation conjures up the "special prose" Mansfield set out to write, inspired by Baudelaire's prose poems (Kaplan) and perhaps even by the French poet's theorizing. In his introduction to his translation of Edgar Allan Poe, Baudelaire lauded the formal innovations and intensity of the short story genre, and in his introduction to *Le Spleen de Paris*, he stated his desire to create a poetic prose devoid of a rigid rhythm or rhyme, yet musical, suited to the movements of the consciousness. Gallant's supple metric pattern aligns itself with such attempts to extend the boundaries of prose expression, and it calls up Shklovsky's enlightening distinction between prose and poetic speech: "Poetic speech is *formed speech*. Prose is ordinary speech" (20, original stress).

There is nothing ordinary about Gallant's apparently simple speech. To explain how Gallant is great, Adderson points to how she writes sentences like the following:

> At five o'clock the skylight over the stairway and the *blank, black* windows on each of the landings were pitch dark – dark with the season, dark with the cold, dark with the dark air of cities. (*GA* 173; *Cost of Living* 202)

Adderson observes that the sentence's power lies in "simplicity, rhythm, and repetition" (79). I want to look closer at this beautiful opening from

"The Cost of Living" and see why it casts such a spell, or rather *how* it casts a spell through the ear, namely through *phonic tropes*. There are schemes of repetition indeed, and they begin right here with the contiguous, similar sounding *blank/black*. The combined full alliteration [*bl*] and assonance ([*a*] nudges the pairing towards slant rhyme, which is actually produced by an arresting *metaplasm*: a figure which involves altering a word by adding, deleting, or inverting sounds or letters. This particular metaplasm deletes the nasal consonant [*n*] from "blank" with two results. It wrenches the meaning of "blank" towards its *darker* cousin. At the same time, it strengthens the impact of the reduplicated plosive [k] in the pared down "black," which then mutates into the similarly ended "dark." The triple full anaphora ("dark with") is intensified by further reduplication ("dark with the dark air"), while the plosive [*k*] in the reiterated "dark" is taken up and echoed by the consonance of "cold." The discourse, doubled and folded over in this manner, remains suspended, rather like a musical performance's last chord.

A second microanalysis from "The Cost of Living" can serve to buttress my point. When the invalid mother she has cared for in Melbourne dies, and Louise is free at age forty, she joins her younger sister (the narrator) in Paris. She brings an old, heavy boy's bike with her, "thinking that Paris would be an *easy dreamy* city, full of trees and full of time" (*GA* 174). The ear picks up the phonic tropes of hypnotic repetition: assonance and consonance. The close vowel [*i:*] is sounded twice in each successive word, first long then short [*i:zi/dri:mi*]. The repetition of the adjectival phrase (full of) is grammatically useless (for the coordinator "and" would do), but rhetorically powerful, producing an effect of amplification. The anaphora (an attribute of grand style) is intensified by the recurrent fricative [*f*], namely the frictional passage of the expired breath. The echo effect is magnified through the consonance (trees/time), a phonic trope which also heightens the haunting poetic syllepsis yoking the concrete and the abstract.

So we can see that like Flaubert's prose, which the French writer subjected to the ultimate test of the *gueuloir*,[23] Gallant's poetic, formed speech cannot simply be eye-read. It adheres to Douglas Barbour's observations regarding the radical basis of the most exciting contemporary Canadian poetry: "the spoken word, the chanted word, even the screamed word, but always *the heard word*" (30).

---

23 Flaubert famously read his sentences aloud in his *gueuloir* (shouting room) at the top of his voice to test if they sounded right. The practice allowed him to screen out excessive or infelicitous phonemic patterns.

metre and the art of sinking – & rising again

I shall take my vantage point to a higher altitude later on and study the rhythm of Gallant's narrative. At this point I find it valuable to continue my hands-on microanalysis and focus on still critically unexplored territory: the *technique* of the sentence lit up through a poetic analysis of prose. This concerns the rhythm of the sentence, namely the duration of segments of discourse organized into rhythmic groups of weak and strong time, rising and falling. I shall first select for scrutiny the ekphrastic passage I evoked from "In the Tunnel" in which Gallant gives voice to the mute art object, namely Giovanni Canavesio's fifteenth-century Judas Iscariot fresco, in what is known as the Sistine Chapel of the Alps. This, then, is a verbal representation of a graphic representation exemplifying the apex of grotesque realism paradoxically interlocked with devotional meditation. My questions are: *How does Gallant write this visual art?*; How does she write the grotesque realistically embodied by the iconographic figure, which already materially mediates late medieval local, regional, and international conventions? Canavesio's figure is an anatomically realistic hanged man with twisted neck, bulging eyes, and tongue clenched between the teeth, with, to boot, a ripped-open abdomen spilling out his innards along with his soul – a miniature of his ugly self, quickly grabbed by an even uglier, beast-like devil, the very incarnation of the grotesque aesthetic. This Judas is a double whammy, two grotesques in one. It syncretically combines the two biblical versions of the traitor's death: the version in which Judas "hanged himself" (Matthew 27:5 [KJV]), and the one in which "falling headlong, he burst asunder in the midst and all his bowels gushed out" (Acts 1:18). The Italian painter's excruciatingly realistic details manifest a Nordic influence (Borchert). More importantly for my concerns, the fresco, as Véronique Plesch argues, demonstrates a visual rhetoric connected to medieval religious theatre, in turn connected with the medieval art of preaching, grounded in the rules of rhetoric. The fresco's point is to get across a religious message by structuring the audience's experience: showing and dramatizing the price of wickedness in a shockingly brutal, terrifying way. The strategy, then, involves evoking the sublime, or high (the salvation provided by Christ, presented less obliquely in the rest of the Passion cycle) through the low – the traitor's soul singularly expelled not from the noble site of logos, the mouth, as was customary, but from the belly along with the viscera.

The Gallant story's young innocent Canadian focalizer, Sarah, spending the summer on the French Riviera, has suggested the outing to her older, more cynical English expatriate companions. Arriving in the chapel,

The Hanged Judas, part of Giovanni Canavesio's late fifteenth-century fresco cycle of the Passion. Notre-Dame-des-Fontaines Chapel, France.

Sarah sees Roy and Lisbet glance with some "consternation" at "the life of Jesus spread around for anyone to see."

> They would certainly have described themselves as Christians, but they were embarrassed by Christ. They went straight to Judas, who was more reassuring. (*HT* 113)

A glance reveals a metrical and syntactical symmetry. What does the binary architecture articulate around the rhythmically balanced medial pauses or caesuras? Certainly not the equivalences between protasis and apodosis which we expect, but rather inversions or figures of retort. The double cleavage between the opening topics and their predicates is ironic and, yes, comical. These viewers flee the pictures designed to elevate and stimulate devotion, and rush to the picture designed to trigger horror and fear of the abyss. It is useful to recall that both the programmed pity (for the suffering Christ) and the terror (of the fate which awaits the evil-doers Judas exemplifies) are two facets of the sublime. By finding Judas "reassuring" Roy and Lisbet deactivate the painter's sublime. We shall see through their eyes (and Sarah's) what is left:

> Hanged, disembowelled, his stomach and liver exposed to ravens, Judas gave up his soul. His soul was a small naked creature. Perceiving Satan, the creature held out its arms. (113)

The opening sentence of the ekphrasis reveals a metric pattern unusual for Gallant, who generally operates within the iambic rhythm of traditional spoken English. In this case she keeps her steady duple metre but deploys a strong trochaic pattern mixed with the iambs, which I can depict with the following schemata, in which S represents a stressed syllable and x an unstressed syllable. "Hanged, disembowelled, his stomach and liver exposed to ravens, Judas gave up his soul" sounds the way this looks, divided into metrical feet: {S Sx Sx xS xxS xxS xSx Sx xS xS}. The line is headless, so that the stress falls brutally on the key monosyllabic word: hanged. It is followed by the sledgehammer effect of double plosives [d/b] combined with a double trochee (DIS/em BOW/elled). The line continues in steady iambic and anapaestic metre until Judas erupts in a trochee (JU/das), and concludes with the standard iambic rising metre which drives home to the heart of the matter (gaveUP/hisSOUL). We readers can consequently note the remarkable balance of the sentence construction framed by strong stresses on each end, which pairs the physical and the metaphysical. I find it quite a feat on the part of Gallant to write the grotesque, which by definition seeks to destroy harmony and proportion, with such balance.

I also want to call attention to Gallant's rhetorical mastery in the dynamics of *deflation*. Her characters' inversion of the objects of attraction and repulsion mirrors the shift in modern reception regarding pathos (that which moves the public), a shift grounded in the mutation of our Western ideological belief system. The author keeps the graphic exaggerated expressionism of Canavesio's grotesque realism. But through the diffracted vision of her protagonists, she lowers the sublime into the trivial, and moves the aesthetic from the sphere of the unnatural and horrific to that of low burlesque. Gallant writes with the *comic impact of graphic caricature*, reducing (with one quick line) heinous crime and punishment to a parodic, carnivalesque life of the belly. The line in question is a sardonic one pronounced by her lover, Roy: "Now, *that* man must have eaten Sarah's cooking" (113, original stress). One can note the headless line and medial pause which function theatrically, like the raising of the curtain before the clown enters. The core statement's vocabulary and style ("*that* man ... cooking") collide with the elevated subject, as low burlesque should, but Gallant's art of bathos is even more expert. Visualized, its metric pattern looks like this: {Sx Sx Sx Sx Sx}. In other words, the nub of the joke is delivered in pure trochee, which combines the dramatic demonstrative properties of the initial stress with the weak ending of *falling* metre – formally homologous with the fall from high to low.

An equally reader-friendly example from a much-anthologized, much discussed story by Gallant, "The Ice Wagon Going down the Street,"[24] showcases how on the contrary Gallant tends to favour the strong beat of rising metre. She generally deploys trochees sparingly for sentence variety and emphasis, but rarely places them in a concluding position, which the final unstressed syllable would weaken (an effect sought and deployed to advantage in the extract analysed above). In "The Ice Wagon," the feckless Canadian expatriate protagonist Peter Frazier resents a new higher-up who arrives in his office in Geneva. The young and earnest Agnes, who

24 "Ice Wagon" has recently been the subject of controversy, namely as to whether Sadia Shepard's story "Foreign-Returned," published in *The New Yorker* in January 2018, is a plagiarism of or homage to Gallant's 1963 story (see Gavron). Readers can decide for themselves, for Gallant's story, which was first published in *The New Yorker* on 14 December 1963 and was included in two earlier story collections, *My Heart Is Broken* (1964) and *Home Truths* (1981), is now available in the reissued *Home Truths* (2001) and the recent collections *Paris Stories* and *Montreal Stories* (2002), as well as in her *Selected Stories* and now reissued *Collected Stories* (2016).

reminds him of a mole, comes from a Norwegian immigrant family in Saskatchewan,[25] and shows her modest origins through the things she brings with her to the office. These range from a framed university degree she hangs on the wall and her ostentatiously brand-new scarf, shoes, and purse, to the objects she puts on her desk in the absolutely symmetrical, altar-like arrangement Mavis once remarked was favoured by the lower classes. The story's poetic prose displays the same degree of regularity in principal stresses as we find in free verse and song. The accentual contour, namely the use of a rhythmic, quasi-metric measure, particularly rising metre, is evident in the following extract which sketches Agnes's portrait. The method initially follows the traditional convention consisting of moving from the external to the internal. The accumulation of regular measures serves a general pattern which plays with accumulating and stripping away, in turn part of a rhetorical strategy of *Delay*, of suspending, deferring, and metamorphosing meaning. I shall once more capitalize the strong accents to showcase the mix of iambs and anapaests, which two vigorous trochees interrupt.

> Her VOICE/was NA/sal and FLAT/. She had TWO/WORK-ing/COS-tumes/, both DULL/as the WALL/. (*PS* 15)

We can sense that the stress shift to the double trochee "working costumes" avoids monotony and keeps the beat alive; it also underscores a growing reflection on representation and authenticity through overtones of disguise. In the sentences which follow, readers also learn that "She dressed for no one; she dressed for her desk" (15). The rhythmically balanced medial pause or caesura is once more noteworthy. As both metrical boundary and semaphore – lighting up the connectedness of syntax and sense and of formal and intellectual activity – the caesura commands a breath-stoppage interrupting the melodic curve in the manner of the breath marks on wind instrument scores. But while the oboe's resulting musical phrase does not "signify," the textual pause engineers the breath-groups of signifying rhetorical cells. It actually plays out in the scale of the half-line (a-verse plus b-verse) in traditional alliterative verse (Weiskott 46): one idea per half-line, foregrounding complexities which would have been smoothed out by an

25 The choice of place guarantees an instant effect on readers. In an essay on Canadian humour Margaret Atwood pointed out the conventional assumption that there is something intrinsically funny about Saskatchewan, "viewed as overwhelmingly provincial, prohibitively lacking in 'culture'" (Atwood, "What's So Funny?" 182).

orientation towards the line-end. The beat of Gallant's steady duplets and the rapid triplets carries the thought on smoothly as if one were skimming along in a skiff before the wind.[26] But the breathing period, pregnant with pathos, accompanies a fall in intensity in which the weak syllable of "no one" floats suspended, as in music. It floats just like the vantage point oscillating between the scornful protagonist, Peter, and the more benevolent narrator who travels into and out of minds. The breath breaks what could otherwise be an overly regular metrical pattern, as the author drives us to the loveless "desk," a symmetrical substitution for the missing lover. It can be useful here to showcase the metric measures of the full sentence enumerating the objects on display on the desk, evoked above, which continue ontologically the resonance set up by the echoic arrangement of the opening parallelism, "she dressed/she dressed":

> She DRESSed/for NO/one; she DRESSed/for her DESK/, her JAR/of FLOW/ers, her BI/ble, and her/BOX of/KLEEN-ex. (15)

The device of enumeration generally obeys an amplifying metonymic function and serves to expose the paradigm in a small space. The list above clearly serves to equate the owner with her three prized possessions, all the while setting up an ironic internal equivalence among the things themselves. A glance at the rhythmic metrical pattern {xS xS xxS xxS xS xS xxS xxx Sx Sx} reveals a rhetorical function which collaborates with the intonation to mark the boundaries of textual articulations for expressive and interpretive purposes. With a remarkable correspondence between the visual and the acoustic, the iamb opening the segment following "desk" emphasizes the unaesthetic choice of a cheap glass jar (rather than a vase) – a jar which, we have previously been told, occupies the star central position of the desk. The list begins, then, with Gallant's favoured rising metre (namely two iambs and two anapaests, subsequently duplicated), but it continues with a cluster of small note values and concludes on a falling metre, conventionally perceived as weak. Yet the first trochee ("BOX of") attacks with a punch that reinforces the

26 One of Flaubert's definitions of an ideal style is imaged in just such a way: "un style ... qui serait *rythmé comme le vers*, précis comme le langage des sciences, et avec des ondulations, des ronflements de violoncelle, et où *votre pensée enfin voguerait sur des surfaces lisses, comme lorsqu'on file dans un canot avec bon vent arrière*" [a style as rhythmic as verse, as precise as scientific discourse, with the swaying, roaring voice of a cello, on whose shiny surface one's mind can sail as smoothly as a boat with a strong tail-wind] (*Oeuvres complètes et Annexes* 5092).

alliterative link with the word "Bible" to its left on the page. It gleefully mirrors formally our informed spatial image: the box of Kleenex serving as "a *counterpoise* for the Bible on the right" (14) – a balancing act which neutralizes the distinction between two planes: the trivial and the sublime. The similarly plosive attack of the final trochee, "KLEENex," consolidates the comic dynamics of deflation, and the weak ending of the falling metre (which concludes deliberately on an unstressed syllable) empowers a bathos which matches in wit and elegance Alexander Pope's art of sinking.[27]

One of the marks of Gallant's greatness, moreover, is her ability to *sink and rise again.* "Ice Wagon" remains an ideal case study. Francine Prose has dubbed it "Compressed, dense, and beautifully written" ("The Ice Wagon Going down the Street by Mavis Gallant"). I want to take this impressionist view further, much as a music critic takes a musical performance so virtuoso that it looks easy, and shows how it's done. Prose declares Gallant's enigmatic ending to be "mysterious, profound," and "wildly original," and she leaves us to mull this over for ourselves. The profundity of Mavis's vision and the lightness of her hand are manifest in the story's epiphanic disclosures behind apparently pedestrian situations. I shall start by gesturing to the food fraught with socio-cultural frictions. Peter's wife, the Liverpudlian social climber Sheilah, careful not to drop her aitches, has invited Agnes to their house for dinner to sound out her connections. The fancy restaurant food she has ordered to impress her (lobster, kirsch-soaked pastry, wine) appals the young woman from Saskatchewan, who makes do with plain bread and butter, sliced tomatoes, and ginger ale. Peter subsequently has a flash of insight at a high-life costume party[28] where plain vanilla Agnes feels out of place, unlike his beautifully groomed but shallow wife, adept at pretending what she is not.[29] When he helps Agnes home, and her mirror reflects their images together,

---

27 I refer to Pope's own practice, naturally (such as in *Rape of the Lock* [1712], in which he sinks the epic genre), and not to his tongue-in-cheek satire of poets who sink because they don't think (namely his essay "Peri Bathous, Or the Art of Sinking in Poetry" [1727]).

28 The costumed guests Gallant dressed as "*the* ghost, *the* gypsy, *the* Athenian maiden, *the* geisha, *the* Martian, and *the* apache" (21), as the generic definite article underlines, are signs or emblems pointing to the paucity of the human imagination, and are redolent with the modernist preoccupation with the original and the copy, the authentic and the spurious.

29 "I'd be like Agnes if I didn't have Sheila," he thinks (21). Light touches have shown us that Peter, too, is out of place, always on the outside of closed, laughing circles which contain Sheila and men with whom she has private understandings.

Peter's world cracks,[30] and the uncanny emerges from the homely. The sudden thought of careening into a parallel reality with his "shadow self" (Prose, "The Ice Wagon Going down the Street by Mavis Gallant"), living another life stripped of simulacrum, erupts in an oneiric register of cosmic, even apocalyptic, terms:

> He saw floods of seawater moving with perfect punitive justice over reclaimed land; he saw lava covering vineyards and overtaking dogs and stragglers. A bridge over an abyss snapped in two, and the long express train, suddenly V-shaped, floated like snow. (*PS* 24)

The extended metaphors of the phenomenological experience pulsate in an anagogic manner and link up with the core objective correlative, the ice wagon heading down the street, which the young Agnes would get up at dawn to watch alone, in rapt communion with a universe yet unmarred by domestic noise and muddle.

visual overlays: page & screen

For film lovers like Mavis, Agnes's wagon resonates with the translucent overlay of its stylized spectral ancestor in Victor Sjöström's iconic expressionist film *The Phantom Carriage* (1921)[31] – a huge influence on Ingmar Bergman's oeuvre. Suffice it for the moment to note that at readerly first sight the wagon and the dawn (of life, time, rebirth?) clearly embody beginnings or beginning anew, just as the first snow for Peter ("the first clean thing in a dirty year" [*PS* 20]), which he equates with the first day of spring, is a form of beginning again. The visual correlatives of the wagon and the dawn both highlight and counterpoise the Calvinist "ashes in the mouth" which Peter "recognised and tasted" (14) as soon as

30 The mirror, like the eye and the circle, is a transcultural symbol with conventional metaphysical resonances as well as the more recent psychoanalytical ones. The node through which ideas rush in Gallant's short novel *Its Image on the Mirror*, the mirror is a phenomenological image particularly dear to Arthur Schopenhauer and his Kantian preoccupation with the perception/reflection/distortion of the Idea, the eternal, perfect form or essence. Schopenhauer notably calls the pure knowing subject lost in contemplation both "clear eye of the world" and "a clear mirror of the essence of the world" (109).

31 The original title, *Körkarlern*, signifying "wagoner," refers to Death's Driver. Sjöström's carriage of death is notably the ancestor of the hearse that comes for Isak Borg in *Wild Strawberries* (in which Sjöström himself stars), and the Driver inspired Bergman's figure of Death in *The Seventh Seal*.

he saw Agnes's black Bible.[32] The seismic imagery fissures the ideology of predetermined paths and leads to a metaphysically tinted Bergmanesque dénouement and a numinous open ending.

The ending has Peter back where he started. Back in the space (Toronto) and time (the narrative present) of the story's opening, he thinks back to the Agnes he has "lost," and thinks of her ice wagon going down the deserted street. But then, with the abrupt discontinuity of a cinematic jump cut, he "*sees* something he has never seen in his life – a Western town that belongs to Agnes" (28). He sees the whole morning scene, complete with all the sensual details, in the manner of Edmund Husserl's primary memory or retention enabling us to "see" or rather experience the past in a presentative way, rather than through the representative mode of secondary memory.

> Here is Agnes – small, mole-faced, round-shouldered because she has always carried a younger child. She watches the ice wagon and the trail of ice water in a morning invented for her: hers. (28)

Or rather in the manner of modernists like Proust,[33] Faulkner, and Bergman – notably in the uncanny dream sequences of *Wild Strawberries* (1957)[34] – Peter's imagination takes him (and us) back to origins.

> He sees the weak prairie trees and the shadows on the sidewalk. Nothing moves except the shadows and the ice wagon and the changing amber of the child's eyes. The child is Peter. He has seen the grain of the cement sidewalk and the grass in the cracks, and the dust, and the dandelions at the edge of

---

32 Peter is a wastrel and a wastrel's son, who dissipated the hard-earned fortune of his "granite Presbyterian" immigrant forebears from Scotland. The young man was left "the rinds of income, of notions, and the *memories* of ideas" (11). These generate a shock of recognition: upright ethical Agnes, he feels, embodies origins. While he is last in line, she – the one who gets up at dawn – is first. She is "the true heir of the men from Scotland," where he would be if he could "choose his *reincarnation*." She was at the *start*," sent by ghosts to tell him "You can *begin*, but not *begin again*" (14).

33 As Proust's I-narrator remarks in his final volume of *Recherche*, by introducing the past into the present without modifying it, just as it was when it was the present, memory suppresses the dimension of time in which our lives unfold (*Le Temps retrouvé* 422–3). The writer accomplishes the feat by conflating *sensations* and memories (249). One naturally thinks of Proust's opening volume, in which he dips a madeleine into his tea. A feeling of pure joy and of essence or I-ness surges over him at the taste of the blend on his tongue, and out of his teacup arise the solid shapes of the town and gardens of his childhood, complete (*Du coté de chez Swann* 55–8).

34 *Wild Strawberries* was released the same year as *The Seventh Seal*, just a few years before "The Ice Wagon" was first published.

> the road. He is there. He has taken the morning that belongs to Agnes, he is up before the others, and he knows everything. There is nothing he doesn't know. (28)

Gallant translates Peter to another space-time through the device of *anamnesis*, the conjunction of two periods in time in which reminiscences of a past event are substituted for the expression of a present feeling or idea, and which takes the extreme form in which the past events are re-experienced rather than remembered. The hybrid passage mixing narrative scene and descriptive pause – by nature meditative – is drenched with light, just as Bergman shot old Isak Borg's dreams of childhood summers (both metaphors of Arcadia) in poetic black and white and, more specifically, in bright white light on fast, light-sensitive film. Gallant's hypnotic lexical repetitions can be compared to Gunnar Fischer's mesmeric camera style.[35] But they are not alone in producing an incantatory effect designed to engineer a dream-like phenomenological dimension that pulls us up and beyond the external physical world even as it pulls us inward into the psyche. Gallant's rare use here of parataxis and polysyndeton (all the litanic "ands") serve to do so as well, all the while they produce the flow and continuity of experience. In *Wild Strawberries*, Bergman compresses two space-time locations eerily by projecting Borg into his own childhood scenes still anchored in his present septuagenarian body. The uncanny arises from an overlay of a flashback blended with dreamscape onto a natural, realistic setting figuring a subject at once same and other.[36]

Mavis often confronts a younger and older version of one and the same self (more on this in the next chapter), but here careens even more radically into a marvellous parallel universe. For Peter metamorphoses into the child he never was. Plugging into the ancient dream vision convention charged with allegorical undertones, the moment is a Pauline, epiphanic one which transforms "this is *like*" into "this *is*," seen through a glass darkly.[37] The ex-static quality of an eternal "now" is conferred,

---

35 Fischer's mentor was significantly Sjöström's cinematographer Julius Jaenzon, famous for his ability to change modes and moods and to set up a correspondence between landscape and mindscape through an extraordinary use of light and darkness, depth through camera angles, and long-held close-ups.

36 This agenda is manifest in the opening dream sequence (nodding to Murnau's *Nosferatu*) in which Borg encounters a horse-drawn hearse and finds himself being pulled into the coffin by his own dead body.

37 *Through a Glass Darkly* (1961), the first film in Bergman's Silence of God Trilogy, also plays with the Christianized Platonism of I Cor. 13:12, which most famously encapsulates the patristic recourse to Plato's parable of the cave, rendered compatible with the ideology of the Fall.

and the reader, along with the character, "is *there*" (28), transported into what the philosopher Paul Ricoeur terms "l'ek-stase de l'être-là" (*Temps et récit III*, 139), arguably coterminous with Martin Heidegger's *Dasein*, or Being-there, stressing the site for the disclosure of being (*Being and Time*, 1927). It is as if Gallant has her protagonist sidestep Heidegger's world time and accede to *originary temporality*, an inseparable unified whole which cannot be partitioned into the temporal ecstasies of future, past, and present.[38] Interestingly, Mavis herself at times experienced intense flashes of pure being, when the world would become as static as a film still, and – her mind and senses heightened – she would graze an epiphanic breakthrough.

As in Sjöström's *The Phantom Carriage*, a cousin of Charles Dickens's well-loved *A Christmas Carol* (1843), the wagon is a *memento mori:* a reminder of mortality inciting the protagonist to review his life, repent, and begin again. For Peter, after his first epiphany, still as feckless as Sjöström's David Holm, has drifted around the world "picking up microbes and debts, always on the fringe of disaster, the fringe of a fortune" (28). Gallant's dénouement unfolds within the framework of several dominant modalities which imprint the narrative. One can detect the alethic, governed by operators of possibility/impossibility/necessity. The modality is at the heart of modernist preoccupations with the self – free or constituted. These in turn led to the Sartrean existentialist positioning which – borrowing from Heidegger's *Dasein* as potentiality-for-being or *Seinkönnen* – privileges the existence one *constructs* rather than any predetermined essence, and plays down the historically conditioned habitat which limits the space of possibilities, as Gallant does not. An extended metaphor from a later story I have already alluded to, "Baum, Gabriel" encapsulates the fraught existential dynamic in the concrete readymade:

> A woman can always get some practical use out of a torn-up life, Gabriel decided. She likes mending and patching it, making sure the edges are straight ... A man puts on his life ready-made. If it doesn't fit, he will try to exchange it for another. Only a fool of a man will try to adjust the sleeves or move the buttons; he doesn't know how. (*PS* 183)

38 An analogy comes to mind with Janet Frame, that antipodean late modernist who was born the year after Mansfield's death – while Mavis was born a few months before – and who grew up in the shadow of the early modernist trailblazer. Frame's novel *Faces in the Water* (1961), with its predominance of water, glass, and mirror motifs, sets out to deconstruct clocktime, observing that "using tenses to divide time is like making chalk-marks on water" (Frame, *Faces* 35).

Back in "Ice Wagon," one can also note Gallant's use of the epistemic in its Socratic, Scholastic, and transcendental variants. The first, handed down by Plato, holds that morality is an affair of knowledge: Peter sees the good, knows it, and will do it. The second, informed by the Fall, posits that even in the presence of truth the will can fail – as the open ending allows us to suspect it may. The transcendental variant invites the subject to give the whole power of his/her mind to the perception of a natural object, *lose* himself in the object to the point that the perceiver and the perception – Peter and the child – "become one" (Schopenhauer 102). The individual who has "lost himself" in this way becomes "a pure, willess, painless, timeless *subject of knowledge*" (102, original stress): "There is nothing [Peter] doesn't know" (*PS* 28).

an ellipsoidal narrative rhythm through which ideas rush: where import lies

"Ice Wagon" is remarkable for its sinusoidal[39] structural convolutions – namely intermingling and overlapping circles (or more oval ellipses), complete with repetitions, parallelisms, and intersecting flashbacks and flashforwards caught in an unending tension-resolution spiral. Never coming full circle around a single centre, and forever moving towards an end which is always a variation of a beginning, the structural convolutions in turn house ethical convolutions. Since a helix usually pursues a vertical, upward course, Gallant's winding discursive curves lead readers beyond the physical to the metaphysical. They also suggest a roundelay of failures, a circle dance whose steps forward invariably loop back, as we can see in the passage below. It is set the morning after Peter took Agnes home and nothing happened except the metaphorical tsunami, so it precedes the dream vision. But in the author's trademark use of parenthesis (which I highlight), it flashes forward in space-time to after the dream, on (or back) to the beginning's narrative present (also highlighted) and careens back again, framed by a looping ocular reference, the same but not quite:

> [Agnes] put down her hand. There was an expression on her face. *Now she sees me, he thought.* She had never looked at him after the first day. (He has *since* tried to put a name to the look on her face, but how *can* he, *now*, after so many voyages, after Ceylon, and Hong Kong, and Sheilah's nearly leaving him, and [...] the money owed, the rows with hotel managers, the lost and

39 I borrow the term from Eco, *Role of the Reader* 132.

> found steamer trunk, the children throwing up the foreign food?) *She sees me now, he thought.* What does she see? (26, italics added)

The free-floating "What does she see" superimposes two viewpoints and blends two voices, in the manner of an *in-camera double exposure* which superimposes *a base image and its overlay*. As free direct discourse (unlike free indirect speech with its modulation to the preterite), the viewpoint and the interrogation are Peter's, unreported, unmediated, simply there. As an unmediated present free of any formal markers of direct or indirect speech, it overlaps with and turns into a rhetorical question, one of many, emanating from an invisible narrator with her own recognizable voice sustaining an overarching monophony, who abdicates omniscience when convenient.[40] So the double-voiced utterance is also a perlocutionary speech act, pragmatically designed to affect the projected reader and produce a relation of complicity. The amplifying rhetorical list has rendered visible the continental rift which separates Peter from the only other being on earth he – that morning – has quietly shared views with on sublime issues: being and nothingness, choice, guilt, faith, right and wrong.[41] The axiological and deontic modalities unfurl before our eyes just as they do in Shakespeare's *King Lear* and *Hamlet*. What is goodness or badness; are they relative or absolute; what is permissible or reprehensible; are we agents or patients of prohibition and obligation?[42]

Gallant's dénouement dream vision offers Peter a second chance at moral regeneration. But after having appropriated Agnes's morning and

---

40 "But what were they talking about that day, so quietly, such old friends?" the narrator wonders. She gives us some answers, only to reiterate in a feather-stitching fashion ("What did she see when she looked at him?") and then abdicate knowledge and sidestep: "God knows what they were telling each other. Anyway, nothing happened" (27). The sidestepping is structurally ironic, as Mavis is never interested in event, but in consciousness and mood.

41 Agnes, taught all her life to respect the educated, was so violently disabused at the party by the dissipated behaviour of those "worse than pigs" because they "*know* what [they're] doing" (26) that she contemplated ending it all – held back only by ethics and empathy: the fear that Peter might have been blamed, or might have blamed himself for her suicide.

42 "Wisdom and goodness to the vile seem vile; / Filths savour but themselves," Albany tells Lear's daughter, Goneril (*King Lear* IV.ii.38–9), and Agnes would have agreed. But the narrative consciousness in "Ice Wagon" seems closer to the less value-laden statement, "There is nothing either good or bad, but thinking makes it so" (*Hamlet* II.ii.255).

grazed the transcendence of revealed knowledge (the spirit, we know, is willing), Peter draws back (the flesh, we know, is weak):

> He could keep the morning if he wanted to, but what can Peter do with the start of a summer day? Sheilah is here, it is a true Sunday morning, with its dimness and headache and remorse and regrets, and this is life. He says, "We have the Balenciaga." (28)

The Balenciaga dress is a semaphore of illusion/self-delusion which counterpoises the ice wagon, semaphore of revealed truth. Bought in Paris with the last scraps of Peter's squandered inheritance, the haute-couture dress is a "talisman" (6) for the Fraziers of a Paris Paradise Lost. That it is outmoded and soiled by Sheilah's smeared-on make-up makes Peter's declaration superbly bathetic.[43] Building up to the ironic climax is the tiered perspective (overlapping internal and external) of the rhetorical question, and of the declarative "Sheilah is here" – euphoric for Peter, dysphoric for the narrator and the reader.[44] Gallant ends with a trademark anti-closural strategy which suspends resolution and opens out by both doubling back and sidestepping:

> Let Agnes have the start of the day. Let Agnes think it was invented for her. Who wants to be alone in the universe? No, begin at the beginning: Peter lost Agnes. Agnes says to herself, somewhere, Peter is lost. (28)

The care lavished on the final clausula[45] is evident from the viewpoint of rhythm and cadence or fall of voice. The penultimate sentence ending in falling metre leads to a short minor cadence with a final masculine ending, the voice dropping on the one last stressed syllable: "lost." In addition, the focalizer's final defiant rhetorical question, "Who wants ..." sliding into the narrator's injunction, "No, begin at the beginning," displays techniques which will be examined closely. These are Gallant's multivocality and multiview – viewing characters from the inside and the

---

43 A further irony is that Cristobal Balenciaga was a Spanish fashion designer, and that even after he left Madrid for Paris in the late 1930s his designs were inspired by Velázquez portraits or traditional toreador costumes.

44 Readers will remember that Sheilah has a tendency to confer her favours elsewhere (implicit), and has been on the verge of leaving Peter in the past (explicit).

45 A clausula by strict definition is the final member-segment of a structured sentence or period. But in "Clausules," his study of the poetics of narrative closure, Philippe Hamon proposes the finale of a work as a looser definition (509).

outside simultaneously or in quick succession, analogous to the cinematic technique of *eyeliner matching*.[46] Gallant's extra-cranial shifts – when she flits in and out of heads – arguably prolong both dream visions' climate of muted strangeness – a climate novelist Michael Helm describes as "the low heat of an altering force seen there in the bubble and pock." So when Adam Mars Jones objects to Gallant's "drifting between consciousnesses," which makes him as a reader feel "trapped in a dream where every room opens onto another one and there's no sense of home," we can point out that this is precisely the author's intention. It is an intention with a purpose. As I shall demonstrate in the following chapter, *Gallant's multiview locks into the Cubists' agenda* of multiplying viewpoints and depicting objects on the picture plane as if all its facets were visible at the same time – notably combining the horizon of the viewer with the horizon of the object. It is far from being a mere conceptual technique.

Descent dynamics in the "Ice Wagon" passage under scrutiny thus overlap in winding curves which, like a helix, also pursue a vertical upward course, interrogating existential ethical issues and the construction of the self. The concerns are distilled into the *acoustic* leitmotifs and variations which echo beyond the ending (begin, lost), and into the story's central *visual* image. The image of the wagon, the node from and through which ideas rush (and where import lies), is notably freighted with the accumulated meanings of the *topos* which even readers unfamiliar with classic films have been "'programmed' to borrow from the treasury of intertextuality" (Eco, *Role* 21). *The Phantom Carriage* and its source, a novel by Nobel Prize–winner Selma Lagerlöf, both borrowed from the same folklore that generated the variants of the ghost ship, the Flying Dutchman, ranging from Coleridge's *The Rime of the Ancient Mariner* (1798) to Richard Wagner's opera *The Flying Dutchman* (1843), based in turn on Heinrich Heine's retelling of the legend. So readers can pick up from a storage of intertextual competence involving the recognition of *topoi*.

Related *topoi* that roil under the surface of Gallant's seemingly realist story are the parallel dimensions or overlapping worlds manifest in Henry James's "The Jolly Corner" (1908). James's uncanny story conjures up the protagonist's unlived life – the one which would have been actualized if Spencer Brydon had not gone to live abroad, just as Peter's unlived life is the virtual one shared with Agnes, a life of rectitude, belief in work, faith in undertakings, and "the bread of the black Sunday" (14).

---

46 Eyeliner matching, which Bergman practises extensively, involves cutting from a character looking off-screen (at a certain angle) to the focus of his/her gaze (from that same angle, namely her eyeliner), as if the viewer is seeing through the eyes of the character.

Like the dim corridors and shuttered rooms inhabited by a ghostly alternative self which Brydon is determined to confront,[47] the image of the ice wagon going down the street, a threshold point gesturing to a junction pregnant with possibilities, joins with Peter's abdicating imperative "Let Agnes have the start of the day," to nod to Robert Frost's "The Road Not Taken" (whose simplicity and insight Mavis valued).[48]

But Gallant does it the Cubist way, showing the multiple, mutually exclusive roads simultaneously. The writer's visual and acoustic motifs haunted by digested and displaced intertexts make up an anachronous ellipsoidal twisting of numinous moments which concords with the timeless mythic mode setting up contemplation. The contemplative mood which augments in the enigmatic but replete ending is not dependent on the Judaeo-Christian resonances threading through the narrative, supported by the onomastics of a Peter denying the incarnated *Agnus Dei.* The tone connects equally with notions of the self, of rediscovery and return in Eastern cosmologies and their derivative, theosophy, and it oscillates between Sartrean existential positioning and the Idealist currents of thought which so attracted the modernists. (One can evoke Beckett's preoccupation with the disintegrating relations between subject and object in his 1930s Trilogy and in *Watt*, written circa 1943 but published a decade later.) Gallant's ending quietly engages with Kant's influential synthesis of the manifold – developed notably by Schopenhauer – which posits that the mind makes connections among its multiple sense-experiences of phenomena to engineer a coherent representation, but that the world can be known only so far as it corresponds to the forms of time and space, which determine, and limit, the use of the senses (Kant, *Critique of Pure Reason* [1781]).[49] I shall come back to the concept in my next chapter on Gallant's Cubist Realism, but want to underline here to what extent "Ice Wagon" is suffused with a Kantian inner/outer isotopy implying that

47 The alethic and epistemic modalities govern James's story, whose protagonist "wanted to know himself." The supernatural encounter made Brydon swoon or die (and be brought back to life in the mode of folk tales, with a kiss – which never occurs between Peter and Agnes), and in either eventuality "brought him to knowledge" ("Jolly Corner" 233) and made him wiser.

48 When Mavis lost her sight, I was one of the close friends who would read to her. When her strength no longer allowed her to follow sustained narratives, the poet Marilyn Hacker and I naturally turned to her poetry collection. Frost, Keats, Emily Dickinson, and Wislawa Szymborska (whose work she prized well before the Nobel Committee discovered her in 1996) were among the favourites Mavis asked for.

49 Shelley, read religiously till the mid-twentieth-century, had also declared in his Idealist manifesto, *A Defence of Poetry*, that "All things exist as they are perceived; at least in relation to the percipient" (1085).

reality is a mental, culturally conditioned construct, a mindscape or representation.[50] Gallant's text collapses distinctions between the empirical, external, recognizable public world and the inner mental private space of the mind/the mind's eye. Out and in are one territory. I suggest that Gallant's "Ice Wagon" ending is so undefinable yet replete because it melds ethics with aesthetics and merges the metatextual and the philosophical.

By ending with "No, begin at the beginning," Gallant's fiction doubles back on itself and formally questions the origins of the artistic process as well as the byzantine intricacies of knowledge and truth. Orner has observed that for Gallant, "the business of having to begin again, to quote the title of one of her most magnificent longer stories, is 'the cost of living'" ("Introduction" xi). In the eponymous story Orner alludes to, published in *The New Yorker* in 1962, one year before "Ice Wagon," one can indeed remark an analogous poetic. "The Cost of Living," which Mavis's editor William Maxwell compared to a prism, keeps spiralling back to the opening line, and each time we know more. In the opening sentence the first-person narrator announces a first time: "Louise, my sister, talked to Sylvie Laval for the first time on the stairs of our hotel on a winter afternoon" (*GA* 173). The second time the first time comes up, the story unfurls further and introduces perspective: "That winter's day when Sylvie talked to Louise for the first time, Louise was guiding her bicycle down the stairs" (176). The third time the first time comes up, it is preceded by words from someone else's mouth, and we find ourselves not only back to the beginning, but back beyond the beginning:

> "COULD YOU LET ME HAVE SOME MONEY?"
>
> That was the first time Sylvie talked to Louise. Those were Sylvie's first words, on the winter afternoon, on the dark stairs. The girl was around the bend of a landing, looking down. Louise stopped, propping the bicycle on the wall, and stared up. Sylvie leaned into the stair well so that the dead light from the skylight was behind her. (182, original capitals)

Beginning again once again, Gallant delineates the scene more precisely, temporally, spatially, and axiologically. The subject situated at the bend of a landing, looking down, has already been observed by a painterly eye in such a peripheral position, in addition broken up like the preparatory sketches of a nude. Sylvie has already been arrested in a pose,

---

50 It can be enlightening to keep in mind that the French translation of *The World as Will and Idea* (1818), Schopenhauer's appropriation of Kant's concept, is entitled *Le Monde comme volonté et comme représentation.*

hanging over the bannister calling to someone below, the eye noting "the tensed muscle of an arm or a leg, the young neck, the impertinent head" (177). Sylvie is not just compared to a Degas dancer, she *becomes* a Degas dancer through the powerful transforming dynamic of the metaphor, which places Sylvie and the dancer in the same distributional slot: "Sylvie *was* the coarse and grubby Degas dancer" (177). This overlay of pictorial subject on textual subject seems to argue the superiority of one medium over the other, namely the text, which can and does depict the subject in movement and even provide "the voice you imagine belonging to the picture" (177). On an even higher plane, I once more ask the question I put forward in my first chapter: *why* Degas? I argue a convergence in practice, namely that Gallant's textual scene is *the verbal variant of Degas's transgressive canvas composition*, namely a woman placed near the edge of the picture, looking out of it, in essence offering viewers a new experience of seeing. Homing in on questions of narrative perspective, namely "the girl around the bend of the landing, looking down" – by which we infer seen from below – can light up how Gallant formally fits with the decentred figures and oblique, high- or low-angle vantage points with which Degas had challenged traditional Western visual perspective.

I find it valuable to pursue the above extract's design and organization of experience and their fit with the visual arts, and I shall return to this passage in my next chapter on dissonance and syncopation. Here I note that, as if she were providing readers with the accumulative structure of seeing, Gallant zooms out with a painter's or filmmaker's eye to provide an expanded perspective. She notably builds on the till-now absent vantage point which gives Sylvie the advantages of light and angle. The narrator, part and parcel of the story, omits what is outside of the deliberately restricted frame, as if she initially chose to wear blinkers. She describes the scene in which Sylvie asks Louise (a complete stranger) for money, in the vivid manner of *hypotyposis* (which renders a scene as visible as a picture). But the vantage point on the stairs is at first absent. It is clarified as the perspective expands in a *cinematic zoom shot* (in which the lens is adjusted while the camera – in this case our narrator's gaze – stays put). The narrator progressively appends the key segments missing from the initial restricted frame offered us: the frame of origins from which the story, the encounters, and the climate unfold.

The passage showcases how, in congruence with the tenets of modernism, Gallant privileges the pictorial (hypotyposis) over the verbal (namely realist sustained dialogue), and synchronic moment over diachronic sequence. Her agenda involves a transmutation of strategies of fragmentation and accumulation from *a nondenotational visual* medium (devoid of temporal notions) to a *denotational literary* medium (in which time has always been the nerve centre). By appending a till-now missing segment anterior to the beginning – a stranger directly accosting Louise for money – Gallant notably adds consecutiveness. More importantly, she adds depth via alethic, deontic, and axiological considerations. These are questions of choice, need, and necessity, the permissible and the reprehensible – analogous to the "work and debt and obligation" which make up the world view of Agnes and her "white-hot Protestants" in "Ice Wagon" (*PS* 12). We learn in "Cost of Living" that "giving money away to strangers was not the habit" (182) of the narrator's middle-aged sister, who wrote all her expenditures down in an account book containing two columns: Necessary and Unnecessary. Was Sylvie right to ask? Should ethical, thrifty Louise "put her hand in her pocket" for someone "who had no claim on her at all"? Will she choose to oblige? If she does, in which column should/will she record the expense?[51] The choice of a first-person narrator with, by definition, insider but limited knowledge and a spontaneous storytelling style which spirals back and keeps spiralling ahead, allows the author to send us readers back and forth like rats in a maze, as seen in works from Laurence Sterne's *Tristram Shandy* (1760), which writes beyond the beginning,[52] to Nabokov's *Pale Fire* (1962) and its obsessed narrator/editor-cum-commentator Charles Kinbote.

The narrator of "Ice Wagon" is an omniscient one, unlike "The Cost of Living"'s first-person intradiegetic narrator, who is part and parcel of the story, and who chooses to disclose or reveal what she sees and knows. Yet "Ice Wagon"'s self-conscious narratorial intrusion, "No, begin at the beginning," similarly proclaims the artist's control of his/her material. As do the still lifes of modernist and postmodern painters ranging from Chaïm Soutine to Francis Bacon,[53] Gallant's stories commingle the physical and

51 Louise does give, and keeps on giving, from petticoats and dentist bills to a costly necklace which she marks under "Necessary" for a fifth of the true price. The giving entails cheating to absorb the balance in the rest of her accounts: "She charged herself an imaginary thousand francs for a sandwich and two thousand for a bunch of daisies, and inflated the cost of living until the cost of the necklace had disappeared" (192).

52 Sterne's narrator defies Horace's advice to begin *in medias res*, and decides to relate a juicy episode predating the beginning of the story proper. He playfully suggests that readers who wish to may skip the rest of the chapter beyond the door – which the visual layout outlines typographically (12).

53 Soutine's *Le Boeuf écorché* [*Carcass of Beef*] (1924) and Bacon's *Crucifixion* (1965) represent objects of the real world and critique their contemporary habitat (notably the carnage of the world wars), but retain and nod to the numinous resonances of the biblical/mythical overtones of their predecessors – notably Rembrandt's *Flayed Ox* (1657) and both Pieter Aertsen's and Joachim Bueckelaer's *Meat Stall* and *Butcher Shop* (1551 and 1568 respectively), which humbly suggest a Crucifixion connection – to question an existence in which man has become meat.

the metaphysical, all the while addressing their own medium. Alongside this metatextual plane, the injunction to begin at the beginning also functions on a generic plane. It posits that not only is a story never really completed, but that it never really starts. It is always a continuation of another story, fitting into a network of *intertexts* whose pre-existing patterns of thought, motif, and form serve to engender and prolong.[54]

The notion of beginnings fraught with the tension between past and future and connecting old and new was part of Mavis's DNA. This is manifest in the extract below, taken from a letter she sent me (along with two of her well-loved books) following a particularly meaningful get-together. The lines she quotes by the Polish poet Wislawa Szymborska (namely the stanza closing the poem "Love at First Sight") and the fact that she knew them by heart are what light up her work here.

Paris, Sunday, 1 September (2002)[55]

Dear Marta,
After I got home last Friday a scrap of poetry kept running through my head: "Every beginning after all / is nothing but a sequel / and the book of events / is always open in the middle," but I couldn't for the life of me remember the name of the poet or the first line of the poem. So instead of going straight to bed I began to put into some sort of order my messy poetry shelves,[56] *thinking the poem would just emerge. By the time I got*

54 Postmodern writers would intensify such metatextual interrogations, at times resonating with ontological overtones. In Margaret Atwood's *The Handmaid's Tale*, for instance, the ending is ingeniously suppressed by equating it in multiple ways with a new beginning. The end of what we are to learn is a framed tale opens out onto the virtual beginning of a new story. An open-ended structure leaves the story on a deliberately inconclusive note: "Whether this is my end or a new beginning I have no way of knowing (...) I step up, into the darkness within; or else the light" (307).

55 The year is unmarked (as was sometimes the case when Mavis had sent a note or card shortly before), but the letter arrived after a belated 2002 mutual birthday dinner together in which we talked about my new relationship and future wedding (as a mother with grown children). The note was nestled in a package containing two books from her shelves, a French translation of Joseph Roth's iconic *Hotel Savoy* for my new partner, Patrick, and for me the new English translation of the Szymborska poetry selection, *Miracle Fair*, from which she quotes.

56 I have already mentioned that Mavis had begun by writing poetry and continued to read poetry (usually in the morning), facts clearly connected to the compression and intensity of her writing, as well as her sensitivity to tone and rhythm. I share this letter's particular detail with readers to show that the way Mavis had organized her library pointed to the very special status she continued to grant poetry. She generally

down to the letter S I knew it had to be Szymborska. (You will find it on p. 30.) The volume is in good condition simply because I already had most of the poems in other editions. I wonder what she (Szymborska) thought of Norton's putting a Russian painting on the jacket. It takes an American publisher to think that any Slav is any Slav.[57] (...)

Love,
Mavis

I shall come back to Mavis's dialogue with Szymborska's closure (in chapter 5), but for the moment will focus on pre-closure and absence of closure. Breaking beyond our recognizable historical, spatial, and temporal axes, "Ice Wagon"'s pre-closure – the point where the text "*could* end" (Lohafer 3) – allows us to recognize its "narrative wholeness," which short story theoretician Susan Lohafer calls "storyness" (3). Both its pre-closure and its absence of closure show the primacy of narrative as a method of understanding, and show "storying" to be "one of the elemental cognitive processes that make experience intelligible" (3). Mavis sets out to transcend through the imagination our understanding of the nature of society, of the human mind, of the world, and of knowledge itself. Science grounded in reason and consequence can never attain a final goal, the truth, Schopenhauer has famously argued. But the powers of the imagination extend the artist's horizon "far beyond the limits of his actual personal experience, and thus enable him to construct the rest of the picture out of the little that comes into his own actual apperception" (110). The isolated minute detail "becomes for art, a representative of the whole, an equivalent of the endless multitude in space and time" (108). While Ricoeur sees stories as configurations which confer a retrospective vision and articulate an understanding of human time (*Temps et récit I*, 130–1), Schopenhauer argues that all great art removes us from the stream of the world's course and "stops the wheel of time" so as to apprehend "the essential, the Idea" (108).[58]

Gallant's story "Irina" contains a phenomenological quest which addresses such immanence. Objects tremble, and the writer, along with her

filed her books alphabetically, regardless of the genre, period, or author's nationality, but she kept her poetry collection grouped in a separate section of shelves in her entrance hall.

57 I shall return to this valuable comment which showcases Mavis's keen eye for fine distinctions (in this case political) – distinctions which often escape even professionals, in this case editors and book cover designers.

58 Specialists of closural theories such as John Gerlach, Frank Kermode, Michael Trussler, and Lohafer could undoubtedly discuss "Ice Wagon's" dénouement structurally from different angles.

elderly mouthpiece, pushes language to its limits, beyond what words can designate, to Being itself. Using letter writing as is her wont to move in and out of minds (and also to establish immediacy and a truth effect), Gallant has recently widowed Irina write a letter to a favourite son. She confides she is "homesick," not for a place but for a time – childhood, when "nothing had crystallised and mistakes were allowed" (*PS* 36). At present, in old age, she ponders the visible and invisible:

> Every thought had a long meaning; every motive had angles and corners, and could be measured. And yet whatever she saw and thought and attempted was still fluid and vague. The shape of a table against afternoon light still held a mystery, awaited a final explanation. You looked for clarity ... and the answer you had was paleness, the flat white cast that a snowy sky throws across a room. (36)

The motive with measurable corners opens a succession of conceits which surreptitiously slip beyond subjective perception and suspend the referential functions of language. The form or essence of the table seen as a question sets up a state of contemplation in which epiphanies occur. Gallant the ironist naturally sees to it that Irina's meditation on this life and a possible one beyond – the neoplatonic paleness – are misunderstood. The son, a banker, "told his wife what he thought [the letter] contained, and she told a sister-in-law what she thought he had said" (37). They send Irina their little boy as a pet, having concluded that she craves

> a symbol of innocent, continuing life. An animal might do it. Better still, a child. (37)

Part of an overarching narrative consciousness, the rhetorical punchline, engineered by the clausula consisting of a nominal sentence and clinching masculine ending, underlines a double irony: equating a child with a poodle, and reducing a metaphysical yearning to a desire for a pet. The ironic edge is aimed at what Bakhtin terms "the common view": society's normative approach to people and things, "the *going point of view* and the going *value*" (301–2, original stresses).

The novel *Green Water, Green Sky* also interrogates the going point of view and the going value, and grapples even more clearly with *essentialism and the perceiving subject*. The symbolic dimension subtending the surface of events invites reflection on the way the history of thought from Darwin to Sartre has dismantled the neoplatonic myth of the idea. Right from the opening pages, the novel engages not with event but with the human brain, and investigates the problematic relations of the self with a mentally constructed and culturally conditioned reality. As in many modernist works preoccupied by the relations between the original and the replica, the genuine and the spurious, neoplatonic motifs point to a world of appearance dependent on the vantage points of inner consciousness and body: the rotting vegetables floating in Venice's Grand Canal, "black under water, green above" (1), the overlay of two disparate memories placed "one on the other, glass over glass" (7) like "water under sky," one "reflecting the other" (19). Although Mavis herself had not read Frame until I gave her a copy of *The Lagoon* in 2011, her images dialogue with Frame's *The Lagoon and Other Stories* (1951) and *Faces in the Water* (1961), which also interrogate the relations between the percipient and the perceived, at times through an explicit intertextual nod.[59] As in Frame's ventriloquistic takeover of Matthew Arnold's waterworld (itself a reconfiguration of Homer's *Odyssey*), in which the whales which sail "with unshut eye round the world for ever and aye" are glimpsed from the "porthole" of an insane asylum (*Lagoon* 132), Gallant's opening Venice in August space-time vanishes, resurges, refracted by another's memory, governed by another's perception. Notions of space, time, and event are shown to be functions of the way the human mind shapes and organizes sensory material. A sidewalk surges up seismically, but the earthquake is in Flor's mind, with no independent existence as a substance of reality. A glass bead the child George salvages and keeps as a token from a necklace his cousin Flor wilfully broke years before contains whole worlds: Venice's pigeons and bells, Flor herself and the mutually reflecting "twin pictures" of love and resentment (19) – his for her, and hers for a divorced American mother who transformed her from a "person" to a "foreigner" (29). Flor is a walking metonym of what a human is when all the layers of individuation have been peeled away like onion skins. Become a young married woman, Flor has inhabited books and her mind for so long that she is not sure she really exists. She watches herself in shop windows to make sure she is "still there," and imagines life as "a brightly lighted stage with herself looking on" (29). For Mavis, her own mindscape was as real to her as the cityscape around her – in her own words, she "lived in writing, like a spoonful of water in a river, for more than forty-five years" ("Preface" to *Collected Stories* 3). Mavis and her persona Flor would both agree with Proust's narrator-mouthpiece, who explains that representation,

59 One of Frame's narrators finds herself in Matthew Arnold's neoplatonic poem, "The Forsaken Merman" (1849), with its two worlds above and below water, each invisible to the other but for some transgressive figures (Frame, *Lagoon* 132).

namely the act of reading, is more powerful than life for essentially two reasons. The images, actions, and emotions played out inside our heads are more intense than any empathy could be for someone living in the outside world. Moreover, the book concentrates in one hour all the joy and misery we would need a lifetime to experience, and which, to boot, would not be as intense because the slowness with which they unfurl dulls our perception (Proust, *Du côté de chez Swann*: 102–3). Flor has thus spent her childhood, girlhood, and marriage reading, "drugged, drowned" in "liquid words" (28), oblivious to the foreign streets on the other side of the window. We readers find ourselves confined inside a collapsing consciousness, glimpsing other consciousnesses in an inner "journey away from shore" (82) analogous to the dying Rachel's in Woolf's first novel, *A Voyage Out* (1915).

Flor's uncertainty as to her own existence points to the posited unreality of the self – linked with Maya or illusion – in Eastern cosmologies such as Hinduism and Buddhism at the level of origins, but also at the level of rediscovery and return (theosophy, transcendentalism). The life/stage analogy mentioned above also clearly gestures to Shakespeare's *As You Like It* – notably to Jaques's famous meditation on reality and illusion: "All the world's a stage, / And all the men and women merely players" (II.7.xx). The play has already been paratextually signposted for us.[60] Gallant has superimposed an epigraph on her novel, like "glass over glass" or "water under sky," one reflecting the other. To orient our interpretive reading of her story, she overlays the lines of Duke Frederick's court jester, whose licensed function is to provide an oblique running commentary on the folly underlying human ventures – the manner (comic wit) oversetting the matter (deadly serious) like glass over glass. This signposted speech from elsewhere, "Ay, now am I in Arden; the more fool I; when I was at home, I was in a better place: but travellers must be content" (II.4.xx), inhabits the novel, double-voiced from the start. It triggers an epistemological and metaphysical questioning which will be taken up by other intertextual tributaries on the boundaries between the self and the world, the foreign and home, the different and the same. In the following chapters I shall pursue this study of Gallant's novel. I shall examine in more depth how she amplifies her vision of the human comedy through a multivocal stratification of language, notably feeding new

60 An epigraph belongs to a category that Gérard Genette identified in *Palimpsestes* (1982) as paratext. In *Seuils* (1987) he develops his analysis of its function as a threshold [*seuil*], an interstitial zone between the text and the off-text, meant to inform the reading.

texts on previously digested ones and introducing "the speech of another" (Bakhtin 303) into her own discourse in concealed form. Suffice it here to highlight how Gallant's displaced expatriates contained in a circumscribed world or microcosm call up Chaucer's peripatetic pilgrims, who in turn remind us to inquire beyond a story's *solaas* or surface meaning, to its *sententia*, import or higher meaning. For the twentieth-century resurgence of allegorical writing to which *Green Water* belongs can operate either in the political mode of national allegory, which Fredric Jameson declared to be the dominant mode of postcolonial texts, or in the classical mode grounded in ethical and metaphysical concerns.

4
Dissonance & syncopation

An artist's practice "comes from the whole of his sensitive life," declared T.S. Eliot (*The Use of Poetry* 148), and Gallant's *mise en oeuvre* does seem to represent "the depths of feeling into which we cannot peer" (148). Mukherjee has observed that, as with good poetry, we need to return again and again to Gallant's unsettling stories – fluid and strange like dreams – to make them yield their meaning (11). Helm, among the many writers who have deplored the relative scarcity of critical focus on Gallant, has also deplored that the tonal shifts and "muted strangeness" of the much-anthologized stories should be half-lost on young readers too inexperienced to appreciate "an observational telling in which the subject is character-in-place, emotion rendered socio-historically." I wish to reiterate the intermedial analogy I made before between Gallant's oeuvre and the "unsettling detached oddness" (Romney) of Tati's aesthetic agenda, capable of superimposing the effect of an ostrich mating dance onto a mundane base image of factory workers filmed from a high angle, or of making a newfangled garage door and kitchen cabinet snapping shut feel like a Venus flytrap. The analogy can provide a visual key to the narrative sleights-of-hand and tonal shifts with which Gallant destabilizes. Counter-expectation is a trademark feature of her pen, just as discrepancy through visual incongruity is the bedrock of Tati's cinematic social satire. Both artists practise situational defamiliarization to critique the larger picture via the telling detail, simultaneously exaggerated and downplayed – like Mme Carette in "The Chosen Husband" looking politely away so that her daughter's suitor, "in trouble with a caramel," can "strangle unobserved" (*VE* 188) or like the man-eating garage door and kitchen cabinet in Tati's *Mon Oncle*.

One of the masterpieces of early jazz, "West End Blues" (1928) – probably the now legendary Louis Armstrong recording with its opening syncopated trumpet solo and wordless scat singing – played the role of Proust's *madeleine* when Mavis called up her childhood in the rented country house in Châteauguay where she and her parents spent the summers:

> If I want to bring back a Saturday night in full summer, couples dancing on the front gallery (Quebec English for veranda), a wind-up gramophone and a stack of brittle records, all I need to hear is the beginning of "West End Blues." The dancers are down from Montreal, or up from the States, where there is Prohibition." ("Afterword," *PS* 373)

When she was a young adult in the 1940s, Montreal danced to the swing music of the big bands, and Johnny Gallant played the piano at the Ritz Café, where he accompanied singers like Suzy Solidor, Celeste Holm, and Jane Morgan, and played to patrons that included visitors like Marlene Dietrich and Maurice Chevalier (Weintraub, *City Unique* 127). The vinyl LPs Mavis later bought in Paris also revealed her taste for the syncopated rhythms of jazz along with high art. Wagner's *Parsifal*,[1] Prokofiev's *Love of Three Oranges,* and Stravinsky's *The Rake's Progress*[2] cohabited with hits by Armstrong, Ella Fitzgerald, Benny Goodman, Dizzy Gillespie, Duke Ellington, Marlene Dietrich, and Charles Trenet, famous for his poetic wordplay. She also enjoyed Georges Brassens's cheeky songs, notoriously offbeat in both senses of the term: unconventional lyrics and melody grounded in hemiolas – rhythmic alterations consisting of two beats in place of the expected three.

T.S. Eliot wrote some of his poetry (*Sweeney Agonistes* notably) as experiments in syncopated jazz and ragtime rhythms. Critics have also detected the influence of jazz on the rhythm of Malcolm Lowry's novella *The Forest Path to the Spring* (1961), a modernist *Paradiso* published posthumously.[3] The jazz-like process that Catherine Delesalle identifies

1 Another interesting Paris interconnection. As Linda and Michael Hutcheon point out, Wagner conceived the opera while living in Paris (*Opera* 22).

2 Mavis was in Madrid when Stravinsky's syncretic opera was first performed in Paris in June 1952, but mobile as she was those first years (moving from Italy and Austria to Spain and Yugoslavia), she may well have attended the world premiere in Venice, which the composer himself conducted in September 1951.

3 Mavis once confided that this novella (just out in the story collection *Hear Us O Lord from Heaven Thy Dwelling Place*) made her homesick for Canada for the first time. It also made her realize that there was so much in Canada to write about, and so much she could say about it that no one else could. With the politically sensitive story "Bernadette" (published in 1957 under her maiden name, de Trafford Young, to avoid outraging her French-Canadian acquaintances) she had already demonstrated her unique – for an Anglo – inside knowledge of a certain French-Canadian community at a time when the two "tribes" lived in two solitudes.

in Lowry's text (whose narrator is a jazz musician composing an opera of the same name) involves the emergence of the unpredictable as well as "a succession of tension and release" (Delesalle 135). This is indeed consubstantial with the musical genre. But the critic also imputes to jazz Lowry's practice of repetition and recombinations of sounds, words, and motifs. While these partake in the process of recursion we find in Gallant's oeuvre as well, I wish to point out that they are tenets of literary modernism in general – the motivic variations of images or leitmotifs substituted for the sequentiality and causality of realist writing, to take but one example.[4] I find more fruitful the question of tension and release, actually common terms for the resolution of dissonant chords to consonant ones. I find it valuable to draw attention to Gallant's agenda of regularity and disruption, and to grapple with how she does it.

I have demonstrated how the writer's fingerprint is a lively steadiness of rhythm which, buttressed by euphonious figures of speech such as alliteration and assonance, engineers harmony. I have analysed how consonance unfolds through rhythmic devices such as rising metre, binary and ternary rhythms, parallelisms, periods, and chiasmus. Yet I have also touched on the author's techniques of avoiding an overly predictable metronome effect. In this chapter I focus on this other fingerprint of Gallant's: recourse to figures of deviation from an established norm. The practices we call syncopation and dissonance create a disturbance. Both terms belonging to music theory are familiar to readers, but I want to delineate their core traits here the better to illuminate their relevance to Gallant's literary practice. We all know that certain chords or combinations of notes sound jarring due to mathematical relations of overtones, namely acoustic frequencies which interfere with each other rather than coincide. Cognitive dissonance is a cousin of this original dissonance applying to sound (as shows the etymology *dis+sonare*). The cognitive dissonance Gallant deploys, as I shall show, is analogous to the grating effect and laser focus of, say, a tonic and perfect fifth[5] combined with a minor second. Dissonance holds a *harmonic* function, either preparing a resolution (the consonant chord that follows), or maintaining an unresolved roughness (desired in jazz and rock as well as contemporary

4 Actually, Gallant's appropriation of the musical leitmotif is quite Dickensian, often serving to identify the character with whom it quickly becomes interchangeable. See for instance the cook's little boy in "Bonaventure": "shut up," the only English expression he knows, is served up indiscriminately whenever he reappears.

5 In *Les Faux Monnayeurs* [*The Counterfeiters*] (1925) by André Gide, much admired by Mavis, one character's idea of heaven consists of one perfect chord drawn out to the end of time.

music). Syncopation, on the other hand, is a *rhythmic* invention which also involves a displacement from common practice. It interrupts and radically transforms the regular flow of rhythm by casting the stresses to where they do not normally occur: the weak or unaccented beats. I shall investigate how Gallant wrong-foots us with words, and what purpose the off-beat results serve.

"silent, flickering areas of light": making strange

At the beginning of Gallant's story, "Bonaventure" (1966),[6] the omniscient narrator presents to us Douglas Ramsay, a gifted young protagonist (who quickly becomes the focalizer) and the parents who have always submerged him with stories of his conception (a possible nod to Laurence Sterne's *Tristram Shandy*), and who have sent him to Europe to pursue his musical studies:

> The father was more reticent than the mother, perhaps more Canadian. He could say what he thought, but not always what he felt. His memories, like the mother's, were silent, flickering areas of light, surrounded by buildings that no longer exist. (*HT* 157)

This passage is extracted from a narrative anchored in the realist aesthetic. The story is set in contemporary times, provides verifiable social, historical, and geographical details, and contains plausible events and characters compatible with our identifiable world. The beginning of the extract shows in addition a discourse organized into the logical, coherent, unified segments of realist writing, such as the half-playful equation between "reticent" and "Canadian," and the balanced antithetical parallelism encapsulating the commonly acknowledged masculine psyche (say/thought; not say/felt). What then should we make of the tonal shift which propels us via an extended conceit into the abstract and unreal? What are we to make of the buildings which no longer exist? The step to the side, an *estrangement-effect*, disrupts our habitual ways of seeing and thinking. It breaks the automatism of cognition and ordinary speech which Shklovsky denounced: "Habitualization devours work, clothes, furniture, one's wife, and the fear of war" (16). One can question the pertinence of the equivalence he draws between wives and furniture, but the *ostranenie*

6 The manuscript was initially a novel Mavis was working on in the 1950s, set aside when the idea for *Green Water Green Sky* (1959) came to her. She rediscovered it years later and reshaped it into a short story.

(making strange) the formalist advocated was precisely what the modernists admired in Chekhov and Tolstoy. Mavis had several translations of the Russians, and would gift her close friends books off her shelf. Tolstoy's *The Kreutzer Sonata and Other Stories* was among those she gave me. It includes the last novella Tolstoy wrote, *Hadji Murad* (1912); in it a ball at a Russian palace, seen through the eyes of the eponymous Avar warlord, consists of "half-naked women" who turn "round and round in the embrace of men in bright uniforms" (392).[7] The estrangement-effect is often but not always deployed through such a shift in perspective. Tolstoy also has Tsar Nicholas I go to the ballet "where hundreds of women marched round in tights and scanty clothing" (422). Here the defamiliarization of a practice well known to the tsar is clearly authorial.

Gallant, too, likes to sidestep and break step, postponing or deferring the reader's understanding in a strategy which Aristotle called "Delay," and which Shklovsky labelled "Retardation, the general law of art" (20). Like the modernists who appropriated Tolstoy's and Chekhov's agenda of cognitive-estrangement and who made language opaque, she liked to de-automatize perception by not naming a familiar thing or act but describing it instead as an unknown object never seen before, a sort of UFO. Douglas Ramsay's parents keep telling him about how their marriage almost ended at Bonaventure Station at the end of the war, when Douglas "was not conceived, was not present, was not even deaf, blind, and upside down" (*HT* 173). This is clearly *delay or retardation at work, operating like the form of syncopation* which plays a note ever so slightly after a beat. Its manner of suspending readers' respiration is analogous to the hemiola's substitution of two beats for three, a ratio of one and a half to one. It is moreover playfully equivalent to the cinematic double take. Like film's stylized delayed reaction, readers need an extra split second to realize that what the dissonant perception portrays is an unborn baby. The alien quality of the gaze, which prolongs perception and makes readerly identification difficult, makes the process of perception "an aesthetic end in itself" (Shklovsky 16) and allows readers to recover the sensation of the prenatal stage of life – exactly what Shklovsky meant in his famous remark about "making the stone *stony*" (16).[8]

7 This mirrors in a way (inverting the gendered viewpoint) Chekhov's poor little rich girl, Anne, at her first ball with her old new husband; she is invited to dance by a huge officer, who moves "like a piece of meat in uniform" ("Anna Round the Neck," in *The Kiss and Other Stories* 213).

8 The fuller version of the quote by the Russian formalist reads: "art exists that one may recover the sensation of life; it exists to make one feel things, to make the stone *stony*" (16, original stress).

There is similar use of delay in the same collection's weirdly political story, "Saturday" (1968). Here Gallant brakes in order to break a routine, readerly practice which has become unconscious. The protagonist, Gérard, has been brought up an atheist by anticlerical French-Canadian parents who turned their backs on French to escape the Church the language was enmeshed with. Gérard encounters a funeral procession, wonders why he is being scrutinized, and "touche[s] his forehead, his chest, and a point on each shoulder" (*HT* 36). We readers trip over this depiction deconstructing the sign of the cross.

Mavis rejected automatism and the arbitrary, and she felt the surrealists lacked imagination. Still, very early stories like "Jorinda and Jorindel" and "Up North," written in the 1940s and re-excavated from the family picnic hamper containing her writings a decade later, and also later works like *Green Water Green Sky*, *The Pegnitz Junction*, and "Saturday" (1968) show strong traces of the surrealist agenda of making strange. They make use of some of the disruptive devices advocated by André Breton. Breton's tool bag contains an unformatted child's perspective, dream, madness, spoken thought, and the grotesque. It has on the other hand thrown out information, description, transitions, and logic in general. While Joyce and Faulkner seem to have completely appropriated Breton's tool bag, Gallant's vision and technique are qualitatively different. In general she privileges not the modernist estrangement-effect of linguistic opacity but that of mystery, enigma, and the hermeneutic.

In "Saturday" the opening procession I have alluded to veers into the grotesque and disquieting: the sobbing mourners double over with laughter, the realistic space-time dissolves, the coffin (a mere stapled-together carton) falls apart, and a crippled woman asks Gérard to take a white envelope from the hands of the corpse. The dissonant imagery – dissonant because incongruous – propels us towards the uncanny opening sequence of Bergman's *Wild Strawberries* (discussed in my sub-chapter on visual overlays), in which Borg meets a hearse and is pulled into the coffin by the dead body. When Gérard's mother finds him kneeling in the dark with his head against the refrigerator door and a smashed plate of leftover ham beside him, we realize that Gallant has not only been citing but also playing with Bergman's dream sequence.

Gallant injects a Chekhovian grotesque into her autobiographical "Jorinda and Jorindel" as well. As Proust advocated in the posthumously published essay "Contre Sainte-Beuve," she releases from the buried world of unconscious memory the ever-living reality to which habit makes us blind. We shall see how she defamiliarizes to the point of producing readerly unease. The story begins with all the ingredients of Mavis's childhood summers in the French-Canadian countryside: the weekend party, the dancing and the guests up from the States fleeing Prohibition in the 1920s, "the gallery" or veranda, the thinly disguised small Mavis, the devoted French-Canadian *bonne d'enfant* and the distant, all-powerful parents.[9] Mrs. Bloodworth (whose name is already discordantly grimacing), an American practising the Charleston, falls "flat on her behind" (*HT* 21) with her feet pointing upward, squinting through the hair all over her face at the little girl Irmgard (the focalizer) sitting in her nightgown on the stairs:

> "Are you watching the fun?" she said in a tragic voice. "Is it really you, my sweet pet?" And she got to her feet and crawled up the stairs on her hands and knees to kiss Irmgard with ginny breath. (21)

The Chekhovian dissonance emerges from the incongruously "tragic" voice, the weird incompatibility between "got to her feet" and "crawled." When the crawling woman kisses the child "with ginny breath," readers squirm. They wonder if this is a nightmarish "reality" or a floating extension of little Irmgard's troubling dream, which has melded realist elements (her visiting smug American cousin Bradley, a deserted sidewalk with grass in its cracks) with the eruption of a witch from a scary Grimms' fairytale.[10] Through its ingredients of death, spells, and transmutation, Gallant wrenches the realist mode into the uncanny domain of legend, romance, and the demonic. The dark woods, the atmosphere of twilight and terror in the Grimms' *Jorinda and Jorindel* frame and leak into Gallant's story in overlays such as the Mrs. Bloodworth sequence above. The horrific lies in wait in a lateral narrative ellipsis, an omission or hole of sorts. I shall discuss the technique of *paralipsis* (in which the narrative sidesteps an element) in the following sub-chapter "surfeit & lack." Suffice it here to point out that Irmgard's opening dream of Bradley

9 Among the autobiographical elements dialoguing with the retrospective narration of childhood in "The Doctor" is Mavis's parents' habit of blacklisting guests who have displeased. Mrs. Bloodworth here falls into the category Linnet describes in "The Doctor" as "those wretched once-only guests who were put on trial for a Saturday night and universally condemned" (*VE* 79).

10 Mavis's European-born, German-speaking maternal grandmother, Rosa Wiseman, exposed her to the language and to stories less known outside German-speaking countries at the time than tales like *Hansel and Gretel,* such as *Jorinda and Jorindel,* which gives Gallant's story its name.

and an old empty sidewalk – presence and absence – begins to resonate in motifs of disappearance, then terror and death. We decode the clues the author encrypts concerning Freddy, a little French-Canadian playmate that Irmgard spurned when she had her cousin on hand to play with – Freddy who vanishes from her life after a triple betrayal which syncopates into Biblical myth, in which we readers are invited to supply the metaphysical cock crows. The syncopated pattern we slide into when Irmgard denies Freddy thrice transforms and remaps the surrounding text, generating a dénouement in light of the overlaid prosodic rules. Irmgard remembers at the end of the story the dream elements that were initially withheld: that Freddy was sent on an errand down the sidewalk at the edge of the woods.

> He went off down the sidewalk, which was heaving, cracked, edged with ribbon grass, and when he came to a certain place he was no longer there. Something was waiting for him there, and when they came looking for him, only Irmgard knew that whatever had been waiting for Freddy was the disaster, the worst thing. (*HT* 32)

No child should go near a strange forest, we are told. But Irmgard does not know what lies in wait. She is no longer sure for whom the bell tolls: for Freddy, Bradley, or "even herself" (28). Yet we are now caught up in the knowing and have recovered the sensation.

I have drawn attention to Gallant's "retardation," the aesthetic effect of the slow motion with which a perception is constructed, completed, all contours filled in. It is precisely by *combining deferral and syncopation* that the writer engineers estrangement in "Bonaventure." The protagonist cannot bring himself to apprehend the reality of his parents' lives before his gaze brought them into being: "Before he *was* – Douglas Ramsay – the world was covered with mist, palm fronds, and vegetarian reptiles" (*HT* 157, original stress). The cranial shift – viewing the character from the outside, then the inside, in quick succession – triggers a magical time-shift: the two combined make us miss a beat. A dissonant image compressing the abstract and concrete then makes us miss another beat. We learn that a wartime photograph of his father "taken before true history began" came into his mind's eye when Ramsay was confused, his emotions dispersed, or "his intellect, on which he depended, reduced to *water*" (157). The author then changes gears with an unfolding harmonious enumeration whose final clause jerks us onto another plane: "He was in Switzerland, it was a June day, he was recently twenty, and he had to get rid of chocolate wrappers" (158). The chalet expecting him is another agent of *ostranenie*: it is like "a bison, or a bear, *hairy* with vines" (158).

The hairy chalet belongs to the widow of the recently deceased great conductor Adrien Moser. Invited to visit, Ramsay discovers the countryside, he who had known only cities: Montreal and Berlin, which were the same to him "whether their ruins were dark and soft, abandoned to pigeons and wavy pieces of sky, or created and destroyed by one process, like the machine that consumes itself" (159). Language here is incantation transcending communication. It stops, suspends, transports us elsewhere. The modernist preoccupation with war, danger, and death eerily rushes in. In the streets of one place, Berlin, "he walked on the dead, but both cities were built over annihilated walls scarcely anyone could remember" (159). Annihilated walls and buildings that no longer exist frame this story which jumps everywhere in time and space, pausing at a clock "that was stopped forever at six minutes to three" (161).

The young widow, Katharine Moser, crusades for the virtues of nature, claiming that her elderly musician husband did his best work after she removed him to the countryside and a steady diet of larks and wind in the trees. She drives Ramsay to fetch pure drinking water from a spring, which proves to trickle from an evil-looking grotto into an old bathtub. She worshipfully immerses her bottles in the tub and "fill[s] each with typhoid fever, conjunctivitis, amoebic dysentery, blood poisoning, and boils" (177). The discordant list which compresses the abstract and the concrete stops us readers in our tracks. It intensifies a contrapuntal melodic line debunking the romantic notion of art grounded in, even copying, nature. As Gallant's mouthpiece, Ramsay, argues, perhaps against the grain of many readers' convictions, "Painters learn to paint by looking at pictures, not at hills and valleys, and musicians listen to music, not the wind in the trees" (176). Clusters of leitmotifs and mini-parables surrounding Katharine Moser divert her from her self-proclaimed role of muse and earth mother/wife and eerily transmute her into a praying mantis who vampirized her husband and who is now spinning a death-dealing web for Ramsay. The clusters operate like a musical rhapsody, in the sense of *rhapsoidia*, from *rhaptein* (to sew or stitch together) and *oide* (song).[11] The theme and variations of predation notably create

11 The rhapsody, a free instrumental form which George Gershwin's jazz-inflected *Rhapsody in Blue* (1924) made world-famous, seems a closer fit to Dobozy's notion of Gallant's "chaotic patterning of language," which I have mentioned he compares to "the fugue" (79). His analogy with a musical form is instinctively sound, but the patterning of the fugue is anything but chaotic. And after all, as Dobozy himself admits in his conceptual term "designed anarchy" (85), Gallant's patterning is only *apparently* chaotic. It simply requires "an altering of 'cognition'" – of the ways in which we readers "process the text" (86).

an imprint via accumulative repetition. There are the birds Katharine explains "prey on fledglings" (161). There are the trees "devoured by ... a web, a tent of gray, a hideous veil" (140). There are the eyes and the paws of Katharine's cat seen from below attacking a nest, with Ramsay screaming, "Stop him, stop him!" (161). There is "The shadow netted on the breakfast table, on cups and milk and crumpled napkins [which] seemed a web to catch anything– lovers, stretched fingers, claws" (162). The polysyndeton (and/and) contributes to the slow motion, suspends focus on familiar objects redolent with domesticity, and makes more dissonant and ominous the concluding chaotic enumeration. The list telescopes predators and prey ("savage cat" but also "cannibal magpies, cannibal jays" [192]), and arguably equates Katharine's fingers with the killer claws.

Those interested in the act and processes of reading cannot fail to be intrigued by the complex intersections with the ghostly buildings evoked at the beginning of this sub-chapter. These belong to a different continent and a different time frame. Montreal's Bonaventure Station and its surrounding buildings are suffused with a solid presence marking a time and place: there where the father of the still-unconceived Ramsey comes back from the war, mutilated from the Dieppe Raid; where his young wife tells him she wants him out of her life before finally taking him back. Torn down before the boy has ever seen it, the station and its surrounding buildings, which stand only on old postcards and in his parents' stories, were what his parents looked at when they were deciding his existence or nonexistence. While the father's lingering desire "to start again, to arrive [once more] at Bonaventure" (197) resonates with the central trope of beginning again in "Ice Wagon" and "The Cost of Living," the buildings' absence also haunts the family with its associations of the suffering, mutilation, and death humans inflict on one another. These intermesh with Katharine Möser's Swiss space-time in a form of counterpoint analogous to the cinema's technique of parallel editing, which draws parallels or contrasts between two different space-time locations. Gallant's war/wife overlay puts a laser focus on the pain of an aging artist who marries so as not to be left alone, only to have his wife torment him about "being alone in eternity" (162):

> "I told him," she said, putting the wild flowers in a glass of water on the breakfast table. "Unless two people die at exactly the same moment, they can never meet again." With such considerations had she entertained the ill old man. He had clasped her hands, weeping. His headache marched from the roots of his hair to his eyebrows, down the temples, around the eyes. (162–3)

The dissonance between the act of beautifying and the act of inflicting pain lingers, prolonged by the unlocatable voice. Does the implicit value judgment ("with such considerations ...") meant to guide readers emanate from the focalizer being addressed or the omniscient narrator occupying the authorial vantage point? Do the additional details Ramsey has not witnessed emanate from the narrator's omniscience, or does the widow casually or clinically mention them? As flies are we to the gods, or to our partners, the writer seems to suggest in this exploration of power, cruelty, and pain which showcases the banality of evil at a breakfast table.

Yet throughout the story, the unfolding grimness syncopates into farce and back again. Ramsey learns that Katharine removed Moser from his well-loved concert halls and museums to the backwoods, where she deprived him of the sweets he craved and bribed him with forbidden caramels to take the fastidious walks he loathed. Discovering Moser's collection of empty caramel boxes, his labelled containers of screws and tacks and elastic bands, the young Ramsey is brought to produce an effect analogous to the backbeat of jazz, in which the percussion stresses the even-numbered beats instead of the strong first and third beats. Gallant's juvenile protagonist shifts the accent unexpectedly from the main, strong beat (the renowned artist) to the weak beat (his own unknown self). He notably pulls out of his pockets the things he will leave behind for admiring posterity:

> when Douglas Ramsey died, his Yo-yo and the plastic marbles would be placed on a shelf and labelled and dated, and dusted every day. (168)

Farce for Mavis is the other side of the grim, like the two sides of a translucent sheet of paper. I have already raised the issue, and will discuss it at length elsewhere, but it is already clear in this story that *the grim and the comic participate* in one and the same process, which finds its point of departure in incongruity. When Ramsey is moved into Moser's pavilion, he muses,

> the old man had been sent here, with a curé's bed and a doll's piano, and told something: "You will be alone in eternity," "Don't eat sweets." "If you think you are dying, ring that bell." (169)

The comic surges out of dissonance, namely the discrepancy between the two statements placing eternity and fudge on the same plane (or plate), as well as the internal discrepancy of the final sentence, which equates dying with ordering a meal. In addition, Gallant exploits discrepancies in sound for comic results that participate in a modernist absurdism often identified with her well-loved Camus (*L'Etranger*, *La Peste*)[12] and Beckett. Katharine Moser's daughter, Anne, has a fat fourteen-year-old friend visiting from England who pronounces the half-open vowel *e* as a short *i*, transforming cow bells into cow bills and her own name into Piggy. On the other side of the Atlantic, decades earlier, Ramsay's mother meets her wounded husband at Montreal's Bonaventure Station and tells him she refuses to live with an invalid. He is so stunned that he forgets his name and what he is doing there. Yet the author mentions a Salvation Army band playing a well-known hymn, which she parodies as "Lamb of God, *Sheep of God*" (172). Along with this Shklovskyesque stone/stony sidestep to an incongruously cumbersome variant which makes the liturgical lamb sheepy, the author specifies that the hymn was "taken up by a drunk woman sharing their bench" (172). In a similar discordant parallel, the cosmological plane of death and dying is twinned with a Lilliputian counterpart. Ramsey, as damaged from a car accident as his father is from war, unheroically plays the role of exterminator at night in the composer's too short bed, battling a moth with a can of pesticide which poisons his own air and creates scores of collateral casualties dropping from the ceiling.[13] Night after night,

> he fought flies, midges, mosquitoes, and moths, most of which expired on his pillow or on the white bedsheet. They seemed determined to perish upon a white expansion – some mountaintop of their insect literature and mythology – instead of going and dying in a corner where Ramsey need never see them again. (177)

In a nod perhaps to Mansfield's miniature study of power and evil, "The Fly" (1922), Gallant throws in a dying fly which thrashes and buzzes in the wastebasket and keeps Ramsey awake all night. When the young man complains the next morning, Katharine's daughter calmly telescopes the banal and the horrific: "All you had to do was squash it" (177) – precisely what we Westerners did with our invented engines of mass destruction during the last world war.

---

12 *The Stranger, The Plague*, respectively.

13 This particular mix of comedy and social realism anticipates Woody Allen's offbeat cinematic technique. It notably anticipates the spider scene in *Annie Hall* (1977), in which the inept, out-of-step comic persona, Alvy Singer, tells Annie, "Honey, there's a spider in your bathroom the size of a Buick," calls for a snow shovel, and wrecks the bathroom battling the beast with a tennis racket.

"tougher than bulldogs": the odd man out

In previous chapters I have shown the degree of regularity in Gallant's rhythmically accented language, a steadiness in measure which poetic prose shares with song and dance, and which we can best feel by beating time. In this chapter I have been engaging with the occasional change in beat or syncopation with which Gallant avoids the automatizing effect of predictability. Setting up a harmonious effect via a steady tempo, parallelisms, echoes, and figures that proceed by addition and repetition, she then upsets the steadiness that would result in a military march. The writer never disrupts her rhythmically arranged patterns systematically or even predictably, for "the rhythm of prose is an important automatizing element; the rhythm of poetry is not" (Shklovsky 20). In this sub-chapter, I shall explore another syncopating device with which Gallant provides fresh flexibility. In discourse, the stress or strong time (which rhetoricians call *thesis*) is displaced onto the weak time (*arsis*) by a sort of change in step (which only dance makes visible). Especially interesting is how the writer *combines syncopation with dissonance* for maximum disruption.

I have shown how Gallant often resorts to lists built like crescendos, which flow on until they hit an odd man out. The term refers to an incongruous element not of the same nature which wrong-foots us by derailing the innocent ordering principle. In "In the Tunnel," Mrs. Reeve had not waited for her husband to die "before starting her widow's diet *of tea and toast and jam and gin*" (*HT* 95). The regular iambic metre I have italicized for clarity sails ahead, carried along by the twinning double alliteration: tea/toast, which is cognitively as well as phonically congruent, and jam/gin, which is not. The artists' widows in "Speck's Idea" are labelled "vain, greedy, unrealistic, and tougher than bulldogs" (*PS* 141). The enumerated set of abstract qualities unfurls and expands, moving from one syllable to two, then more, and on to a comparative which syncopates onto a dissonant element, leading us in a rush to collide with the very concrete, jarring bulldog. The technique operates very much like the harmonic function of chords in music, serving to create a larger style-specific harmonic progression. Gallant's discursive units, like the chords in question, obey collective tendencies and work together to form a foundation for a phrase or theme. Just as a chord's function concerns not only its internal characteristics (namely the notes that belong in it) but also where it is employed (namely the chords which precede and follow it), Gallant's bulldog feels "wrong" and serves to trigger the startling effect of caricature. One finds an incongruent snoring bulldog clinching another list in Gallant's review of Nabokov's short novel, *Transparent Things* (1972). Gallant describes the hero's Belgian-Russian wife with a trademark crescendo culminating in a clashing chord: "Armande is stupid, conceited, cold-hearted, and she snores like a bulldog" (*Paris Notebooks* 201).

In the daringly provocative story "Bernadette,"[14] the title protagonist, an illiterate French-Canadian Catholic maid terrified by an unwanted pregnancy, is employed by a well-meaning, well-off left-wing Anglo suburban housewife, Nora, who battles for "birth control, clean milk, vaccination, homes for mothers, homes for old people, homes for cats and dogs" (*GA* 50; *The Cost of Living* 130). Gallant's irony nestles unnoticed in the first three terms of the unfolding list of noble causes. It emerges in the second ternary set, whose anaphora (homes) and common preposition (for) creates an equivalence, even escalation, in worth (mothers/old people/...). Readers then careen into the unexpected final rubric (cats and dogs), which contaminates and trivializes Nora's preceding held-up banners and casts doubt on her ability to discriminate. The sentence which follows shows how the writer can catch readers off-guard with a double change in step: "She fought against censorship, and for votes for cloistered nuns, and for the provincial income tax" (*GA* 50). Readers can note that this time the syncopating chord or odd man out is in the middle.

"tum titty": adjacency pairs

In my sub-chapter on visual overlays, I remarked that in "Ice Wagon," the year's first snow for Peter resonates powerfully. Like the early morning ice wagon for Agnes, it embodies a new start, an escape from the roundelay of compromises and failures, the promise of a higher plane of existence. When Peter takes his wife, Sheilah, to the Burleighs' Mardi Gras party, he has to overcome punishing conditions: driving an unknown rented car with right-hand drive through the year's first snowstorm, being unable to locate the windshield wiper switch to see where he is going, having endless trouble finding a place to park in unknown streets packed with snow-covered cars. Yet when they stand at last on the pavement, Peter waves all this aside. His only words are: "This is the first snow" (*PS* 19). Sheilah responds with "Hurry, darling. My hair." (19) This sequence of two utterances by two different speakers illustrates how Gallant unsettles the unit of conversation which linguists call an *adjacency pair.* In a typical exchange of one turn each, the first turn calls for a certain

---

14 Originally published in 1957 under Gallant's maiden name to avoid outraging her French-Canadian acquaintances, as I have stated in a previous note, the deliberately politically incorrect *New Yorker* story is available to readers in *The Norton Anthology of Short Fiction* (2000), and is also collected in *My Heart Is Broken* (1964), *Going Ashore*, and *The Cost of Living*).

type of (preferred) response. The adjacent pair of utterances are related and even mutually dependent, in predictable patterns such as complaint/apology or blame/denial. In "The Ice Wagon" passage, the first turn resonates through its concluding celebratory spondee ("first snow"), but the second turn or utterance ("My hair") deviates from expectation and is thus made salient. The author emphasizes the dispreferred response[15] by repeating the sequence – the same but not quite:

> "It's the first snow."
> "You're repeating yourself," she said. "Please hurry, darling. Think of my poor shoes. My *hair*." (19, original stress)

Peter's litanic reiteration reinscribes the plane of aesthetics and metaphysics, delaying dissonance by offering his wife a second chance to give a preferred response. But Sheilah's yet again dissonant reply rides roughshod over the hoped-for response and derails us onto the track of domestic trivia. When the feet along with the lacquered hairdo become primary considerations, we drop from high to low through the void Peter finds himself in without a helpmeet by his side. The conversational implicatures (Grice, S. Levinson)[16] are multiple. We infer that Sheilah's utterance buttresses a Chaucerian anti-portrait in which the positive signifiers of her outer beauty are in inverse proportion to the negative signifieds regarding her inner shallowness and questionable authenticity.[17] We also presume from the mismatched exchange that the dissonance would not have occurred with Agnes.

Conversational sequencing disfigured by a variety of torsions occur frequently in Gallant's well-known Linnet Muir cycle. The twist in "Between Zero and One" (1975) is a fine example. Young Linnet, working in a Montreal wartime agency, finds herself under the orders of a new arrival from Toronto, Mrs. Ireland, who is determined to expose her lack of qualifications. The benevolent General Manager intervenes, ostensibly because his father knew Linnet's father and asked him to paint a mural for his plant in Sorel. But Mrs. Ireland goes on clamouring her outrage at "a girl" (*HT* 292) having been hired: "'I know there's a shortage of men,' Mrs. Ireland would

15 I borrow the term from pragmatics, the branch of linguistics dealing with language in use and in context, namely the relations of sentences to their habitat. See Harvey Sacks.

16 The Gricean term implicature refers to what is suggested in an utterance even if it is not expressed or even strictly implied by the sentence.

17 Following the aborted exchange, Sheilah shielded her head to signify that Peter did not "understand her beauty," but took his arm to show him "she treasured him and was not afraid of wasting her life or her beauty" (20).

suddenly burst out" (294). The choice of verb ("burst out") and its frequentative aspect indicate that the character recurrently indulges in rhetorical conversational sequences with herself, or rather with a collective audience not intended to talk back. Her statements about the scarcity of men rest on general, admitted truth, but conceal a presumptive meaning, namely that Linnet otherwise would never have been hired. Although Mrs. Ireland does not require or even expect a response from the cowed office workers, her utterances are adjacently paired with disguised fragments from popular ribald songs (prohibited on site), ostensibly addressed to no one:

> "I know there's a shortage of men," Mrs. Ireland would burst out.
> "Oh umptee tum titty," sang Bertie Knox.
> "And that after this war it will be still worse ..."
> "Ti umpty dum diddy."
> "There'll hardly be a man left in the world worth his salt ..."
> "Tee umpty tum tumpty." (294)

We can see that the Ireland/Knox pairs of utterances are talk in interaction, but that they deviate from the classic pattern of turn-taking. Mrs. Ireland is monologuing rhetorically, and Knox's timed bits of chanted monologue are actually insertion sequences syncopating with hers. The two turns are not mutually dependent; the second is not even related to the first, thus flouting the maxim of relevance which is understood to regulate conversation, along with clarity, brevity, and truth (Grice). Gallant's adjacency pairing here *returns to the source of literary counterpoint and operates like musical counterpoint.* While literary counterpoint juxtaposes or commingles independent episodes which are separated either by time or space so that they mutually illuminate each other, musical counterpoint simultaneously combines two or more harmonically independent melodies (here Ireland/Knox) into a single harmonic texture in which each retains its linear character, independent rhythm, and pitch contour. Bernie Knox's natural-sounding but semantically meaningless syllables form a curve that tracks the sound over time, from *tum titty* to *dum diddy* and from *umpteen* to *umpty* and *tumpty*. The polyphonic weaving of the distinct utterances operates in a discordant fashion in which the second turn grates against and overpowers the discourse rather than responding to it harmoniously. In the rest of the out-of-tune passage below, one can note how the utterances which carry no meaning structure the discourse and construct the tension of cognitive dissonance:

> "But what I do not see ..."
> "Tee diddle dee dum."

"Is why a totally unqualified girl ..."
"Tum tittle umpty tumpty."
"Should be subsidised by the taxpayers of this country ..."
"Pum pum tee umpty pumpee."
"Just because her father failed to paint ..."
"Oh umpty tumpty tumpty."
"A mural down in ..."
"Tee umpty dum dum."
"Sorel." (294–5)

We have seen that Mrs. Ireland is not allowed to arrive at the completion point of her syntactic units, and that the second speaker's utterances are actually synchronous with the first speaker's. The *tum titties* are in fact discourse markers which combatively take and hold control of the floor. The implicature is one of defiance – against censorship, against authority. The *cognitive dissonance* consists of Bertie Knox's compressed, conflicting beliefs, values, and behaviour. His provocative debunking of his female superior's thesis and, in essence, his defence of Linnet, clash with the paternalistic views he holds along with his co-workers (and most of his generation), namely that women are "trouble" (244). Bertie Knox's dissenting sounds and, more generally, the sequence's experimentation with communication and language behaviour, can catch readers off balance. Yet readers are simultaneously initiated into the process of preferred interpretations when the writer revisits meaning and nudges them to presume by default there where *general* principles are involved, or to infer meaning from *specific* signals implying intention and context. The effect is as remarkable from the communicative as from the aesthetic perspective.

frame-breaking: the real & the reel

Incongruity and counter-expectation make up the core of the dissonance and changes in step I have examined in the above three sub-chapters. Illustrations abound of Gallant's multifarious eruptions of disrupted and disrupting language. Mousy Agnes from Saskatchewan in "The Ice Wagon," for instance, explains that she feels uncomfortable in Geneva with the worldly Burleighs: "Their friends are too rich and I'm too Canadian" (*PS* 18). The balanced chiasmus (their friends/I; rich/Canadian) is inhabited by a syncopating figure which narratologists call *metalepsis* or *frame-breaking*, one of the rhetorical figures or tropes of discursive displacement as radical as irony and metaphor. We can see how it transforms terms not of the same nature ("rich" and "Canadian") into an antithetical binary positing an impossible interchangeability. It discordantly compresses the ontologically dissimilar concepts onto the same ontological plane (thus equating "Canadian" with the term it has implicitly replaced: "poor"). I have also discussed "Ice Wagon"'s complex climax, notably analysing how the focalizer's final rhetorical question ("Who wants to be alone") suddenly jumps to the narrator's injunction ("No, begin at the beginning"). The disrupting figure which gives readers the impression of veering from inside to outside is another instance of frame-breaking.

A cinematic analogy can be helpful: a frame can signify a picture area on a strip of film, but can also signify the perimeter or boundary line of the picture area. Just so, the "altering force" Helm has sensed in Gallant's writing involves points of intersection between different levels of narrative which unexpectedly break through the frame or logical established structure of points of view in the text. This produces a delay in readerly understanding and a corresponding estrangement-effect. In the concluding sequence of "Bonaventure," Douglas Ramsey has fled Katharine Moser and settles down to eat in a Swiss pension dining room where television accompanies the supper:

> Chairs were arranged so that everyone faced in the same direction. A girl who looked like Sabine lay on a piano and sang. Every few seconds, though the song continued without interruption, the girl wore different clothes. Now she stood with her hand on the pianist's shoulder; he looked up into her eyes, and the pair posed that way. (*HT* 196–7)

Readers inevitably trip over the young woman lying on the piano. They may also stumble over her magically changing clothes before realizing that the writer has jerked them from world to screen. The cognitive estrangement arises from the absence of transition between the logic of the real world and the logic of televisual representation. Placing both in the same slot first disrupts readerly understanding, then makes us see through new eyes the absurdity of a convention which has been naturalized, and finally puts perception rather than story onto centre stage.

It can be enlightening here to engage at more length with a story I have repeatedly brought into the discussion, which rests on the mingling of two distinct story levels: "Baum, Gabriel, 1935–( )." Gabriel, whose family in Bavaria was apparently wiped out in the war, with the exception of an uncle who left in time for Argentina, ekes out a living in Paris playing bit parts (often the victim disposed of in the first scene) in films and eventually television, the Occupation being a favourite theme. We know he had fulfilled his military service in the Algerian war and was discharged, and we are told that his friend Dieter "had begun as a private, had been promoted to lieutenant, and expected to become a captain soon" (*Paris Stories* 179). The ternary rhythm balancing the trio of plausible, temporally coherent verbs with the trio of escalating ranks is followed by a metaleptic binary which pulls the carpet out from under readers' feet: Dieter "had two good facial expressions, one for victory and one for defeat" (179). Gallant here breaks the frame: she *snatches us out of the real and drops us into the reel.* Dieter is indeed a ranking officer, but in the world of make-believe, not our world. The metalepsis operates as *a Trojan horse* from which satire erupts. The historically verifiable act of military ranking swings over into a ranking of movies and television, ostensibly grade B. Farce is once more interchangeable with the grim – haunted by the casual, backhanded mention that "*Unlike Gabriel's father and mother*, Uncle August had got out of Europe in plenty of time" (*PS* 171).

Gallant as critic misses nothing of the film industry's codes, staple ingredients, and recipe-like substitutions and combinations. Her 1979 story is about memory and change; it deconstructs the development of the screen all the while it depicts the protagonist growing older and Paris going global. The old Montparnasse train station for instance has been torn down and "a dark ugly tower" put up in its place. Gabriel moreover no longer sees Paris as it was, but as it has stayed in his mind: "he still saw butchers and grocers and pastry shops, when in reality they had become garages and banks" (184). One thinks of Federico Fellini's autobiographical *Roma* (1972), in which the cameras and gazes of a contemporary film crew engineer a collision between the city's past and present. The audience witnesses the tunnelling process of Rome's first subway line, which breaks through to ancient palace walls covered with splendid frescos, whose bright tints vanish before our eyes from the rush of air. Fellini's movie, however, adheres to a grimacing grotesque, while Gallant's story spins a gentle farce. In its telescoping of the micro and macro, inscape and cityscape, "Baum, Gabriel" also calls up Giuseppe Tornatore's *Cinema Paradiso* (1988). The movie inserts archival footage of the great film classics, even as it shows their screening venues. Kirk Douglas, but no, the Ulysses of Greek myth, strides into Toto's realist but just as fictional frame, and we viewers stumble over characters who have slipped from one fabricated system into another. In Tornatore's framing realist world, we move diachronically from the village in Sicily, where the parish priest makes the projectionist of the moving pictures cut out all the kisses, to today's recognizable, standardized, homogenized movie theatres. An even closer intermedial analogy with Gallant's story would be Ethan and Joel Coen's *Barton Fink* (1991), whose playwright protagonist has been hired to write a wrestling picture, but cannot bring himself to simply apply the standard formulas a successful scriptwriter's "secretary" kindly supplies. Yet the Coen brothers' movie, which lampoons the pretentious New York theatre scene as well as the Hollywood film industry, is so dark and disquieting that viewers squirm. Gallant oversets her parodic deconstruction, involving derailing from "life" to film reel and back, onto a thoughtful social and political meditation, but makes it fun. We learn that

> Gabriel had been shot, stoned, drowned, suffocated, and marked off for hanging; had been insulted and betrayed; had been shoved aboard trains and dragged out of them; had been flung from the back of a truck with such accidental violence that he had broken his collarbone. (*PS* 182)

The Joyce-like seriation, calling up Jacobean tragedy's predilection for varying the methods of putting to death, is briskly propelled by an initial asyndeton eliminating copulative conjunctions as just so much rice pudding. The seriation is then energetically carried forward at a pace rendered reader-friendly by binaries which engineer a horizon of expectation (shoved aboard/dragged out; train/truck). The comic tone lies in the ambiguity the author maintains between Gabriel and his screen roles. We gather that his multiple deaths are not for real, but that his broken collarbone is. We then read:

> His demise, seen by millions of people, some eating their dinner, was still needed in order to give a push to the old dishonourable plot – told ever more simply now, like a fable. (182–3)

Gabriel's generic death expropriates the real via the millions of eye witnesses, while on the plane of simulacrum it confers a hero's aura. Yet the narrator's parenthetical remark on the diners and dinners situates Gabriel inside the frame of a small box in a million living rooms filled with the sound of masticating jaws. The geopolitical and economic context at this point in the story is grave: it takes place after the 1973 Yom Kippur War, which has triggered the OPEC oil embargo and subsequent international oil shock. The bar where the "real" Gabriel and his equally hard-up fellow actors hide out decides not to allow its customers to linger more than thirty minutes over a single order. The climate of entropy, fuelled by economic decline, is metatextually equated with "the old dishonourable plot," and treated metonymically as the dumbing down of the film and television industry – which tells "ever more simply now" (183).

Gallant gleefully takes us on a tour of the latest television project based on the French Occupation, foregrounding the accumulation of social stereotypes which passes for plot. A group of Resistance fighters being deported would jump out of a train. The group would include

> an anti-Semitic aristocrat, a Communist militant, a peasant with a droll Provençal accent, a long-faced Protestant intellectual, and a priest in doubt

> about his vocation. Three Jews will be discovered to have jumped or fallen with them: one aged rabbi, one black-market operator, *and one anything*. (185)

Gabriel, a real-life Jew, assumes he will be the reductive one anything who gets in a rowboat with the other caricatures and makes for the maquis. But Dieter tells him he is now "the wrong age to play a Jew" (186), and asks him to become a surrendering Wehrmacht officer, seen in the last episode instead of vanishing after the first. An orgy of frame-breaking follows, blurring the genuine and the simulacrum. Dieter is expected at a wedding in Bavaria, but the shooting of the last scene has been delayed:

> Dieter had to call and explain why he could not be at the wedding; he was held up waiting for the surrender. (188)

The binary parallelism places on the same plane the contemporary "real" wedding and the make-believe surrender. Gallant intensifies the incongruity through the underlying historical resonances connected to an incompatible time frame (the 1940s resurging into the 1970s). The resulting hilarity gains in scope through the author's use of what narratologists call *aspect*, namely the relations of frequency or of repetition between the telling and the story. Here a one-time only event is treated iteratively, as if it happened again and again.[18] Following "an infinity of surrenders" (192) which had preceded this one, they were finally "*able* to surrender" (189). My added italics foreground the source of another metaleptic syncopated beat: the adjective signifying competence is incompatible with the verb which follows it, requiring none. Dieter and Gabriel in German uniform before the Delacroix monument wait for the camera to start turning and hear an elderly couple passing by ask them in German, "What are you doing here?" "Waiting to surrender," says Dieter (190). The effect on the reader can be provocatively compared to the sudden glottal closure of the hiccup. Less prosaically, the figure is analogous to the polka, namely the skip and half step which follows the opening hop-step-close-step. The half-step in the air houses a slide and turn, a moment of suspension when the movement tilts in the other direction. For the two-step veering from the real to the reel culminates in another slide and turn in which the

18 Elsewhere, the author creates ontological confusion via grammar. She submits the fictive through the mode of the real when she presents the surrender through progressive aspectuality, namely as an ongoing process rather than a completive action viewed perfectively, as a whole: "They surrendered *all the rest of the afternoon*" (191).

two frames are radically compressed: "The man tried to give them cigarettes, but *neither colonel* smoked" (190). A snapshot then completes the fusion and confusion, by putting the inhabitants of both worlds at a further remove and on an equal (and equally blurred) footing on a two-dimensional picture plane. "The couple took pictures of each other standing between Dieter and Gabriel, and went away" (190), and "*Dieter and Gabriel led some Turks and Yugoslavs and some unemployed Frenchmen into captivity*" (192).

surfeit & lack

The frame-breaking from "Baum, Gabriel" which I have italicized above operates rather like an odd man out, in which the end of the segment ("into captivity") jars with the middle (Turks, Yugoslavs, unemployed Frenchmen). The discord between two distinct diegetic levels moreover dovetails with the disruptive weight of *paralepsis*: a transgression of the focalization code governing the narrative via a sort of information *surplus*. As we can see in the italicized sentence quoted above, Gallant has adopted external focalization: the subjects Dieter and Gabriel are third person and thus are ostensibly not the speaker but somebody else. Yet Dieter in a preceding passage has complained that unlike his pool of extras in the 1960s – proper Germans authentically endowed with the "right" nationality or identity – at present there "were no real Germans among them, but Yugoslavs, Turks, North Africans, Portuguese, and some unemployed French" (*PS* 189). So when the author then passes up neutral, congruous terms such as "Dieter and Gabriel led *their troops/men* into captivity," in favour of a list of extra information, a breakdown of the bedraggled cast's real, incompatible nationalities, the knowledge and terms are Dieter's, and we have sidestepped into his head. Under the syncopating paralepsis roil the writer's multivocality and her multiview.

It can be enlightening at present to return to the story "The Cost of Living" and its first-person narration, which is favoured by modernists (and their postmodern successors) who think contemporary readers feel traditional omniscience to be manipulative. Gallant's eye/I-narrator, who is named properly only once, in a picture (as the child Patricia), and who is addressed occasionally as "Puss" by her older sister Louise, remains essentially the camera eye: "I had often watched her and seen the pattern" (*GA* 179), she explains. She also has an ear, and thus learns certain insider information, but by definition, her knowledge remains limited. The author adheres on the whole to the narrative's governing code of plausibility, and has her narrator offer many a precautionary remark on scenes she has not witnessed or thoughts she cannot know:

> "It would be presumptuous of me to say what she was thinking, but I can guess" (176)
> "she probably looked at his hands" (180)
> "Louise may have looked out of her window; I would rather not guess" (195)
> "That was all Louise could tell me later on" (183)
> "That is all I can tell you: I am not Louise" (192)

Yet the narrator often tells us much more than she should – more than the focalization code would allow her to. It is Louise who tells her sister about the reception where she met her future lover, Patrick, who turns out to live in the same hotel as they do (and who we learn is Sylvie's lover). But the narrator relates the encounter complete with a profusion of dialogue she did not hear and could not possibly have heard so accurately second-hand, much less remember. The narrator's following remarks show how she takes on a semi-omniscience. Stretching the truth effect, she notably reports knowledge beyond her years, and even the thoughts of other characters:

> "most women think a man's character is shown in his hands" (180)
> "He was young, but old enough to know what that sudden silence meant" (181)
> "They had seen each other across the room, and each of them had thought 'I wonder who that is?'" (178)
> "Unable to squander, she wondered where to deposit her treasures of pity, affection, and love" (185)

Gallant also deploys the mirror opposite of paralepsis, namely paralipsis (in which, as we have seen, the narrative sidesteps an element). Rather than tripping over the former's unexpected ridge (that information surplus) on an otherwise even terrain, we readers stumble into a hole: the *omission* of paralipsis. The analogy of derailing might be even more apt, as the figure of paralipsis involves a lateral ellipsis: the narrative does not pass over a moment in time but sidesteps it. I broached this device of lateral omission when I discussed the *partial* rendition of Irmgard's dream in "Jorinda and Jorindel," in which the cracked sidewalk image is left deliberately incomplete. In "Ice Wagon" as well, as I have pointed out from another angle, the omniscient narrator empowered to view her characters from the inside suddenly withholds information, forbidding herself a cranial entry and flaunting a posture of limited knowledge: "But what were they talking about?"/What did she see?" (*PS* 27). The narrator does not omit mentioning the event. She merely steps to the side of the segment, the components of which go unaccounted for, and leaves readers in a state of want. With "The Cost of Living"'s first-person narrator, such questions would be compatible by definition with the focalization code, which is transgressed rather by bouts of too much information. Still, the author does at times rake the transmission of information by fits and starts. In the preceding chapter (in the sub-chapter "an ellipsoidal narrative rhythm"), I discussed how the story repeatedly careens back to the opening meeting between Louise and Sylvie, three steps forward and one step to the side and back. I noted how the intradiegetic narrator, an actor in the story, omits what is outside of the deliberately restricted frame, as if she had blinkers on. The scene in which Sylvie asks Louise for money is depicted in the vivid manner of hypotyposis. But the vantage point on the stairs is at first absent. It emerges as the perspective expands in an unfolding cinematic zoom out, which shortens the focal length to give the appearance of moving away from the subject. The widening field of view progressively appends the segments missing from the frame initially provided.

The discordance strikes when we learn that the narrator, our camera eye, was not present at the scene she represents so graphically.[19] The *backward zoom shot*, which exaggerates depth relationships, is first experienced as a paralipsis, information withheld and slowly relinquished, but suddenly derails into paralepsis. The narrator has been filling in details she cannot have seen, and could not plausibly have heard second-hand: Sylvie looking down from around the bend of the landing with the light of the skylight behind her, Louise propping the bicycle and staring up, her arm aching, even the "touch of winter light upon [Sylvie], on the warm skin and inquisitive eyes" (*GA* 182). The scene is suffused with a surfeit of information coming from a non–eye witness. "Puss" reports not only the exact dialogue she did not hear, but also the tone and manner, complete with an analogy and conceit displaying an appraisal and interpretive act. But whose appraisal is it? Whose voice? Who has taken the measure of Sylvie?

> This was not said plaintively but with an intense vitality that was like a third presence on the stairs. Her warmth and her energy communicated so easily that there was almost too much, and some fell away and had its own existence. (183)

---

19 "That was all Louise could tell me later on" (183), the narrator confesses.

The slippage in gaze is signalled implicitly at a higher, authorial level, when Gallant has Louise talking about Sylvie (who now uses her as an open bank account) in "a new, breathless voice" (188). When Patrick disappears from her life, Louise begins to haunt Sylvie, and pleads with her not to talk about her, "never to disclose – she did not say what" (196). That Louise, who belongs to the type of client the hotel-keeper classifies as "the foreign, interfering, middle-aged female," has fallen in love with a young, French would-be actress is left unsaid. Facing a world "growing deaf to the unsaid" (Hutcheon, *Irony's Edge* 8), it nestles in the choice of an innocent adjective.[20] It lies concealed in "the giving and the lying": in the gifts Louise pays for and disguises in her account book by listing a bottle of aspirin under "the price of a five-course meal" (193). It lies unnamed in the narrator's "revulsion," in her conviction that the new expenses in the life of Louise (who never sees her sister's needs) "were waste and pollution," and that "what had been set in motion by her giving was not goodness, innocence, courage, or generosity but *something dark*" (199).

In the following chapter I shall discuss how Gallant withholds and encrypts much more in "The Cost of Living" than the storied experience of a love triangle. I shall examine how her I-narrator is at the heart of a game confronting depth and surface, *the latent and the manifest* – in line with Picasso's definition of Cubist art: painting not what you see but what you know is there (Flanner 3: 146). Having investigated the modernist figures of dissonance and syncopation which erupt and fracture the classic consonance of Gallant's poetic style, I shall go on to explore more specifically the rhetorical techniques which dovetail with Cubist Realism, such as multiview and narrative rhythm (what narratologists also call tempo, speed, or duration). I have mentioned how in his review of Gallant's collected early stories, *The Cost of Living*, Adam Mars Jones accuses her multiple perspectives of unmooring the reader. In the review in which Jones considers Gallant's mixed perspectives to be flaws, Mavis almost converts him with "Bernadette." He is notably astonished at the blend of a satirical tone for the liberal employers with "a disorientingly deep understanding of the reality of their pregnant maid's existence." Jones admits that this "destabilisingly fierce attunement to a relatively remote life" makes what he sees as the "fault" of mixed perspectives "almost enviable." Nonetheless, Jones prefers "tethering" the point of view. He explains that the reader needs to know if the main character is being viewed "from the inside or the outside," and makes an interesting

20 The hotel-keeper complains that Sylvie often has someone over at night, and that when the police come around to check, he has to pay a fine. "'Do you mean men?' said my *wretched* sister. Do you mean the police come about men?'" (198).

analogy: "It's as basic as a time signature in music." Yet Jones has forgotten how – well before free jazz – modernist composers like Bartók and Stravinsky exploded the time signature at the beginning of the stave,[21] just as they shattered the key signature (which J.S. Bach well before them had disrupted: after umpteen modulations, we no longer know where we are).[22] Jones objects to Gallant viewing her characters from the inside and the outside simultaneously, and states that "to be in two places at once is really to be nowhere at all." In the next chapter, I will pursue my argument that, on the contrary, her multiview takes us everywhere.

---

21 In the *Danse sacrale* which concludes *Le Sacre*, for instance, Stravinsky moves from 2/16 to 3/16 and 5/16 in every bar (a huge challenge for the choreographer Vaslav Nijinsky).

22 More recently, Beethoven's dumbfoundingly dissonant *Grand Fugue* (1827) was actually acknowledged by Stravinsky to be "absolutely contemporary" (Stravinsky in Craft 24).

5

Text/image borderblur & Cubist realism

Grâce à l'art, au lieu de voir un seul monde, le nôtre, nous le voyons se multiplier et autant qu'il y a d'artistes originaux, autant nous avons de mondes à notre disposition, plus différents les uns des autres que ceux qui roulent dans l'infini.[1]

Marcel Proust, *Le Temps retrouvé* [*Time Regained*] (895)

In Gallant's oeuvre, in a tendency reaching back to premodernists such as Henry James,[2] thought displaces event, the mind supersedes the world, and the lens supplants the object. As Hemingway suspected when he chose Cézanne as a model for his writing, and as Arthur Danto has theorized in *Beyond the Brillo Box: The Visual Arts in Post-historical Perspective*, visual artworks are dense with latent properties that are often appreciated later, through modes of consciousness of which their contemporaries were not necessarily aware (89). The picture, once envisaged as the transfer to a canvas of a reality external to the individual (artist or viewer), has in our modern era become linked to the phenomenon of consciousness and inner vision (Francastel 28–9). This radical transformation from world to brain underpinning the whole of modernist production was naturally

1 "Thanks to art, instead of seeing one world only – our own – we see that world multiply, and we have at our disposal as many worlds as there are original artists: worlds more different from one another than those spinning out there in infinity" (my translation).

2 In the 1908 edition of *The Portrait of a Lady*, Henry James reiterated the aesthetic concepts of his 1884 essay, "The Art of Fiction," namely that he was not interested in action or plot but in consciousness and in the study of memory, imagination, and motive. He posited that the portrait sketched of his heroine's long "meditative vigil," the simple "representation" of her "motionless *seeing*," is as interesting as the surprise of a caravan or the identification of a pirate" ("Preface," *The Portrait of a Lady* xvii.)

accentuated by the Freudian revolution, but actually reaches back to the foundations for empiricism laid down in John Locke's *Essay Concerning Human Understanding* (1690), namely that all knowledge derives from experience, that ideas result from the arrangement of materials derived from sensory experience and lodged in the memory. With his famous use of anamorphosis in *The Ambassadors* (1533),[3] Hans Holbein the Younger had already demonstrated that reality is determined and limited by the perceiver's position in time and space, or to boil it down further, that reality is dependent on perspective. The interest in perception as an open synthetic process was irrigated by Kant and by the phenomenological studies of Edmund Husserl, who pointed out that we never see all six sides of a die simultaneously, and that what we call a cube is actually the synthesis of multiple successive apparitions which we mentally assemble into a unit. Hence Picasso's agenda to paint the sides of the cube hidden from his (and our) vantage point, which he (and we) know are there.

This is of course in radical opposition to Joyce's initial definition of *integritas* or wholeness, according to which the aesthetic image must first be "luminously apprehended as self-bounded and self-contained upon the immeasurable background of space or time *which is not it*" (*Portrait* 192). I have explored how Gallant adheres to the principle of wholeness, notably through a high altitude vantage point showing the bigger picture of the human comedy. Yet other authorial techniques *lock into the agenda of synthetic Cubism*: multiplying viewpoints and depicting objects on the picture plane as if all its facets were visible at the same time. In *A Fairly Good Time*, the focalizer-turned-narrator Renata, Shirley's friend, who has just had an illegal abortion, lies in bed, and her "kneeling gnat" lover Karel (196) lies down on top of the counterpane with his boots on, facing her. Shirley, who in the dark room has just "noticed a sleeping fox that turned out to be a pile of ski boots" (196), observes, "An eye fixed to the glass roof would have seen two seahorses, but no one ever watches from that direction" (197). When I addressed essentialism and the perceiving subject in chapter 3, I already pointed to analogous motifs of Cubist refraction which erupt in Gallant's texts. I have shown these can occur in an enigmatic open ending such as that in "Ice Wagon," housing a quiet apperceptive interrogation of the Kantian manifold. Or in the phenomenological imagery (mirrors, water, glass) of *Green Water, Green Sky*, which

3 In the foreground of Holbein's portrait of power – secular, political, religious, and economic – a flat, distorted image lies in the foreground. When seen from a vantage point to the right of the picture, the distortion is corrected and the image – with a *vanitas* dynamic – revealed to be a human skull.

suggests a vision beyond *eikos* or perceptible reality, collapsing the ontological structures of the real which are interlocked with vantage point and perspective. Cubist diffraction occurs even when an invisible overarching narrative consciousness, such as in "The Cost of Living," obliquely discloses knowledge the subjective narrative voice conceals.

"you paint not what you see but what you know is there"

At the end of the preceding chapter I alluded to how Gallant withholds and encrypts much more in "The Cost of Living" than the storied experience of a love triangle, a recipe as old as the sun, even if the fluid ménage à trois gives it a modernist imprint. I posited that her choice of a first-person narrator is at the heart of a game in line with Picasso's concise manifesto of Cubist art, which turns on its head J.M.W. Turner's credo – which is actually Lockean, sensualist, and thus (pre)Impressionist rather than realist. While Turner stated, "My business is to paint what I see, not what I know is there" (Turner qtd in MacCulloch 160), Picasso claimed that his Cubist art involved "painting not what you see but what you know is there" (Flanner 3: 146). Gallant's game in "The Cost of Living" is precisely to play with the manifest and the latent, surface and depth, seeing and knowing. The winding structure of the story spirals both backward and forward in recurrent tellings which intermesh, in the same way as the women's common lover and would-be lover, Patrick, is depicted in the replicative manner of a Cubist portrait "in which there are three eyes and a double profile" (*GA* 188; *CL* 219).

Quite like Jean, the narrator of *Its Image on the Mirror*, Puss watches and tells, but no one watches her. She shows us a world, but does not give free access to her mind. The paralipsis or concealment works in the manner of Agatha Christie's famous mystery, *The Murder of Roger Ackroyd*, in which readers fail to divine the identity of the murderer because he is the narrator and chooses not to tell us. Such a strategy disrupts the standard reading pact which views the confessional first-person pronoun as offering the truth of subjectivity. Just what truths does Gallant withhold with one hand – through the obstinately blind angle of the controlling vantage point – and encode into her story with the other? *How does she paint the invisible*? Our first clue is embedded not in event but in the description of a picture, the sepia studio portrait taken over two decades before, when the narrator was eight and Louise thirteen:

> Here is Louise, calm and straight, with her hair brushed on her shoulders, and her pretty hands; there am I, with organdy frock, white shoes, ribbon, and fringe. Two little Anglo-German girls, accomplished at piano, Old

> Melbourne on the father's side, Church of England to the bone: Louise and Patricia – Lulu and Puss. (*GA* 175; *CL* 204)

The word picture is idyllic. All the components work together in stillness and silence to suggest concord: we *see* that these are like-minded, well-cared for children brought up to be good, familiar with the consonance of music and religion. But the truth erupts in the description's dissonant concluding sentence – a sentence visually buttressed by a paragraph break, which sidesteps into readers' minds and breaks to a halt: "We hated each other then" (175). Cleanliness is not next to godliness, music does not soothe the savage breast, and under the peaceful surface – unseen – roils the untamed, wild and fierce. Surprised readers may want to hunt for clues in the verbal representation of the graphic representation. They will find an ironic strategy of surfeit and lack which suspends meaning and displaces. Louise, we learn, has pretty hands. As for Patricia, the details listed operate in the mode of the anti-portrait, namely in what is said and what is omitted. The list unfurls with an ironic dynamic, pointedly mentioning only the little girl's accoutrements. Louise is pretty, then, and Puss is plain.[4]

The older Puss tries to imagine how Patrick seemed in Louise's eyes:

> I doubt if she could have told you. From the beginning they stood too close; his face was like a painting in which there are three eyes and a double profile. No matter how far she backed off, later on, she never made sense of him. (*GA* 188; *CL* 219)

The analogy, disclosing a slippage between the perceived and the percipient, could not plausibly be emitted by anyone other than the percipient herself. Is this a case of semi-omniscience, or is it Puss substituting herself for Louise in a situation of desire? When Patrick leaves her, Louise collapses, conflating his departure with an ancient loss. We learn that

4 Written and published close together, both "Cost of Living" and *Its Image on the Mirror* explore the dynamics of domination, desire, and rightness. Plain Puss lights up and in turn is illuminated by her intratextual doppelgänger, Jean – both narrators placed in the same distributional slot of jealous subordination with respect to a resented, better-favoured sister. But Jean conceals less from us readers, openly confessing her relief at the belief her sister Isobel would die of a kidney infection: "Her death would remove the ungovernable daughter for my parents and the unattainable for my husband. Dead-and-buried Isobel, under a heap of snow, or a rectangle of grass, would be harmless Isobel, *the pretty Duncan sister*, taken too soon to her Maker" (*My Heart Is Broken* 62).

she had been married at eighteen to a young man, Collie, who was then sent to Malaya with his regiment and killed. The narrator tells us, "I was thirteen and they were the love of my life" (196). One trips over the pronoun "they": how can boiling envy and resentment have turned into such intense love? One needs to backtrack and reread the passage to decode a cryptic phrase, a signifying *lateral omission* which beautifully illustrates Gallant's high degree of subtlety:

> I knew it was not Patrick but Collie who had gone. It was Collie who vanished *before everything was said, turning his back, stopping his ears*. I was thirteen and they were the love of my life. (*GA* 196; *CL* 228)

To be remarked is the cunning use of the agentless passive ("before everything *was said*"), which leaves the agent performing the telling unknown. The locution erases the narrating self; it leaves no room for "Puss" in the experience. All the while the narrator sidesteps her role in the event, the pronoun "everything" throws an indiscriminate blanket over just what things were said. But through Collie's body language of outrage disclosed in the contiguous segments, we *know* what was said: "*You* are the love of my life." We know what is invisible: a girl's passionate love for a young man who has preferred an older sister.[5] An older sister who now has been in the arms of Patrick, a new young man the narrator is careful to call insignificant, but a man she watches ever so closely, down to his long eyelashes and grave smile. Most of all, a narrator who is not only unreliable but devious.

What invisible thing nestles in sentences such as "I sat until the room grew dark" or "Everything was still, as still as snow, as still as a tracked mouse" (*GA* 202, 203)? The first sentence I quote concludes an episode of deceit. After Patrick has left Paris for good, Puss notices his handwriting on a letter to Sylvie in the basket of mail. She takes it to her room, opens it, and begins to read it: "The first words were '*Mon amour*'" (201, original stress). The thunderclap is never acknowledged. The narrator misses a beat which corresponds to the blank paragraph break, and veers into a purely informational utterance stated independently of its virtual value: "The new tenant of his room was a Brazilian student who played the guitar" (201). I shall come back to this paragraph analogous to a Pointillist painting, which ends with Puss picturing herself going to meet

5 In the twin but loosely inverse story of domination and secrecy, *Its Image on the Mirror*, the narrator, Jean, is the older sister, whose husband would have preferred to marry the younger sister she envies.

Patrick, and in her mind's eye, seeing his dismay. Sylvie finds her sitting with the purloined letter in the telling dark, which suggests an inner darkness echoing the "something dark" (199) the narrator found in Louise's heart. Sylvie vanishes, and when she comes back much later for her belongings, asks Puss casually if she has ever heard "from him" (203). There follows another missed beat, another drop to a new paragraph, and the statement which sidesteps and suspends: "Everything was still, as still as snow, as still as a tracked mouse." The echoing, alliterative triplication emphasizes the strategy of concealment, as does the analogy between Puss and the "tracked" mouse. This single-sentence paragraph is thick with the unsaid. The narrator is determined to disclose nothing. When prying Sylvie, who we have been told knows everything about everyone, tells Puss she no longer minds she opened her letter, having realized that "A person in love will do anything," Puss retorts "I was never in love" (203). The rhetoric of denial Gallant has substituted for lateral omission unsettles the authority of the affirmation. This final sleight of hand draws attention away from event or content to the act of uttering, and to the invisible climate of the speaker's mind. Through the words we divine the half-embodying of thought which sustains a correspondence between an outness, a reality *sui generis*, and images and movements within.

When Duchamp shocked New York's Armory Show with his *Nude Descending the Staircase*, he was actually borrowing from technology, which had extended the powers of the human eye through time and space. Eadweard Muybridge's zoopraxiscope, a camera modelled on the revolver, could capture a moving object synchronously from various vantage points (Solnit 222); the first moving images of Thomas Edison's kinetoscope (which Proust evokes in the very first pages of *Du côté de chez Swann* as a marvel of deconstruction and recomposition) enabled a Parisian to watch a jockey riding a horse in Kentucky. These forerunners of the movie projector allowed people to experience events in entirely new ways. More profoundly, they collapsed a reality rooted in the space we are melded to and the time or speed it takes to tear us away to another point. By exhibiting disjunctive spaces synchronously, Duchamp was among the modernists who spurred the painter and photographer David Hockney to theorize and investigate the structure of seeing. In Hockney's terms, vision consists of "a continuous accumulation of details perceived across time and synthesised into a larger, metamorphosing whole," and the general perspective is "built up from hundreds of micro-perspectives," explaining in turn why "memory plays a crucial role in perception" (Weschler 63). Interestingly, composers, too, were exploring the perceptual relations between sound, space, and time. By adding one sound at a time to the soundtrack in a quasi puff-pastry technique, Bresson had already foregrounded sonic objects in *Les Dames du bois de Boulogne* (1945), an experimental approach which would later converge with R. Murray Schafer's critique of schizophonia (the split between an original sound in a natural soundscape and its mediated electroacoustic reproduction).[6]

Gallant's practice of superimposing micro-perspectives on the page – as in "The Cost of Living" – reveals a photographer's eye. It calls to mind Hockney's analogous composition through decomposition, notably his Cubist-inspired series of Polaroid composites and photo collages (joiners). The Polaroid portraits generate an impression of disjunction, distortion, and fragmentation through a double, contradictory movement of expansion and contraction which foils the viewer's quest for a congruent fit. The multiple individual snapshots of body segments arranged vertically and glued together to make up the whole figure of a single subject are separated by both white frame and by space between the snaps. Viewers are further challenged in their attempt to scan the collage and fuse the composite into a unified whole. The artist blurs through a strategy of overlay: each framed and separated body segment overlaps anatomically with the contiguous framed image, producing an effect of stretch which the viewer must contract and correct. The pictures are in addition taken from different vantage points and at slightly different times, producing further distortion as well as a friction between stillness and the sensation of movement through space-time.

I have already addressed a textual equivalent in "The Cost of Living," when Gallant's narrator, who operates as a camera eye, describes the first meeting on the stairs between her sister Louise and Sylvie. I noted first of all that Sylvie looking down from the bend of the landing had already been observed by a painterly eye and portrayed like the fragmentary preparatory sketches of a nude. I further noted that Puss delineates the meeting scene with temporal and spatial precision within a restricted frame and from an initially unlocatable standpoint. I demonstrated how the perspective expands in a sort of backward zoom shot, which widens the field of view and exaggerates depth relationships; it gradually appends the segments missing from the frame initially provided. I finally pointed out that our narratorial camera eye turns out not to have witnessed the scene she presents so graphically. *She paints not what she saw but what she knows was there.*

6 Bresson went on to over-foreground sound in *Launcelot du Lac* [*Lancelot of the Lake*] (1974), in which the Arthurian knights' chain mail in the battle scenes sounds like pots and pans being bashed around. While most period films use pots and pans to sound like armour, Bresson decided to use real armour, which sounds like pots and pans. Quite a statement on realism and illusion.

When Gallant foregrounds our accumulative structure of seeing, she, like Hockney and the Cubists before him, effectively explores the way human vision works. I can demonstrate this with a further example from the trail-blazing *The Pegnitz Junction* (1973), which addresses post–Second World War Germans' struggle to shed their past. The writer notably constructs a continuous accumulation of details in terms of phenomenological readerly time.[7] Right from the opening statement, she embraces and blends the referential visible and audible external world with the awarenesses of mental landscapes:

> She was a bony slow-moving girl from a small bombed baroque German city, where all that was worthwhile keeping had been rebuilt and which now looked as pink and golden as a pretty child and as new as morning. (5)

The slow-moving girl in the slow-moving sentence is included in a rather baroque rhetorical accumulation obliging the reader to switch between the different logics and viewpoints contained in the adjuncts. The epithetical style suggests that all possibilities will be envisaged and pursued, and, as is usually the case with the accumulation of qualifiers, it slows down the pace to generate suspension. As Alice Munro goes on to do when she drifts towards the long short story "Open Secrets," Gallant creates an effect rather like that of chromatic music in the minor mode.

The polyphonic novella is fundamentally constructed as a magical junction, even short circuit, in thought and time in which juxtaposed ventriloquized subjectivities criss-cross exponentially, creating a dizzying crescendo. Mavis always objected to appraisals pointing to the work's stream-of-consciousness approach, for she astutely distinguished interior monologue from Joyce's grammatically unedited, inarticulate expression of internal unspoken thought at the prelinguistic stage. Always articulate, Gallant nonetheless, "as few others, nails the meandering, free associative quality of consciousness on the page" (Orner, "The Way Vivid"). In the novella, when the newly emancipated protagonist, Christine, recklessly leaves for a holiday in Paris with her older lover and his small son, and they settle in an old hotel marked for demolition, the seediness is composed in small movements from inside to outside, like track shots moving forward and back. When our gaze is directed to the view which can be had, the list of items to picture is deliberately composite, compelling us to conjure up an image only to decompose it on account of sets of

7 The work was hailed by critics of the period as generating "the true rediscovery of time" (Woodcock 91).

deflationary afterthoughts whose visual signs or icons it takes time to take in. We read: "The view from every window was of a church covered with scaffolding from top to bottom, the statue of a cardinal lying on its side, and a chestnut tree sawed in pieces" (*Pegnitz Junction* 5). The gist is of course a view of a church, a statue, and a tree. I shall reproduce the quote once more below, in a form which underscores the dysphoric units representing accumulations of detail from fluctuating standpoints, which I light up through analogies to film techniques:

"The view (*from every window*)": a track shot to the side or even cinema's stereoscopic technique of superimposing images taken at a distance from each other
"was of a church (1: *covered with scaffolding*)": a forward zoom to increase magnification, flatten depth, and narrow the field of view
"(2: *from top to bottom*)": a tilt pivoting the camera vertically
"the statue of a cardinal (*lying on its side*)": a vertical tilt which unexpectedly turns into a horizontal panning shot
"and a chestnut tree (*sawed in pieces*)": a second vertical tilt unexpectedly turning into a horizontal panning shot

Announcing a live, erect chestnut tree and then transforming it with one stroke into a pile of lumber showcases how the writer adds yet subtracts. Announcing the view of a church only to conceal it with scaffolding demonstrates how Gallant reveals yet hides, validates and invalidates, composes and decomposes. The writer compels us to ceaselessly adjust, erase, and recompose a world in which nothing holds its shape. Hockney's Polaroid portraits operating within a framework of de/composition naturally spring to mind. So does the agenda of decomposition and recomposition of his admired Picasso, notably the Cubist painter's much translated and often quoted remark to Christian Zervos when discussing the notoriously fractured figures in *Les Demoiselles d'Avignon* (in which, to boot, he dissolved the figure/ground relation): "Chez moi, un tableau est une somme de destructions" (Zervos).[8]

never happier than in an artist's studio: intersections

I have discussed how Mavis attributed her fascination with Paris to films that had marked her as a little girl, such as Worsley's *The Hunchback*

8 The fuller statement from Picasso's 1935 *Cahiers d'Art* conversation with Christian Zervos, reprinted in English, reads, "A picture used to be a sum of additions. In my case a picture is a sum of destructions" (Barr 272).

of Notre Dame and Rupert Julian's *The Phantom of the Opera*. These deployed the same disfigured star and the same byzantine set; more importantly, they wrenched the ordinary, created new worlds, and pointed beyond visible experience. Later (coinciding with Mavis's final high school year in New York), the release of William Dieterle's famous remake, *The Hunchback of Notre Dame* (1939), served as a booster shot to Worsley's screen adaptation of the Victor Hugo novel. It also confirmed the image's faculty to carry the unseen: atmosphere, climate. Above all, it confirmed the image's faculty for worldmaking, in the sense that Proust intended in the epigraph above, which imputes to art the generative power of substituting other worlds for the only one we know. In fact, when praising Bergotte, the writer he passionately admires, Proust's strongly autobiographical Narrator evokes the countless parts of the universe which his own feeble perception would never make out without such literary mediation (*Du côté de chez Swann* 115).

"Wing's Chips," the autobiographical story Mavis admitted was closest to her heart, written with such loving care that half a century later she could recite parts of it from memory,[9] addresses her encounter with the powerful screen, which may well have contributed to shaping the writer's feeling that the role of fiction lies in bringing to life "a distillation of all weathers, a climate of the mind" ("Afterword," *PS* 366). The writer narrates her memories as a child on holiday with her amateur painter father in a rural French-Canadian village. In this disguised Châteauguay of her childhood – just as in Tornatore's Sicilian village in *Cinema Paradiso* – the whole village attended screenings, from grandmothers to toddlers. Gallant in this piece depicts the cinema before the advent of synchronized sound as a wrenching of the senses: notably the eye and the ear, derailed and dislocated. The perception of a gap, presented through the defamiliarizing perspective of a naive (but observant) child, reveals the innate gift of the ironist for spying incongruity, for perceiving two contradictory things folded together. It also may have contributed to shaping Mavis's craft of caricature:

> The pictures had no sound track; airs from "My Maryland" and "The Student Prince" were played on a piano and there was the occasional toot of the

---

9 Mavis selected the story when she happily agreed to do a reading at a conference I was organizing at the Sorbonne Nouvelle in 2012. A few weeks before the conference her macular degeneration worsened significantly, but she knew her text so well that a glimpse of words here and there allowed her to skim on till the ending, which she knew by heart. Her vision worsened as the day approached, as did her fatigue, and we had to give up this one last professional appearance.

> suburban train from Montreal while the screen ladies with untidy hair and men in riding boots engaged in agitated, soundless conversation, opening and closing their mouths like fish. (*GA* 26)

The sensual breach from our current world of synchronized seeing and hearing, noticed with precocious detachment, pointed the nascent artistic mind to what its Latin etymology stresses: the *artifice* (making by skill) of representation in manufacturing a world. I adhere to Goodman's observation that worldmaking consists of "taking apart and putting together, often conjointly" (*Worldmaking* 7). I suggest that these early screen reconfigurations of reality may have catalysed Mavis's awareness of successful illusion-making and its intersections with *composition and decomposition.* On the one hand, the deconstruction process consists of "*dividing wholes into* parts and partitioning kinds into subspecies, analysing complexes into component features, drawing distinctions." On the other hand, the (re)construction procedure consists of "*composing wholes and kinds out of* parts and members and subclasses, combining features into complexes, and making connections" (Goodman, *Worldmaking* 7). Picasso's agenda of decomposition and recomposition once more springs to mind, notably his remark about the fractured figures in *Les Demoiselles d'Avignon*: "Chez moi, un tableau est une somme de destructions" (Zervos). The abstraction of such an aesthetic analysis applied to literature takes on concrete contours if we take a specific example from Mavis's beloved Proust. The adolescent I-Narrator has fantasized about the Duchess of Guermantes and her fabulous lineage, and is thrilled to learn she is graciously attending a Combray wedding. When he catches a glimpse of her, he notes a blonde lady with piercing blue eyes, a red face, and a big nose with a pimple. She belongs to a *type* ("un certain type féminin" [Proust, *Du côté de chez Swann* 210]) which could include any doctor's or shopkeeper's wife, and his deception is huge. But since the young narrator wants and needs the Duchess to remain glorious, he decomposes her face into isolated parts, deletes the unsightly features and recombines the particularities he chooses to keep (the blonde hair, the blue eyes, the throat) into a new whole. The deliberately incomplete Duchess is now beautiful, in congruence with her noble ancestor.[10]

---

10 Proust's narrator declares, "je m'écriais devant ce croquis volontairement incomplet: "Qu'elle est belle! Quelle noblesse! Comme c'est bien une fière Guermantes, la descendante de Geneviève de Brabant, que j'ai devant moi!" ["I cried out in front of this intentionally partial sketch: 'How beautiful she is! Such nobility! What a proud Guermantes, a true descendant of Geneviève de Brabant, I have before me here!'"] (212, my translation).

"Wing's Chips," the Gallant story I have evoked, is the one in which Mavis relates going to see an especially long-awaited silent horror film, Worsley's *Hunchback*. Lon Chaney stars as the deaf, deformed, one-eyed hunchbacked bell-ringer, the very epitome of the grotesque, thanks to artifice. The contact lens blanking out one eye, the brace holding his legs together, the set of false teeth, the putty making his nose and cheeks bulge, and the heavy rubber hump covered with animal fur, all engineer the scabrousness of the grotesque body which the *fabliau* and *fabula* have always relied on – as have modernist writers from Joyce and Nabokov to Céline and Beckett. On another level, they also exemplify the similarity-ordering process I have just evoked: making a different world by sorting into kinds – same or not the same – and putting things together in another way. The medium itself was as powerful as a punch to the young Mavis. The violently huge images – often high angle shots – strikingly exemplify the visual arts' power of emphasis, accent, or *weighting*: the departure from the prominence accorded features "in the current world of our everyday seeing" (Goodman, *Worldmaking* 11). Dieterle's and Worsley's film versions alter the world they represent by visually weighting certain features of stance, line, bulk or light. I take them as examples of the intertextual and intermedial borrowings that the early and late modernists delighted in. They offered Mavis lessons in isolated seeing, visually performing Hugo's Romantic aesthetic agenda: the melding of extremes analogous to one unfurling oxymoron all in chiaroscuro. Significantly, she would go on to practise a mixture of codes, considering inseparable the grim and the grotesque, the grave and the comic – which, as my subsequent book will demonstrate – places her in the ranks of fine ironists and satirists such as Austen, Nabokov, and Beckett.

I can offer some private biographical elements here, notably in the form of a letter, so as to clarify Mavis's central role in my discussion of intermedial dialogical responses:

Paris, 3 May (2008)[11]

Dear Marta,

(...) Like many, many *writers, I never enjoyed the company of writers (as I did of painters, for instance) and my friendship with Anne Hébert came about because Jean Paul Lemieux + Madeleine Desrosiers (his wife), both painters, had asked me to call on her in her hotel in Menton.*

11 The year, which Mavis at times did not bother to write on her card, is indicated on the corresponding envelope postmarked 5 May 2008.

Once in the cultural capital which staged the Cubist rupture with traditional figuration and spatial perspective, Mavis met seasoned artists like Max Ernst and Man Ray (and became close to Man Ray's wife, Juliet). Never happier than in an artist's studio, she also encouraged young painters, from the Hungarian Béla Kondor and French Alexis Gorodine to the Canadian Joseph Plaskett, throughout their experiments with style.[12] These included departures from and returns to figurative art, nonetheless stripped of perspective and shadows. Her praising the "jewel-like" quality of objects seemingly vibrating on their own in the flat, shadowless still lifes of Gorodine and Plaskett (Plaskett 293) interestingly calls up Mukherjee's analogy comparing Gallant's stories to "little gems, perfectly cut and glittering" (11). Mavis famously asserted that her stories began in a flash with a fixed image, and that a haptic, sensualist mental image of the lost Sherbrooke Street of her childhood was the starting point of the Linnet Muir sequence, a sort of *recherche du temps perdu* ("An Introduction," *HT* xxii).

Mavis also had a vast collection of artwork and art books including fifteenth- to eighteenth-century Flemish and Dutch drawings and prints of genre scenes, interiors, and portraits. I consider their brief strokes of shading or hatching and their pared-down contours to be the non-linguistic semiotic equivalents of the light strokes or "series of sketches" Ondaatje noted by which Gallant "will have circled a person, captured a voice, revealed a whole manner of a life" of a world "in shadows" (x). Under Gallant's brushstrokes, *scribal variants of the swift suggestive outlines of the sketch* and the pastel which modern painters favoured over the ponderousness of the oil painting, characters come to life in mid-gesture, "in the zone between thought and possible action" (x). The story I analysed in the previous chapter, "The Cost of Living," demonstrates the life-making power of Gallant's draftsmanship – such light strokes and fine contours conferring such thickness. "Think of draggled laces, sagging hems, ribbons undone; that was what Sylvie was like," begins the portrait Gallant draws through Puss's painterly eye (*GA* 176). Beyond Sylvie's forever open door, anyone can see "her furrowed bed and the basin, in which underclothes floated among islands of scum" (177). Sylvie sits in bed, "with her back to a filthy pillow, eating *pain-au-chocolat* (...) crumbs on the blanket and around her

12 In *Almost Nothing*, Karpeles relates how Mavis also befriended Józef Czapski, the Polish painter in exile who had written a text she admired on Proust (16–17; 144–5). In fact, Karpeles found out about the little-known Czapsky thanks to Gallant. She mentioned him and the circle of Polish expatriates she frequented in her *Journals*, and literary agent Steven Barclay, who was preparing the diaries for publication, tracked down Czapsky's lectures on Proust (delivered in a Soviet prison camp) and sent them to Karpeles.

chin" (186, original italics). When Louise sets her thermos down on Sylvie's table, it finds itself "between a full ashtray and a cardboard container of coagulated milk" (187). This last image is finely delineated by sound: an apparent triple alliteration (c/c/c) which turns out to be a quaternary consonance framing the extended image with the same plosive, from the initial "cardboard" to the final "milk." All are images which on one plane operate as a guarantor-discourse of verisimilitude in congruence with a realist aesthetic agenda. Yet on a higher plane they are images through which ideas rush, regarding the right way to live in the world.

Gallant's portrait of Sylvie speaks to Alice Munro's first story collection, *Dance of the Happy Shades* (1968), from the men in undershirts and the women in slovenly dresses torn under the arms in "Walker Brothers Cowboy" to the house's dirt and smell of decay evoking carrion under the verandah in "Thanks for the Ride," operating as semaphores for the moral decay of the grotesque figures pandering their own daughter and granddaughter (see Dvořák, "Dailiness"). Both Munro and Gallant delineate things to concretize the concepts of civic and moral righteousness (in the original etymological sense of rightwise) and transgression. Sylvie's slovenliness is indeed the vice that John Wesley famously denounced,[13] namely *acedia*, the apathy of physical and spiritual sloth – tragically death-tainted in the case of Munro's "The Time of Death." Gallant, however, brandishes no signs of a transcendent determinism or evil, but simply, with a glance, interrogates a way of being. Like Munro, but to a different degree, she can be said to operate within a representational realism, in which characters can serve to embody or concretize qualities that the reader perceives as both personal and universal. The mode is rooted in turn in the philosophical realism of authors such as Charles Dickens and George Eliot, who aimed more earnestly to improve their readers.

Such image clusters privileging the pictorial over the verbal and synchronic moment over diachronic sequence form a spiral pattern of recursion and free play in which signifiers are deferred and reconnected to manufacture cohesion. Actually, motivic variations engineering connections belong to a process of recursion already practised by Impressionist painters like Monet, and taken up by American Cubist Realists like Joseph Stella, notably with his numerous paintings of Brooklyn Bridge. Proust, the writer Mavis reread most, wondered about a possible writerly emulation of such artistic iterations – a series of the same cathedral or lily pond in different sorts of light, for instance, the same but not quite – creating

13 I naturally refer to Wesley's famous declaration, "Slovenliness is no part of religion (...) Cleanliness is next to godliness" (qtd in Thomas 56).

a powerful overarching sensation. He vigorously promoted what he saw as the vindication of effect over cause (Karpeles 18–19). I detect in Gallant's work a literary congruence with the Cubist Realists or Precisionists, who depicted modernity in delineated geometrical forms verging on the photorealistic in a highly stylized manner. I have in mind not so much the pictures of technology-mad Joseph Stella and Charles Sheeler (respectively *Old Brooklyn Bridge* [1941] and *Wheels* [1939] for example). I rather have in mind the affiliative graphic backdrops of Oliver Smith, famed for his designs in the cult theatrical productions and screen adaptations Mavis adored, from *Guys and Dolls* and *Porgy and Bess* to *The Sound of Music* and *West Side Story*. An architect and painter who exhibited at the Museum of Modern Art and the Art Institute of Chicago, and who also involved himself in opera, the versatile Smith won the Tony Award for Best Scenic Design for the original 1957 Broadway production of *West Side Story*. His décor for the sordid urban milieu of *Guys and Dolls* is a marvel of meticulous detail with a sheen, precisely what we find in Gallant's pages.

Informed by the philosophical aesthetics of Goodman, Danto, and Levinson regarding the common parameters of fine visual art, which Goodman calls the manifestations or "symptoms of the aesthetic" (*Worldmaking* 67), my discussion illuminates Gallant's distinctive work by identifying and exploring the *analogous perceptual substructure* which supports it. I have repeatedly shown how the writer's expressive aural devices allow the lexical sphere to operate semantically, and serve a referential and semantic intensity. I now argue that *the parameters Gallant's prose shares with visual art involve syntactic and semantic density*,[14] relative *repleteness* (when many aspects of a symbol are significant), *exemplification* (when a symbol serves as a sample of properties), and *multiple and complex reference* (where a symbol performs several [integrated and interacting] referential functions) (Goodman, *Worldmaking* 67–8). These jaw-breaking terms can be visually illustrated by *Pot de fleurs* (1930), an oil on canvas by the Chinese Montparnasse painter Sanyu, which sold for almost 7 million euros at a Paris auction I attended at the Hôtel Drouot in December 2017. If Sanyu's potted peony is so coveted by the art market, it is precisely for its density and repleteness in

14 Chapter 2 provided definitions for syntactic density, which manages to represent the finest differences, and for semantic density, which can tell apart and provide symbols for things ever so finely distinct. In chapter 3 I have offered a personal example of Mavis's eye for distinctions where others fail to see them, notably in the letter dated 1 September 2002 in which she discusses the Polish poet Szymborska: "I wonder what she (Szymborska) thought of Norton's putting a Russian painting on the jacket. It takes an American publisher to think that any Slav is any Slav."

line and colour (reduced to three tones), and for the way it exemplifies all flowers,[15] serving both referential and symbolic functions. Goodman's terms will become even clearer as I unfold my analysis of Gallant's fundamental stylistic properties, properties I see as the painterly dynamics also identified by Goodman: *deletion and supplementation, division and reordering, weighting and distortion* (*Worldmaking* 101). My argument rests on and develops the ideas unpacked in chapter 2's section on condensation and expansion, in which I suggested a writerly correspondence with poetry, allusive but "supercharged with significance" (Wimsatt 231). I adhered to Francine Prose's observation on Gallant's *Collected Stories* that "No one writes more compactly, more densely, with more compression" ("Introduction" xiv).

Gallant's gnomic concentration, her "taut sentences" (Besner, *Light of Imagination* 43), her "rhetorical stinginess" and "parsimonious descriptions" in which "nothing goes to waste" (Manguel xii), her "uncanny ability to distill" (Lahiri, "Introduction" x), are manifest in "The Concert Party" (1988) in which one-third of a sentence sums up Harry Lapwing's view of conjugal relations: "he turned away to look for Edie, to find out for certain what she was doing, and ask her to stop" (*VE* 308). They are manifest in the metonymic word pictures configuring a future domesticity which appals the frivolous bride Lily in "Let It Pass": "She saw herself driving children to basketball practice. Saw a row of tiny shoes, cleaned with liquid whitener, on a kitchen windowsill, drying in the sun. Saw icicles dripping and snowy backyards" (*VE* 246). They are manifest in "In a War" (1989) in the portrait of the not-quite-poor Quebec Irish-Catholic Quale family, who never stayed put but kept packing and unpacking "their bedsteads and their chamber pots and the family washtub" (*VE* 273). Each new place carried constants such as a cold water pump, a privy in the backyard, a glassed-in cube of a veranda around the front door, and a back storm porch of unpainted planks "meant for brooms and pails, old newspapers, overshoes, rubber boots, stray scarves and mittens, jam jars without lids, hockey sticks" (273). The enumerated objects, many linked to lack, call up the whole lives of generations of tenants, and contrasts them with those of homeowners on the right side of the tracks, in this case the river, who have covered verandas or galleries

15 Known as San-Yu in the 1940s, the painter defined his minimalist artistic approach as "simplicisme" or simplicism, a term which contemporary critics replaced with "essentialisme" or essentialism (Joffroy 25). If the prices of Sanyu's paintings have skyrocketed in the last decade, it is also on account of a double exoticism. Asian art is in great vogue with Western connoisseurs, and the Chinese who now invest in fine art are interested in the Paris connection.

running round all three sides of the house. The concluding observation zooms in in ever-smaller units: the specific Quale family and then the son: "It was the place where the Quales shed snow from their outdoor clothes and where Leo sat down on a broken chair to take off his skates" (273).

The broken chair, metonym of a life entire, is soon followed by the lightest of pathos-free brushstrokes to suggest a life cut short: when the war comes, Leo enlists enthusiastically, "leaving behind his civilian life and his life altogether" (280). These are examples of writerly decanting which separates pure substance from sediment; like Sanyu's peony they bring us up against the semantic and syntactic density which Goodman claims are symptoms of the aesthetic. The stylistic cornerstones of Gallant's fictional world are indeed *reduction, essentializing, and exemplifying*: the pictorial medium's reduction to simple forms (especially the pared down, stylized shapes of Cubism) transmuted to the page. The almost haiku-like properties first call to mind Turner's definition of the task of a landscape painter: "To select, combine, and *concentrate*" (qtd in Halloran 75), then Cézanne's famous paring down to the basic forms of the cylinder, the sphere, and the cone. Yet they are also analogous to the swift brushstrokes of a Gen Paul cityscape which manifests certain intrinsic formal properties through kinaesthetic patterns.

I can highlight Gallant's techniques fusing the compressed stillness of haiku with the sensation of movement by taking a look at a simple but subtle, little-known early story, "About Geneva" (1955). A woman living in Nice has sent her small son to Geneva to visit his father, who has left her for another woman. The little boy, Colin, communicates his experience in an essentializing way, shouting "I fed the swans" (Gallant, *The Moslem Wife and Other Stories* 14). An image resurges in his mind: "a gray sky, a gray lake, and a swan wonderfully turning upside down" (14). The same words conjure up in his mother's mind edenic connotations of sunshine, a blue lake, and boats heaped with coloured cushions. The clash in mental images and subjectivities concludes the story, with an enumeration whose principle of odd man out encapsulates the extent to which Gallant's process of expression (of loss, forlornness, and phenomenological questioning) goes far beyond simple denotation to the substance of the message, ostensibly added as a mere afterthought: "Perhaps ... one day Colin would say something, produce the image of Geneva, tell her about the lake, the boats, the swans, *and* why her husband had left her" (16).

"taking apart & putting together"

This chapter investigates how Gallant engineers *a fictional world as reshaped and multidimensional as a Cubist picture*. This can intrigue readers who have observed how Gallant's textured factual detail and crystal-clear syntax interlock with a realist tradition which has fashioned a large part of Canadian cultural production, derivative of a society fascinated by history as well as by social observation, and which has long been renowned for the documentary or expository material of its film, poetry, life writing, and historical or historiographical fiction. The oil lamps, drinking pails, chamber pots, oil cloths, rolled cigarettes, and homemade dresses that stud Munro's *Dance of the Happy Shades* (1968) engineer a reality effect which establishes credibility and reinforces the story's veracity, buttressed by the spoken-tongue prose complete with repetition, parataxis, and colloquialisms. Yet the objects also make up a repertory of signs. These leave open the domain of the signified, and nudge readers beyond the things designated to concepts or belief-systems which have been encrypted within the frameworks of selected modalities: truth, knowledge, necessity, values, or rightness (see Dvořák, "Dailiness").

I have already called attention to how in Gallant's *Its Image on the Mirror* the jealous orderly sister, Jean, hovers around Isobel's improvised bohemian life, and to how the sisters' relation to things draws up the antithetical portraits of their inner selves. Similarly, in *A Fairly Good Time*, which dips into life writing's devices of realistically staging the self, such as the journal and the letter, through scriptors such as Shirley, a Canadian expatriate in Paris recently married to a Frenchman, Gallant measures the distance between individual and cultural subjectivities on the axis of neatness. Until her marriage, Shirley, very much like the author, never bothered to make her bed: "Why make what you were bound to unmake in a few hours?" (11). The rhetorical question in which the author-creator's voice overlays the focalizer-creature's generates a sense of collusion with the reader – Peter Orner, for one, falls in love with the untidy (and yes, logical) character that "bursts forth" ("Introduction" viii) from the page. Shirley, like Mavis, liked to pile her clean sheets and clothes on a chair and wait for the pile of dirty linen between the bathtub and the wall to grow larger than the other pile. Then she would take the heap in a taxi to "a laundry on the far side of Paris" (*FGT* 12) – a step apparently illogical, but actually sensible, grounded in Mavis's real-life reasoning and practice: Parisian taxi drivers tend to refuse passengers requesting short, cheap rides.[16] Philippe, the bourgeois French husband,

16 When we had dinner together at her favourite cafés and restaurants on the Left Bank, Mavis would then insist on dropping me off by taxi at my apartment on the Right Bank before circling back to her Left Bank apartment, giving precisely the reason above.

put a stop to this system, and replaced it with an ostensibly rational one. The irrational aspects of his system dawn on us readers as the process unfolds from a standpoint which the sympathetic implicit author shares with her focalizer. A boy took away the washing every Saturday and

> brought it back torn, worn, stiff as the kitchen table, and reeking of chloride bleach. Every face cloth and pot holder had to be counted, examined and checked against a list ... the clean linen, corseted in hard brown paper, held with murderous pins, had to be undone, sorted, placed on shelves she could barely reach only to be taken down again; a repetition of gestures that seemed to her lunatic but that Philippe assured her were almost the evidence of life. (12)

The table, bleach, face cloth, pot holder, paper, pins, and shelves are drawn from the real world. The rhyme (torn/worn), the simile (stiff as), the ternary and quaternary enumerations foregrounding the quantity of alternative drudgery and effort are the stuff of fiction. As in the other stories I have discussed, the objects tremble, but none tremble more than the personified, soul-killing "murderous pins." They house an ontological stance which challenges Philippe's definition of life, and they foreshadow the death of the couple's married life.

One can see that, like Munro (a decade younger), Gallant excels in representing a recognizable world. Readers are lulled into an impression of a comfortable realism via the ingredients of contemporary experience, language grounded in an authentic spoken idiom, and homely objects which have no structural or narrative function (for no one will be stabbed by the above pins), but which constitute far more than an index of atmosphere. Shirley and Philippe's clash over laundry unfolds in the manner of classic White Clown–Auguste pairings, which have inspired artists from Bertold Brecht and Beckett to Roberto Benigni. Philippe (like Oliver Hardy or Vladimir/Didi in *Waiting for Godot*) would seem to correspond to the White Clown who wants to impose order and is convinced he understands things better than his partner. Shirley (like Stan Laurel or Beckett's Estragon/Gogo) is the Auguste who does not understand her partner's normative reasoning. I posit that Gallant and Munro thus exemplify two different senses of realism which Goodman identifies: Munro and her "comforting fictions" (Boyagoda) epitomize realism in the sense of "habituation" (correct under the accustomed system of representation), and Gallant in the sense of "revelation" (correct under a system strange to us, disclosing unseen aspects). Both are "right" representations respectively reflecting the factors of inertia and initiative, notably in the case of categorization (*Worldmaking* 130–1).

A Fairly Good Time's heroine wandering through life and the novel, its small-scale action, lack of obvious focus, and substitution of a random cascade of incidents for a clear narrative line, all point Gallant's special brand of realism towards the filmmaker Tati's (which I have already suggested borrows from the joyous silent clowning tradition). The two share an exceptional ability to make strange the objects that surround us. I would apply to Gallant what Sean Axmaker remarks of Tati's visual art: the imaginative observations, the small details which "erupt with lives of their own but fit together like a clockwork's mechanism with a human heartbeat." As a case study for the notions above, I shall take one of the last narratives Gallant published in *The New Yorker*, "The Fenton Child" (1993). It has a thoroughly disrupted time frame, but the illusion of reality is nonetheless strong. Montreal in the 1940s, divided along the fault lines of language and religion, arises complete, just as the solid shapes of the town and gardens of Proust's childhood rose out of his teacup.

The point of view provides both an outsider's gaze and insider's experience, held as it is by the bilingual, culturally hybrid Nora Abbott. She has a French-Canadian mother who pretends to understand no English and a (now-converted) Methodist father from Prince Edward Island, where all the neighbours are "called Peters or White" (*VE* 24). As in the story "1933," showcasing another uneasy domestic alliance in which only the dog is bilingual,[17] the writer judiciously analyses the historico-political complexes of the two solitudes and *breaks them down into component features*. She uses the limited view of the young focalizer, Nora, to delete or weed out certain information, only to provide the supplementation needed for a bigger picture through an overarching narrative consciousness. Fenton, the man who adopts a mysteriously unclaimed baby who Nora has been asked to help bring home, is "some sort of Protestant – another race" (5). The author presents even more reductive generalizations through Nora's eyes: Mr. Fenton is a "typical Anglo-Montrealer gladhander, the kind who said 'Great to see you!' and a minute later forgot you were alive" (5). Here is the "touchstone of realism," as Goodman describes it (*Languages of Art* 36). The portrait of Mr. Fenton as a type we recognize from habit may have a component of truth to it. But the illusion of reality it gives stems not so much from accuracy as from its mode of representation: the stereotype – the

17 Nora's father, Ray Abbott, is a rare exemplar of metaphorical border-crossing, uprooting himself from his community and rooting himself in another, finding it "no more difficult than digging up irises to put in tulips" (24). "1933" discloses the intricacies of negotiating identity by featuring a francophone husband and his Irish wife, who is the Same (Catholic) but also Other (anglophone).

more commonplace, the more easily accepted – here rendered delightful through the exaggerated weighting of "forgot you were alive." Other commonplaces are added through Nora's partial gaze (in the double sense of limited and biased), overlaid by the narrator's amusement. When registering the birth of the baby (in a suspiciously late, irregular way), Mr. Fenton gives his name as Boyd Markham Forrest Fenton, and Nora concludes he "was *one of those Anglos* with no Christian name, just a string of surnames" (*VE* 33): another instance of simplifying, deforming, and naturalizing a subjective reality.

Nora's uncle, Victor Cochefort, is an associate in a firm of engineers named Macfarlane, Macfarlane & Macklehurst. After the senior Macfarlane retires, "Cochefort" is to figure on the letterhead, a promotion instantly deflated by supplementation: the narrator specifies the name will be "a bit lower and to the right, in smaller print" (21). As we lower a musical note by marking it with a flat, the signs (in triplicate: lower, smaller, differently aligned) of Cochefort's "different" status are validated by supplementary details: a total of three other people with French surnames are on the firm's staff, namely "a switchboard operator, a file clerk, and a bilingual typist" (21). Like the stationery, the occupations the narrator takes care to supply are samples of subordinate positions in a vertical society, functioning as exemplifying symbols of a glass ceiling for francophones. All the realist filling in actually flattens metaphorically. It ostensibly makes us see, but it also makes us see *beyond*. It conjures up a world rife with sensitive issues of power, territory, (de)possession, and appropriation. It also points to a historical, geopolitical irony: the dominant socio-economic ranking in Quebec of the Scots: formerly conquered and annexed by the English, then sent out to take control of other territories ranging from Canada to India. The irony is brought home through the weighting of enumeration. Victor ponders the retreat and obscuration of the English:

> "The English" had names such as O'Keefe, Murphy, Llewellyn, Morgan-Jones, Ferguson, MacNab, Hoefer, Oberkirch, Aarmgaard, Van Roos, or Stavinsky. Language was the clue to native origin. He placed the Oberkirches and MacNabs by speech and according to the street where they chose to live. (21)

The second level of irony results from the authorial relations of distance regarding how social perceptions negotiate similitude and otherness, notably the widespread amalgamation of language and native origin. On a first ironic level, though, breaking down a monolithic entity, "the English," serves a reshaping, corrective function, taking a territory composed of separate, homogeneous fish ponds and mapping it more finely to arrive at a more intricate, complete world than the one habitually perceived. The one habitually perceived is described in an autobiographical story also set in Montreal, "The Doctor": the parents' habit of mingling guests from the two major communities produces an exotic school of tropical fish. For

> most other people simply floated in mossy little ponds labeled "French and Catholic," or "English and Protestant," never wondering what it might be like to step ashore; or wondering, perhaps, but weighing up the danger. To be out of a pond is to be in unmapped territory. (*VE* 79)

Gallant's strategy in "The Fenton Child" of decomposing a whole (the English) into parts (from Dutch to Slav), consisting of sorting into entities and kinds and of ordering by proximity, is an epistemological act engineering identification. What is the same or not the same? What is or can be lumped together? What properties, precepts, convictions, and prejudices do they share? In a flashback to when Nora is nine, her English-Canadian father, Ray Abbott, tries to enlist after the German invasion of Poland. He explains, "in my family, if Canada goes to war, we go too" (*VE* 22). Nora's French-Canadian uncle, Victor Cochefert, declares at the same family gathering that he will "shoot his three sons rather than see them in uniform" (21). This provokes both a round of weeping by the sons in question (one of whom is three years old) and a readerly smile at such an earnest reaction to a threat so exaggeratedly emphatic. Serious questions do hover, however. How do the subclasses of "the English" in Quebec feel about Canada's support of Great Britain; what do they think of the issue of conscription which we readers with hindsight know tore Canada apart and contributed to the rise of the Quebec independence movement?[18] Are the two "tribes" truly monolithic? And are there other minor tribes or even hybrids on a wider scale than individuals like Nora?

Mordecai Richler garnered fame with his portrayal of a third "tribe" (neither Catholic nor Protestant), and Gallant liked to draw attention to "everyone's minority" (*VE* 262), namely Quebec-Irish like the Quales in "In a War" and "Let It Pass," who "seemed wedged like a piece from the wrong puzzle between English Protestants and French Catholics, matching neither in coloration or design" (*VE* 226). "In a War" notably features the I-narrator's Anglican aunt, who told the Irish-Catholic grocery

---

18 In April 1942, 73 per cent of Quebec residents voted against conscription, while in the other provinces 80 per cent voted in favour. ("Conscription," *The Canadian Encyclopedia*, http://wwwthecanadianencyclopedia.ca/en/article/conscription/. Accessed 1 September 2017.)

delivery boy Leo Quale that war "brings out the best in men and nations" (*VE* 264). Gallant here carries out an almost Céline-like denunciation of nationalism and warmongering through a double ventriloquism. The multivocal technique overlays the author's voice imprint onto the narrator's already sarcastic borrowing of voices filtered through his Aunt Elspeth's. We hear, couched in the free indirect speech which mixes the inner and outer pictures and reminds us that "the word in language is half someone else's" and that we get our words from "other people's mouths" (Bakhtin 293–4), that:

> Folded inside the masculine psyche there had to be a bright yearning to suffocate face down in a flooded trench, to bleed from wounds inflicted by England's enemies, even to be done in by a septic flea bite, if a patriotic case could be made against the flea. (*VE* 263)

The young Leo Quale, who had a father who "hated the English" (264), interestingly told Aunt Elspeth, "England forever!" and exhibited that very yearning or "eagerness to perish" (263). Language is apparently thicker than religion. When Aunt Elspeth suggested to Leo that he would be better off in a French Catholic school with his "own kind" (273) rather than in her nephew's English Protestant school, he "stared at the demented lady who did not know there were Catholics and Catholics" (273). The connector designating similarity serves instead to signpost Homi Bhabha's "the same but not quite" (86); it epistemologically orders by proximity so as to engineer the multiple, and at times conflicting, identifications which we find in "The Fenton Child."

Additional serious questions arise in "The Fenton Child" at the family gathering celebrating the Cochefert grandparents' golden wedding anniversary, notably around the five-tier pink-and-white cake. The only one of Victor's children old enough to get into uniform and "be gunned down by her father" (22) is his eighteen-year-old daughter, just out of her French convent school. Nora's older cousin, Ninette, whose historical essay, "Marie-Antoinette, Christian Queen and Royal Martyr," has won a graduation medal,

> could read and speak English, understand every word of Latin in the Mass, play anything you felt like hearing on the piano, in short, was ready to become *a superior kind of wife*. (22)

Ninette proceeds to demonstrate her skills by wiping her wailing little brothers' snotty faces, picking up the big silver cake knife, and slicing the whole five-tier edifice from top to bottom:

> She must have been taught to do it as part of her studies, for the cake did not fall apart or collapse. "There!" she said, as if life held nothing more to be settled. (23)

At the end of the cake operation, Victor remarks that it is "no use educating women" any further: it "confuse[s] their outlook" (24). He hopes that Ray has "no foolish and extravagant plans for Nora" and her sister Geraldine. In the past, Victor has already accused Ray of a "well-known Anglo reluctance to show deep emotion": no one knows what he thinks or feels about anything (21). At present, Ray's only response to Victor's manifesto on female education and gender roles is to eat quietly and steadily and be the first to finish his cake. Through his English inscrutability and the textual hints we sense he is of a different mind, even if he finds it no more difficult fitting in to French Catholic life than digging up irises to put in tulips. The gardening analogy I evoked previously suggests an equivalence between the two "tribes" and a corresponding relativity regarding values.[19] Are the values equally patriarchal? A flashforward to the end of the war informs us that Ray does send Nora to an English high school, where we expect she will learn more than Church Latin, piano, and cake-cutting. We find out she knows "who George Washington was and the names of the Stuart kings but not much about Canada" (25). At least the information deficit is not gender-oriented, we console ourselves. The "English" have a higher idea of women's roles, we think. Then we piece together certain exploitative facts: her father has told Nora she is to mind the mysterious baby as a favour and not expect payment, but he has actually already pocketed her payment. Finally, other clues start falling into place with respect to what women are for.

When Mr. Fenton arrives at his front door with Nora carrying the baby they have picked up at an orphanage, Dr. Marchand, a French-Canadian friend accompanying him, asks, "Boyd, isn't that the alley where *the* girl was supposed to have been raped?" (*VE* 15). Gallant's strategy is a hermeneutic one: the definite article carries an identificatory requirement which is met for the male speakers in the know, but not met for Nora or us readers. What girl? Why "supposed"? The climate has been set by the ribald memories the men have been sharing in the car, and by Nora's

19 In a flashback Ray even stands up for Quebec in reaction to his rigid Methodist mother, notably the freedom to have a beer when one feels like it. No organized religion or form of zealous constraint goes unscathed when the protagonist's voice melds with the omniscient narrator's to point out that "The rest of Canada was pretty dry, yet in those parched cities, on a Saturday night, even the telephone poles were reeling-drunk" (25).

mother's warning that "having relations" consists of "a source of dirty stories for men and disgrace for girls" (5). We learn that a young woman taking a short cut home through the neighbouring dark alley came banging on the Fentons' door screaming: she had not seen the face of her assailant, who was never caught. Fenton, our exemplar of "the English," remarks that "something like that going on just outside" (16) was hard on his *wife*, Louise, home alone with her maid. He reassures Nora that his street is "safe for girls who don't do dumb things" (17). Nora had inferred that the baby named Neil had been the result of an accident, a mistake, on the part of the Fentons.[20] Now it dawns on her, and us, that Neil was the result of an entirely different "mistake": that of being female and alone in a public space.[21]

We have once more fallen into a hole, the lateral omission or paralipsis discussed at length in the previous chapter, notably the subchapter "surfeit & lack." Our narrative does not pass over the event of the rape as would a conventional ellipsis, but sidesteps it. The omniscient narrator mentions the incident, but decides to step to the side of the segment, many components of which go unaccounted for. Readers, nostrils flaring, are left in a state of information deficit by an all-knowing narrator who paradoxically flaunts a posture of limited knowledge. The narrator has namely reduced her space to that of her focalizer's head, and deletes whatever is outside of the deliberately restricted frame. The strategy calls up the trick Hemingway claimed in *A Moveable Feast* to have learned from Cézanne. In the chapter "Hunger Was a Good Discipline" the writer tells us about a story in which he had omitted the real end (the old man hanging himself) on the grounds of a "new theory": "you could omit anything if you knew that you omitted and the omitted part would strengthen the story and make people *feel* something more than they *understood*" (71). The writer would be one step behind the painter, but one step ahead of his audience: "they will understand the same way they always do in painting" (71). This modernist aesthetic of omission or deletion to which Gallant adheres can clearly be connected to *the pictorial medium's reduction to*

20 Told that a nanny was sailing over from England, Nora supposed that the Fentons "could not tend to an infant without outside assistance, and for that reason had left Neil to founder among castaways for his first twelve weeks" (5).

21 To drive the message even closer to home, certain clues point to the possibility that the young woman Fenton assaulted and impregnated may have been Nora's cousin, Ninette, who was sent to an unidentified place in the Laurentians for an alleged case of tuberculosis, but came back strangely having gained weight, no longer marriageable, to keep house for her father. Only Ray Abbott and Dr. Marchand know Neil's mother's identity, Fenton admits to Nora, but when at the end of the story Nora asks her father for the truth, his answer is to whistle a tune like "Don't Let It Bother You."

simple forms and unsettling of traditional perspective, transmuted to the page. It moreover connects both painting and film[22] with the notions of literary vantage point I have been discussing. Like pictures, then, and like the moving pictures which suggest beyond the visible, as I have argued, Gallant in the story under scrutiny makes her readers feel more than they technically understand. When Dr. Marchand mentions another case of rape in which "an old maid ... set the police on a married man (who never did anything worse than say hello)" (*VE* 16), our feelers quiver at a rhetoric of denial serving a monolithic patriarchal system. The writer has *dismantled the Anglo/French binary and remapped it* on quicksand along the lines of gender – powerful predator at the male end of the axis, and powerless prey at the female end.[23]

Yet mistakes abound in a pattern of theme and variation lighting up the issues of freedom and chance, the karma or loaded dice we are born with and the kismet or personal destiny which we can shape. Dr. Marchand has made "a 'th' mistake in English, saying 'dat' for 'that'" (19), a slip which signals a subordinate positioning. But Nora hands the baby to the maid, mistaking a subaltern in a white apron for the wife who has shut herself up in her room to show the child is unwanted. Fenton laughs noisily at the "mistake" (19) in class distinctions, all the more absurd in his eyes as Missy's non-normative speech ("heavy accent") points to yet another kind of subaltern. Nora senses she has "spoiled Neil's entrance into his new life," as if she "had crossed the wrong line." For interrogating the writer's preoccupation with beginning again (which I mapped out in chapter 3), we read

> The two errors could not be matched. The doctor could always start over and get it right. For Nora and Neil, it had been once and for all. (19)

Through her focalizer, the narrator seems to meditate on the lines by Szymborska so close to the author's heart that she quoted them from memory in a letter I have already alluded to: "Every beginning after all / is nothing but a sequel / and the book of events / is always open in the middle" (Szymborska in Gallant, Letter to Dvořák,1 September 2002). The stanza

22 The aesthetic of omission was notably an essential feature making up the signature of sound film directors such as Howard Hawks. Already in silent pictures, unlike Thomas H. Ince, interested in the "what" of pure action, a director like D.W. Griffith practised cuts to privilege the "why," the metaphorical implications.

23 I say remapped on quicksand because the female gender proves not to be monolithic either. The immigrant maid who lets in the screaming girl and calms her with a shot of brandy says, "Some guy grabs *me* in a lane, I twist him like a wet mop" (16).

concludes "Love at First Sight" in *Miracle Fair* (Szymborska 31), a poem which illuminates Gallant's story when laid side by side. The poet questions the concept of "first sight" and suggests that the new lovers may already have crossed paths, "maybe face to face once / in a revolving door" (30) or through something lost and then picked up, even "doorknobs and doorbells, / where touch lay on touch / beforehand" (31). The way the poem engages with and concretizes the aleatory resonates with "The Fenton Child." Szymborska's persona suggests that for a long time "*chance* had been toying" with the lovers – a chance not quite ready to "turn into their fate," which would alternately draw them together and pull them apart. This chance-cum-fate is personified as a trickster which would cut the lovers off on their path and "swallowing a giggle, / leap to the side" (30).

Gallant's overarching narrative instance, too, wonders if there have been "signs, signals" even if these have been "unreadable" (Szymborska 31). Is the book of events always *open* in the middle – promising the chance to start over? If so, do we have a share of responsibility or is the sequel stochastic, like a series of dice rolls? Or are there redhibitory mistakes that "once and for all" (*VE* 19) cut us off on our path and rule out a satisfying sequel? "The Fenton Child" suggests there may be: mistakes ranging from being born on the wrong side of the tracks to being born a female, or sometimes even being born at all. The implicatures of the mistake motif cluster (operating under the alethic modality of (im)possibility/necessity) link up in a fraught way with those of the journey motif. We shall see below how the two meet up and how their empowering points of convergence take us beyond the physical world of our lived experience to an abstract dimension, comparable to the way Picasso evoked African masks to achieve abstracted faces in *Les Demoiselles d'Avignon*.

Gallant, we have seen, has divided kinds into subspecies, only to scramble their relations with one another and with other kinds or categories. I shall now show how, inversely but conjointly, she recomposes a new whole out of isolated features among which she makes connections. On the one hand she breaks down the big picture, on the other she *zooms in on the small – analogous to a detail in a painting – and builds up*. I can again evoke a meaningful analogy with the cognitive agenda of a painter like Turner, admired by Ruskin for his ability to paint water realistically, but who actually in a pre-Impressionist way set out to represent with precision not reality but his subjective perception of reality.[24] Turner pointed

24 The way Turner depicts water and sun in *The Fighting Temeraire* (1839), for example, remarkably anticipates the technique of Claude Monet in the 1872 canvas which gave Impressionism its name: *Impression: Soleil levant* [Impression: Sunrise].

out that "It is necessary to mark the greater *from the lesser* truth: namely the larger and more liberal idea of nature *from the comparatively narrow and confined*; namely that which addresses itself to the imagination *from that which is solely addressed to the eye*" (qtd in Shanes 23). In a similar way, like the Turner who set out to select, combine, and concentrate from the bottom up, or – to take another visual analogy – from the wrong end of the telescope,[25] Gallant once more plays with the lens of cultural stereotypes. She handles the common knowledge equating economic attributes (rich/poor) with linguistic, religious, and even geographical binaries, notably lumping French Catholics with "the *poor* and improvident, in the *east* end" (*VE* 19).

The writer carefully selects the component features making up the economic complexes we identify as "rich" and "poor." There are property owners and lifelong renters; there are those who occupy a whole original grand house and those who occupy the subdivided parts of houses transformed into flats. There are even finer clothing distinctions between the necessary (winter coats) and the superfluous, the new and the hand-me-down. Nora's mother reminds her she has never gone hungry and that she and her older sister "always had a new coat every winter." Nora points out that Gerry did, but that she "got the hand-me-down" (29). When Nora first meets Mr. Fenton and Dr. Marchand, she notices "their light hot-weather clothes" (32) – seersucker jackets which are an unheard of luxury for those who need clothes for protection from the cold. The distinctions plug into an acute consciousness of social class, but also into the ancient, complex confrontation of need vs the superfluous, a tension which Shakespeare interrogates in King Lear's plea for that which raises us poor forked animals above beasts: "O reason not the need" (*King Lear* II.4.264).[26] Complicating the story's enquiry into deprivation and want vs extravagant excess is a complete scrambling of expected correspondences. Both the Anglo Fenton and the French-Canadian Marchand

25 It is this strategy that Margaret Atwood later adopts to produce pathos and a reality effect in *The Handmaid's Tale* (1985), when her narrator relates the aborted escape during which her small daughter was taken away from her. Lying on top of her little girl to protect her from the gunshots, she notes close to her eyes "a leaf, red, turned early, [in which she] can see every bright vein." When she is torn away from her daughter, "the edges go dark and nothing is left but a little window, a very little window, like the wrong end of a telescope, like the window on a Christmas card, an old one, night and ice outside, and within a candle, a shining tree, a family" (85).

26 Lear goes on to point out, "our basest beggars / Are in the poorest thing superfluous: / Allow not nature more than nature needs, / Man's life is cheap as beast's" (II.4.264–7).

indulge in the unnecessary clothing marking the upper class,[27] and the astonishing clothing motif variant of Queen Marie-Antoinette, which I shall discuss further opens out the story vertiginously.

The features making up the realist complexes of rich and poor thus first seem to be distributed on the sides of the French/Anglo divide which the "common view" or "going point of view" (Bakhtin 301)[28] would expect. Still, alert readers remark how Gallant *selects, scrambles, and recombines the isolated components into new complexes*. Almost all of Nora's French relatives are lifelong renters. Yet Uncle Victor owns not only a large house complete with double garage (plus a weeping willow on the lawn, the narrator gleefully adds), but also some flats which he "rent[s] out to the poor and improvident, in the east end of the city" (*VE* 20–1). The irony of his slum landlord status is intensified through supplementation. We learn that Uncle Victor is "forever having tenants evicted" and has had "beer bottles thrown at his car" (20), and even that at the end of the war he decides to evict all his tenants and rent his flats "to veterans at a higher price" (26). Having damaged many readers' comfort zone, the omniscient narrator goes on to point out that Nora's English father (who works in City Hall where he now has a private office) still lives with his family "in a third-floor walk-up flat" whose undesirability is reinforced or weighted with the addition of extra information: a flat "with an *outside* staircase and *linoleum*-covered floors on which *scatter rugs sli*pped and *sli*d underfoot" (20). Ostensibly there for a reality effect, the details invalidate our going point of view regarding "the English" in Quebec; they function as further exemplifying symbols of low standards and status, which the concluding full alliteration and assonance highlight.

Mr. Fenton does indeed have a prestigious address. He has inherited the grand house[29] where he was born: on Crescent Street, one of old downtown Montreal's most elegant Anglo residential streets with fine Victorian architecture.[30] At the time, I must add. For why does he tell

27 Still, in "In a War," Gallant points out a cultural divide in the matter of clothing. The French-Canadian boys dressed up for Sunday, while the "English" wore comfortable weekend clothes, which to the French "looked like hand-me-downs": "If you didn't know who they were, you'd hand them a nickel" (*VE* 269).

28 A quick reminder that Bakhtin identifies the current opinion or verbal-ideological belief-system of the dominant social group – what people usually believe – as the "going point of view," interlocked with the "going value" (301–2).

29 Nora notes that on her street such a house "would indicate three two-bedroom flats" (15).

30 Actually, as Gallant points out explicitly in "The Doctor," houses like hers were "the work of Edinburgh architects," dating from "when Montreal was a Scottish city"; she notably adds, "it had never been really English" (*HT* 346).

Nora, "This end of Crescent is *still* good" (16)? We learn that his wife, Louise, wants him to sell because "she can't get used to having a dress shop next door" and would prefer "a lawn and a yard and a lot of space between the houses" (14) – the string of elements with extra "and"'s operating as acoustic and visual elements in sync with the spatially sprawling new suburbs. Today's Canadian readers to whom Montreal's Crescent Street conjures up boutiques, bars, restaurants, and nightlife are teleported to a vanished, or rather vanishing, world. For through Mr. Fenton's car windows, refracted by Nora's gaze as they drive the baby of ambiguous origins home, Gallant maps a post–Second World War civilization in the throes of transformation. Nora observes what Louise Fenton deplores: houses with "fancy dress shops on the first floor," while others have been "turned into offices, with uncurtained front windows and neon lights, blazing away in broad daylight" (15).[31] Alex Marchand, the French-Canadian doctor who accompanies Fenton on his mysterious child errand, evokes a fellow acquaintance from the days their ex-Montreal regiment fought in the Italian campaign – a camaraderie that explodes the boundaries of the Anglo/French binary. Mac McIvor, he says, has moved away to Vancouver. Like the Fentons, McIvor exemplifies a once-dominant English-speaking community being disaggregated and displaced – also a central theme in Gallant's short novel *Its Image on the Mirror* (1964), set barely a few years later on the entropic timeline.

The novel's young adult Anglo narrator, Jean, presents the civilizational shift in geophysical terms, equating it to "a new tide" in which "French-Canada flows in when English-Canada pulls away" (*My Heart Is Broken* 58). The imagery shows the tide to be death-dealing. In Allenton, outside Montreal, "all Catholic and all French-speaking now" (60), the parents sell the family home to a seminary, a place for "embryo priests" (60). Selling the house to a religious order amounts to pushing both the past and the family memories of Allenton as an Anglo-Scottish town "over a cliff" (60), and the living vegetable reign soon becomes a dead mineral one.

> A gardener kneels before a row of stones, painting them white. Nearby is the pile of gravel with which the new owners of the house intend to kill the grass. (58)

---

31 When Linnet Muir, 90 per cent Mavis, as she herself admitted, returns to her childhood house on Sherbrooke Street, myth and memory clash with ugly reality (investigated in Dvořák, "Le Montréal de Mavis Gallant"): the house is now "a narrow stone thing with a shop on the ground floor and offices above," the "bare panes" of what might have been the sitting room with its "deep private window seats" now revealing "neon striplighting along a ceiling" (*HT* 271).

Actually, even before the tree is cut down and "the gravel trodden into the dead grass" (58), even before the 1955 sale, the traditional double-porched house with Virginia creeper surrounding the windows – built for the parents' marriage in 1913 – "began to die" (59). Graced with a lawn and vegetable garden, the house was originally flanked by a farm and a cornfield. In a parallel sea-change, the field has become "a development of bungalows" and "nearly everyone in the development speaks French" (59). The shifting linguistic territory is tainted with entropy through its interconnection with the erosion of the agrarian community, subsequently and similarly configured by Alice Munro.

In "The Shining Houses," Munro ostensibly opposes "new, white, and shining houses" of housing estate subdivisions with an old farmhouse the new owners consider a filthy eyesore (*Dance of the Happy Shades* 27). Yet a counter-discursive authorial voice observes that the large new houses in long orthogonal rows are "ingenuously similar" (23). The voice melds with the focalizer's perspective, against the grain, equating the uncut forest and disorderly jungle of wild blackberry bushes running around unpainted "surviving houses" (24), like Mrs. Fullerton's, with liberty – a liberty threatened by the uniformity and standardization of the housing developments, which echo regimented utopian visions from Plato and Thomas More to Huxley and Orwell (see Dvořák, "Alice Munro's 'lovely tricks'"). Through the filter of her Anglo narrator who in turn refracts the viewpoint of a bewildered, still older Anglo generation, Gallant performs the wondrous feat of naturalizing a bias today's readers consider politically unacceptable. In the following extract from *Its Image on the Mirror*, we can see how the writer manages to present a subjective perspective commonly dismissed as prejudiced in an ironic but non-judgmental, even compassionate way. The structural irony is heavily weighted at the beginning of the double-voiced digression in which the speaker innocently evokes a world hierarchically divided in two. I say innocently, for the narrator is blissfully unaware of the blame the concealed narrative consciousness dishes out: "When my sister and my brother and I were children we thought there was a difference in physical substance between people who spoke English exactly as we did, and the rest of mankind" (*My Heart Is Broken* 59). The satirical distance we are invited to occupy partly dissolves, however, when the viewpoint shifts to the old and vulnerable, whose world has become, in T.S. Eliot's terms, a "heap of broken images" (*The Waste Land* 63).

> I think my parents still believe it, for nothing else can explain the expression of honest dumb-foundedness that comes over my father's face when he meets someone decent, moderate, conservative and polite, and discovers that this acceptable person is not English or Scottish or Protestant – all that one

> can be; and I feel sorry for my father when this happens, for it seems hard to have your views shared by everyone around you all your life and then confounded in your old age. (*My Heart Is Broken* 59)

Such intertextual and intratextual trajectories illuminate the seismic resonances of "The Fenton Child." The grand geological concept of earth-moving tectonic processes applied to carving, scraping, and scouring societal slippages is once more suggested not from above through the lens of the larger picture (the unfurling Quiet Revolution), but from below through *the zoom on the telling detail* (McIvor's move to Vancouver). Gallant moves into an authentic-sounding conversational sequencing between Fenton and Dr. Marchand revolving around staying and going, whose resonances go far beyond the adjacent utterances of two individuals. The pattern of dispreferred responses, rife with cognitive dissonance and the tension of home and other, is once more that of the adjacency pair (discussed in the previous chapter). When he learns McIvor uprooted himself so radically, Fenton replies that "He'll crawl back here one day," and adds that he himself was born on Crescent and intends to die there (*VE* 14). "Crescent's a fine street," the doctor concedes, only to switch obliquely to a mismatch: "He's buying a place. Property's cheap out there" (14). Adjacent utterances fuse in a soon predictable call-and-response pattern that takes on the contours of an ideological sparring match. Who would want to go such a long way off, no wonder it's cheap, my father hung on to the house all through the Depression, it's now worth a hell of a lot more. Dr. Marchand's dissenting sequence of utterances – Mac's got a fair-size garden, out there there's no winter, you stick something in the ground it grows – offers the centrifugal view of modernity: the flux of geographical and social mobility unfolding in concentric circles of city, province, nation, empire, and planet. While Louise Fenton represents the residents cringing at the unfurling invasion of tradespeople, her husband declares, "It'll take a lot more than a couple of store windows to chase me away" (14) – the cry of a centripetal belief system valuing rootedness and pride of place.[32]

Mavis was born the same year as T.S. Eliot's *The Waste Land*, the "radical text of a wounded culture" (Kaveney). It was radical for its protean free

32 In "The Chosen Husband," too, the Carettes notice that a seamstress has set up shop in their residential street, Rue Saint Hubert, and take it for a sign that the chic neighbourhood is "in decline" (*VE* 180). The structural irony allowing a fuller reading is available only to readers who know from the linked story "1933" that Mme Carette herself once made her living by sewing. This in turn intensifies the irony of the contiguous statement equating the arrival of "a family of foreigners" (180) as another marker of decay.

verse, collage of non-linear sequences, abrupt shifts in time and place and simultaneous multiple viewpoints, which were the Dada-tinted verbal equivalents of what the avant-garde Cubist painters had been doing. Contributing to what was in the air, it preceded Eisenstein's invention of filmic montage: creating a whole from isolated fragments. Most important to my discussion of "The Fenton Child," Eliot mourned a disintegrating Europe, a dying world order, and a crumbling set of Old World values and cultural practices.[33] The "voices dying with a dying fall" which Prufrock hears "beneath the music from a farther room" (*Collected Poems* 52–3), arguably the expiring aesthetic norms and belief systems from which new cultural and ideological forms must emerge, also haunt the works of other writers Gallant admired, from Elizabeth Bowen to Joseph Roth.

Mavis's maternal grandparents, who migrated at a young age from a territory that was then part of the Austro-Hungarian Empire stretching out to today's Romania, Poland, and Ukraine, may have buttressed Gallant's affinity with the poet Szymborska and triggered her passion for Roth and his tales of entropic crumbling empires. Her fervour for the Eastern European Roth (represented with that hallmark *energeia* of hers) is discernible in the extract below, which is the second half of the letter she sent along with a gift of books – a letter I quoted from in chapter 3 and above (125, 136–7) regarding Szymborska and issues of chance and fate.

Paris, Sunday, 1st September (2002)

Dear Marta,
(...)[34] *Hôtel Savoy was one of Joseph Roth's first novels, written (I think) in 1922. The French translation was out-of-print for years*[35] *until*

33 Although Eliot worked with anti-establishment little magazines, he declared, "I am an Anglo-Catholic in religion, a classicist in literature, and a royalist in politics" (qtd in the non-nominative "T.S. Eliot, the Poet, Is Dead in London at 76," *New York Times*).

34 Readers may remember that this letter began with "After I got home last Friday a scrap of poetry kept running through my head." The opening paragraph concluded with the remark I commented on: "It takes an American publisher to think that any Slav is any Slav."

35 Roth's *Radetzky March* (1932) was translated immediately into English. Yet while a French translation of the Kafkaesque short novel *Hotel Savoy* appeared in 1969, the first English translation (by a man Mavis had loved) came out only in 1986. It arguably influenced Kazuo Ishiguro's oneiric *The Unconsoled* (1995), also set in a Central European city, unnamed and thus universal. J.M. Coetzee (who had a doctoral degree in Germanic languages) needed no translation from the German; the topographical and temporal vagueness of allegorical import in Roth's dark novella already haunts the South African-born novelist's *Waiting for the Barbarians* (1980).

Gallimard reprinted. I picked it up just a few years ago to compare with the English translations and (as well as I could) a few pages of the German original. Roth is one of my favourite writers, intrinsically European. I've read this particular novella I don't know how many times. He died in Paris in 1939, from a mixture of alcoholism, poverty, exile, + malnutrition. Otto v. Hapsburg sent a wreath to his funeral, but a cheque in an envelope might have been more in order – before *his death. [original stress]*
I hope you don't mind receiving books from my shelves. The jacket of the Roth shows a little fatigue but the inside is spotless and in any case I'm not sure the translation is still available. Besides, it is the only way of getting any such thing done. Otherwise a whole sheaf of slips of paper marked "Patrick – Hôtel Savoy"[36] *and "Marta – Szymborska" will remain taped to the lid of the typewriter, along with an enigmatic "Charlie – umbrella" – an umbrella I returned by mail a week ago.*

Love, Mavis

I can surmise which qualities made Roth, "this cousin to Kafka and Milan Kundera" (Gold), one of Mavis's favourite writers. I can evoke his Chekhovian-cum-Surrealist brand of the absurd and the incongruous (a brand which suffuses Gallant's own work). I can call up the Expressionism privileging mood over story (as hers does). I can point to the way he suspends space-time (as she likes to do, catching readers off-guard). I can gesture to his use of sustained caricature and satire (which underpin Gallant's writings). Finally, I can call attention to a modernist aesthetics of breakage combined with a classical, balanced, periodic style (precisely what I have been disclosing with respect to Gallant's own work). Yet on a different plane, perhaps what appealed to Mavis most strongly was a kinship (through her mother's side) in origins, as well as a writerly kinship grounded in the notion of borderlands. A political exile in Paris, Roth was born on the northeastern edge of the supranational Austro-Hungarian Empire,[37] whose collapse he configures in

36 It was the French translation that Mavis sent, meant for my partner Patrick, along with the Szymborska poetry book for me.

37 The empire's two million Jews, among them Roth, who had no nation within the territory, had much to gain by this unification of multiple ethnicities within one stable entity. The "fatherland," as Roth termed the double monarchy in his untranslated foreword to *Radetzky March*, made him feel like "a citizen of the world" (Roth, trans. & qtd by Coetzee, "Emperor of Nostalgia"). Once atomized, it gave way to the rivalry and tensions of multiple competing nationalisms, as did the collapse of the neighbouring Ottoman Empire.

Hotel Savoy (1923) with a dark absurdity which blazes the trail for Kafka's *The Castle* (1926). Roth sets his novella in a seven-storey hotel "at the gates of Europe" (*Hotel Savoy* 9), a hotel where no two clocks tell the same time, peopled by grotesque residents exiled in a strange town whose people "look as alike as fish" (76) and who – also anticipating Beckett[38] – are all "waiting for Bloomfield," who, of course, "does not come" (83). In a subsequent novel, Roth evokes the decline and fall of empire in the transcendent mode of Greek tragedy: the cosmic forces closing in are represented as "the sombre beating of vulture wings (...) hovering above the double eagles of the Habsburgs" (*Radetzky March* 187). The shattered empire which Eliot configured as a "heap of broken images" (*Collected Poems* 63) is reconfigured in Roth's short story "The Bust of the Emperor" as a "home" or "large house with many doors and many rooms for many different kinds of people" which has been "divided, broken up, ruined" (Roth, qtd in Coetzee, "Emperor of Nostalgia").

The more textually specific connections with Gallant are multiple and fraught with aporia. Gabriel Dan, the first-person narrator of *Hotel Savoy*, is a late-homecomer, a soldier on his way back from Russia after years as a prisoner of war, then odd-job man. One senses a dialogue between two generations and two world wars, palpable in Gallant's "Gabriel Baum" (complete with unhelpful rich uncle) and with her "The Latehomecomer," whose young first-person narrator is released from captivity in the Soviet zone in 1950 and returns to his mother in post-Nazi Berlin. While Roth's narrator is clearly an authorial mouthpiece, Gallant performs the feat of changing shoes or even skins three times. The I-narrator, as a male, a German, and a former member of the Hitler Jugend, is three selfs away from the "passionately anti-Fascist" (Gallant in Hancock 34) Canadian female writer, but triggers the readerly identification and empathy which a normative approach would obstruct.

On another level of correspondences, as that other exile, Coetzee, has pointed out, the elegy of the Habsburg monarchy novelized in *Radetzky March* (1932) was ironically composed by "a subject from an outlying imperial territory"; it was "a great German novel by a writer with barely a toehold in the German community of letters" ("Emperor of Nostalgia"). Similarly, when Geoff Hancock asked Gallant if she would call herself

38 Beckett sojourned off and on in Germany between 1931 and 1936, and could not have failed to come across Roth's work.

a Canadian writer or an international one, she replied, "I'm a writer in the English language. Was Katherine Mansfield a New Zealand writer to you?" (Gallant in Hancock 61). Noteworthy here is Mavis's substitution of language for country (just as Roth considered himself a writer in the German language), and also her spontaneous analogy with a *colonial* writer who participated in European modernism to the extent of provoking Virginia Woolf's admiration and envy. Mavis, also born on the edges of Empire, pointed out that when she was young "there was no such thing as a Canadian," not until "about 1935" (Gallant in Hancock 36). She was of course loosely referring to the Statute of Westminster. On a small individual scale, her doppelgänger Linnet Muir refracts the brand-new nation of Canada when she returns there from New York in 1940, when Canada was already "in Hitler's war"[39] but America "still uneasily at peace" (*HT* 255; *VE* 109). One can grasp the political parallels between individual and national identity construction suggested in the border-crossing passage in "In Youth Is Pleasure":

> I was entering a poorer and curiously empty country, where the faces of the people gave nothing away. The crossing was my sea change. I silently recited the vow I had been preparing for weeks: that I would never be helpless again and that I would not let anyone make a decision on my behalf." (*HT* 256; *VE* 109)

What Linnet-cum-Mavis finds, however, is the Montreal of "The Fenton Child," namely "a series of air-tight compartments" of "race and language and religion and class, all shut away from one another" (Gallant in Hancock 25), miniatures of the nationalisms and allegiances which had begun colliding there three centuries before. Gallant's high altitude, supranational positioning generates an epistemological and even existential questioning of borders and belonging in a manner analogous to Roth's. It is spearheaded by an unexpected, juxtaposed correspondence with the Habsburg Marie-Antoinette in "The Fenton Child," a technique of proximity comparable to Paul Signac's Divisionism, which exploits a phenomenological given, namely that a colour placed next to its contrast becomes more vivid.[40]

"Marie-Antoinette, Christian Queen and Royal Martyr" (*VE* 22), as I have mentioned, was the topic of Ninette's graduation essay, whose angle and point of entry showcased how French Catholic convent schools

39 Canada had entered the war of its own accord, after deliberating for only six days.

40 The French term *couleur complémentaire*, or complementary colour, signposts more clearly why red appears more intense next to green, or blue next to orange.

operate in transmitting verbal-ideological belief systems. Nora, now seventeen, meditates on how at the age of fifteen the daughter of Emperor Francis I had to leave her family, country, and language for an alien people and place. Gallant has her focalizer place historical Marie-Antoinette's actual displacement at the heart of an image cluster grounded in staying and going, the contiguity on the page linking the factual event with the fictional developments of two characters. On the one hand, there is the baby taken from the orphanage, hot, tired, hungry, soiled, and bewildered at the shift from static cot to moving car. Mr. Fenton remarks that infants have "these huge peckers," Dr. Marchand declares they are only "a digestive tube" and the brain is "still primitive," trying to "catch up with the soul," but Nora is convinced Neil is trying to "understand where he's going" (13). The child who is either "being rescued" or "taken captive" – a "hairline divide" (11) – has not a stitch to his name other than the clothing on him, fit only "to be burned, not worth a washtub of water" (13). On the other hand, there is Nora's sister, Geraldine, who has left home and family to become a nun, leaving behind everything she owned. Just like the baby, she "had gone through an open door and the door had swung to behind her" (13). The door is where the motif clusters of the mistake and of the journey intersect with the clothing motif – clothes notably separating humans from beasts, but also basic need from excess. The convergence reveals the story's higher, anagogical level. Calling up Shakespeare's clothing dynamics of deprivation, notably regarding Poor Tom/Edgar and Lear – naked as worms, divested of their costly raiment and trappings of power, pondering the *quidditas* of humanity – Neil, someone's mistake, has already given us much to wonder about. What is a life; what is a human? What is consciousness; when does understanding begin? Do we arrive with nothing, John Locke's *tabula rasa*? Is the open door Geraldine goes through, which swings shut behind her, like being born or dying?

The analogy between Neil and Geraldine, leaving one state for another, is drawn explicitly: "*So* [i.e., just so] her sister had gone through an open door." A second, left-field analogy with Marie-Antoinette ("*So* her sister ... *So* Marie-Antoinette") takes the story one stratum higher and invites further meditation.

> So Marie-Antoinette, younger than Nora, had been stripped to the skin when she reached the border of France, on the way to marry a future king. Total strangers had been granted the right to see her nude. The clothes she had been wearing were left on the ground and she was arrayed in garments so heavy with silver and embroidery she could hardly walk. Her own ladies-in-waiting, who spoke her native language, were turned back. (Nora could not remember where Marie-Antoinette had started out.) (13)

The omniscient narrator's final parenthetical remark reminds us that from the vantage point of a young, contemporary Montrealer of mixed background, the powerful Austro-Hungarian Empire is outside the net of stories which organize experience and meaning. A State along with its myth of belonging can not only disintegrate, it can also be erased. What Nora does retain is that the young archduchess must shed all she accumulated in her past existence, as naked as the newborn babe. The line that follows the extract above is from elsewhere, and initiates a polyphonic oversetting. The inserted intertext is a fragment broken off and separated from its source, its context, and its co-text, namely the second half of the line: "*'For we brought nothing ...,'* Nora's Methodist Abbott grandmother liked to point out" (13). As with Eliot and Joyce the quote is not directly acknowledged but so culturally familiar that it sets up a resonant dialogue between text and canonic pre-text. Not quite sure what our cultural baggage consists of, Gallant provides a further clue to the source: the Methodist Abbott grandmother who made the quote is "convinced that Catholics never cracked a Bible and had to be kept informed" (13–14). But Gallant hermeneutically withholds the second half of the quote requiring collocation – the partial quote being a practice stretching back to great satirists like Chaucer. The silence or suppression of the line end, signposted by the suspension marks, is inhabited by resonances with a much consumed Biblical statement which has generated countless spin-off grand narratives, all part of a "discursive dialectic operating along a continuum" (Thieme 2). The full quote, "For we brought nothing into this world, and it is certain we can carry nothing out" (1 Timothy 6:7 [KJV]), effectively enters into dialogue with a planetary cultural continuum, with other bodies of revealed or received truth. These range from the *Bhagavad Gita*, beloved by Eliot, whose Krishna also explains that we came here empty-handed and will leave empty-handed, and Boethius's influential *Consolation of Philosophy,* also advocating contempt for worldly goods and desires, to the medieval morality tale *Everyman*. The miracle play, in particular with its life/journey and staying/going analogies, lights up Gallant's analogies. Marie-Antoinette, divested of country, language, possessions, and acquaintances as she quits one life for another, calls up Everyman, who must leave Goods and even Knowledge behind.[41]

---

41 It is illuminating to recall the play's consonant and dissonant resonances (*guide/ bide*) between the two famous lines delivered by Knowledge and Good Deeds as they accompany Everyman on his journey to the grave. While Knowledge declares, "Everyman, I will go with thee and be thy guide," he must forsake him at Death's door, and only Good Deeds can declare, "I will bide with thee" (*Everyman* 522, 852).

So the passage under scrutiny makes use of multivocality – more specifically, *ventriloquated discourse* thick with the countless collective voices which have pronounced the borrowed words ("For we brought nothing") and their derivatives. Gallant engages with the Judaeo-Christian Scholastic heritage identifiable to a wide Western readership in a sort of joint venture with her focalizer and reader. She teasingly buttresses the dialogization by interpolating a second partial quote Nora dredges up from memory: "'*Naked we came …*' was along the same line" (14). The full Biblical quote which inhabits this double-voiced syntactical structure is "Naked I came from my mother's womb, and naked I will depart" (Job 1:21 [KJV]).[42] Although withheld, the absent words are inscribed in the form of a ghostly presence, fainter than an echo, overlaying the spoken utterance with the philosophical stance of *vanitas*. Gallant effectively performs with the words of her *intertextual web* what Picasso and Braque did with objects in *visual collage*. Her reference is not from words to things, but "from words to words, or rather from texts to texts" (Riffaterre 142). Intertextual dialogism is the agent of not only the mimesis, but also of "the hermeneutic constructions on that mimesis" (142), and produces a text fraught with significance there where a simple linear reading would produce only meaning. A "full" understanding of both meaning and significance, which can involve an ontological reflexion, depends on readers' ability to recognize and collocate.

In this particular story, "The Fenton Child," the dialogism with history and Christian cosmology carries us to a philosophical dimension that resonates with the numinousness of a Rembrandt canvas. I do not mean the manifest metaphysics of, say, Rembrandt's *Supper at Emmaus* (1628),[43] in which the arresting resurrected Christ silhouette in chiaroscuro collides with the very physical plane of the simple table and stunned diner. I refer rather to the quiet numinousness which suffuses the ostensibly realist, low still life *Flayed Ox*, to which I alluded in chapter 3. I suggest that Mavis, too, concerns herself with that which lies beyond experience, well beyond the verifiable physical world comprising the civilizational shifts she depicts, such as Canada's role on the geopolitical world stage, women's role in public spaces, francophones piercing glass ceilings, the break-up and displacement of Montreal's English-speaking

42 A well-known variant can be found in Ecclesiastes 5:15 [ESV]: "As he came from his mother's womb he shall go again, naked as he came, and shall take nothing for his toil that he may carry away in his hand."

43 I am referring not to the picture in the Louvre (1648) but to the different composition and play of light of Rembrandt's lesser-known, sublime earlier version which stopped me in my tracks, the oil on panel exhibited in Paris's Musée Jacquemart-André.

community,[44] and the economic and urban development involving the takeover and fragmentation of its residences by businesses. The writer's poetic operations speak to the succession of identifiable yet anonymous places which the modernists salvaged from the realists,[45] to achieve *a reality effect attaining a degree of abstraction*. In the film version of *West Side Story*, which Mavis and I often watched together, Smith's Precisionist cityscape is apparently natural but actually highly stylized. As Gallant does for Montreal (right down to the Abbotts' third-floor walk-up flat with its outside staircase), the legendary set designer delineates New York's tribal territories, through the Cubist patterns of brick houses and lanes, the orthogonal, fractal, omnipresent wire fences and steel trestles, and the fire escapes which criss-cross the vertical lines in endless diagonals, calling up a haunting Giambattista Piranesi maze. The reality effect is reinforced through a network of clotheslines, but is also aestheticized by the creamy clouds and the clothes hanging to dry: clothes which all happen to be lovely, diaphanous, silky, ice cream–coloured, and as delicate as Maria's feelings. The reddish hues of the brick décor – the perfectly planed buildings stretching into the deep space of the frame – are often highlighted by other objects in the habitat, such as the big shiny flame-red truck serving as a backdrop. As does Gallant's Marie-Antoinette apologue and her fragments of revealed truth, Smith's aestheticizing pushes the realism towards the higher altitude of symbolism, in his case pointing to the tragically inexorable blood and breakage.

a fraught realism

Ms. Gallant had a journalist's nose, a cinematographer's eye, and a novelist's imagination.

Sandra Martin, "Writer Mavis Gallant Dies at 91"

The visual analogies which have unfurled in my mind show through their eclecticism that there is no question of derivative filiations on the part

44 "French Canada flows in when English Canada pulls away," declares the narrator of *Its Image on the Mirror* (*My Heart Is Broken* 58). Gallant scrutinizes the intricacies of identity and shifting alliances of the French-Canadian community also being radically transformed in the cycle of stories linked through the Carette sisters, namely "1933," "The Chosen Husband," "From Cloud to Cloud," and "Florida," which appear together in *Varieties of Exile*.

45 One can evoke T.S. Eliot's chimney pots, vacant lots, discarded newspapers, and dilapidated window blinds in "Preludes," and his factory and bypass, figures of mass production and mass transportation, in "East Coker."

of Gallant, but simply a common "way of looking at things" (Gallant in Hancock 52). When Picasso painted several works live in front of the camera for Henri-Georges Clouzot's documentary film *Le Mystère Picasso* (1955), spectators could see that his brushstrokes were initially mimetic, calling up a recognizable world, and that only then did they become simplified, synthetic lines. Christian Godin remarks that while traditional pictorial art begins with the simple clean lines of the whole picture and then fills in precise details, Picasso moves from figuration to stylization (237). "The Fenton Child" can stand as a case study illustrating that what holds true for Picasso's brushwork holds for Gallant's method as well. The agenda amounts to distillation: using detail from front, side, and back to capture the thingness of the thing. Holding the stable view of the instability of things, whose outlines become transparent, Gallant apprehends the essence behind thing and event: violence, prejudice, power, self-interest. All the while interrogating first principles, which range from being and knowing to time and space, she positions herself on a plane independent of time and space, which as Schopenhauer argues, is the permanent, essential form of the world" (110). Are those individuals of various origins that Victor lumps together under the term "the English" not analogous with the Slovenians, Poles, Czechs, Croatians, Ukrainians, and Germans once united under the Habsburgs and subsequently puffed up with their rival nationalisms? A questioning of the Multiple and the One – countless countries with their own rulers, armies, garrisons, lieutenants – brings Roth's protagonist to reflect that

> the earth is only one among millions upon millions of similar bodies, each a world. That countless suns shimmer in the Milky Way, each with planets of its own. So that one is, oneself, a paltry individual, if not, to speak quite bluntly, nothing but *a little heap of dust*. (*Radetzky March* 195)

Gallant's text resonates with this remarkable centrifugal amplification leading not endlessly outward, as is customary, but ending with a centripetal implosion, in line with Eliot's famous closure of "The Hollow Men": "This is the way the world ends, / Not with a bang but a whimper" (*Collected Poems* 92).[46] The philosophical stance which looks both up

46 "The Hollow Men" in turn famously enters into dialogue with Dante's *Inferno*, Shakespeare's *Julius Caesar* (from which it takes its title), and Conrad's *Heart of Darkness*. Eliot's modernist anticlimactic low-key ending also enters into an intermedial dialogue with Bartók, whose diabolically rhythmic Quartet no. 2, op. 17, first performed in 1918, ends on two soft pizzicati. Still in an intermedial vein, one can evoke Bresson's apocalyptic *Launcelot du lac*, in which Camelot/the world ends not with a bang but with a clunk: from the chain mail of a dying knight's foot.

and down also suffuses Eliot's meditative final quartet, "Little Gidding," which posits that life offers us three conditions, one of which the poet promptly eliminates as a valid choice. The parallel echoic enumeration of the mirror opposites which "look alike / Yet differ completely" have the haunting quality of a litanic chant:

> Attachment to self and to things and to persons, detachment
> From self and from things and from persons; and, growing between them,
> indifference
> Which resembles the others as death resembles life,
> Being between two lives – unflowering, between
> The live and the dead nettle. (*Collected Poems* 219)

Nourished by Krishna's injunctions in the *Bhagavad Gita*, Eliot's poem – published in 1942, in the middle of a bloody world war pitting nation against nation – argues for the liberation of detachment. Significantly, the "love of a country" is disclosed as merely another form of earthly attachment "of little importance / Though never indifferent" (219). Eliot's call for detachment (from nationalism) illuminates Gallant's subtly inscribed suspicion of fundamentalist communal, ethnic, linguistic, religious, or nationalistic passions and their sectarian identity politics. The philosophical stance to which she (along with Roth and Eliot) adheres, a stance which rises up the better to look down, stretches far back beyond the early modernists, and is well encapsulated by a Shakespearean ironic reversal. The canonic sequence which begins "What a piece of work is man, how noble in reason" ends with the satirical lines:

> in apprehension, how like a god! The beauty of the world! The paragon of animals! And yet to me, what is *this quintessence of dust*."[47] (*Hamlet* II.2.315–21)

I have taken "The Fenton Child" as an exemplar of how Gallant interlocks with such cultural predecessors, and of how her narrative consciousness rises to a height disclosing the bigger picture of the human comedy, including both sides of the open door which swings to behind us. Gallant's view from the sky still dialogues well with Tati's hallmark high-angle shots, serving to make humans strange and to generate a "comique démocratique" (Chion 20) – a brand of democratic comedy in which

47 The canonic pre-text common to all is clearly "for dust thou art, and unto dust shalt thou return" (Genesis 3:19).

we are all potentially ridiculous. But her God's-eye view takes us further. Rather like the Platonic dream allegories of the *contemptus mundi* tradition in which the gaze of the subject soars to the vantage point of the immutable eighth sphere, looking down on the empire or nation which is a mere dot on the tiny surface of the perishable earth below, Gallant invites her readers to soar high above the sectarian identity politics of "this little spot of earth" and "hold it vanity" (Chaucer, *Troilus and Criseyde* 307). An aerial view can indeed be a vantage point of power over tiny, meaningless, and interchangeable people: mere moving "dots," as mean Harry Lime (Orson Welles) from the top of the Ferris wheel designates them in Carol Reed's *The Third Man* (1949).[48] Yet there is that other brand W.H. New has called attention to: Gallant's brand of storytelling, "not without wry amusement" but "intensely compassionate" ("The Art of Haunting Ghosts" 155). New admires the way Gallant closes her stories with "one of those magnificent, moodily detached sentences which characterise her writing" (155). But readers looking for direction and the comfort of narratorial judgment are often puzzled by Gallant's impersonal approach, philosophical detachment, and art of ambivalence. They sometimes even subscribe to "the Mean Mavis school of thought" (Wilkshire 904)[49] and find her gleeful irony harshly judgmental – perhaps because her "guns face in every direction" (Enright 110) and none escape unscathed.

Actually, Mavis's detachment was on the one hand completely natural, part of who she was, and on the other hand, shared with Chekhov, Mansfield, Maupassant, and Proust. It can be valuable to apply to Gallant that which Woolf observed about Proust and his alleged absence of direction, namely that "sympathy is of more value than interference, understanding than judgment" ("Phases of Fiction," *Collected Essays* II: 85). For a God's-eye view can actually make it possible – as I find it does in Gallant's case – to see "the tiny, fragile human body" (Benjamin, "The Storyteller" 77) as one small part of a whole, a world or universe, and to deploy an oblique meditation on mortality. A musical analogy can light up and buttress her vertical approach, equally operative in the *cantus fermus*. Comparable to this musical tradition in which a crystalline, higher-pitched, sustained line of half notes evoking constancy hovers over and covers the rapid, agitated lower vocal lines of sixteenths swarming below, Gallant's

48 Reed's post-war film shot on location in the rubble of Vienna homologously engineered the climate of a world out of joint both visually and acoustically: Karas's haunting zither music and Robert Krasker's tilted shots, oblique angles, and distorting wide-angle lenses.

49 Claire Wilkshire gives an overview of critics who find Gallant's pen ruthless, merciless, and even vicious, not to mention gloomy (905).

oeuvre displays the agitation of the sublunar world and puts it into the perspective of a higher altitude.

Such an aerial dynamic can be partly imputed to the fact that the writer's stories share unstable code systems with fable and parable, and that her narrative patterns – grounded in the anecdote and the sketch – tend to operate as social or philosophical commentary. I have shown how her image clusters serve to designate a second meaning; they are Hutcheon's splitting images, which take the measure of what Gallant herself termed turning points:

> against the sustained tick of a watch, fiction takes the measure of a life, a season, a look exchanged, the turning point, desire as brief as a dream, the grief and terror that after childhood we cease to express. (Gallant, "What Is Style?" 6)

As critics have long observed, Gallant, to boot, is a genre-crosser, shifting gears back and forth between narrative modes and the non-narrative modes of essay as well as portrait and self-portrait (characterized, unlike autobiography, by an absence of plot). Mavis, one tends to forget, was an active essayist with a long working relation with *The New York Times*. The combat she waged against prejudice and ready-made or sloppy thinking incited the Québec Writers' Federation to name its annual prize for non-fiction after her. Besner has observed that in many of Gallant's stories actuality and setting appear so transparently accurate, in no way visibly shaped by memory or imagination, that editors and bibliographers "disagree over whether or not these stories are properly essays" and hurt their brains over the boundaries between the two (*Light of Imagination* 17).

Mavis did write early semi-autobiographical stories with a strong documentary edge. Some depict Franco-era Spain, where she chose to live and write in the early 1950s to acquire an insider's view, just as she would sojourn later in Germany with the same purpose: coming to grips with what made fascism tick. With "Señor Pinedo" (1954), set in Madrid, the real time of writing and publishing, dovetailing with the young Gallant's lived experience in Spain, was coterminous with the story time. The understated political satire takes the measure of a life. It portrays a zealous fascist functionary living a peaceful routine in the 1950s, among fellow tenants whose opinions have faded, like the sepia etching of the Chief of State hanging in the entrance hall since 1937, which "now blended quietly with the wallpaper" (*Collected Stories* 193). As the I-narrator is a foreign tenant in the same seedy *pension*, Señor Pinedo is bent on showing her the virtues of the regime. He brings her pamphlets on the drop in infant mortality, the increased production of railroad tracks, soup kitchens for working mothers, and workers' housing projects showing "smiling factory hands moving into their new quarters" (192). When he passes the brochures around in the dining room, the young pseudo-naive narrator notes (with the overlay of the tongue-in-cheek older speaking voice) that "all these people, with the exception of the Englishwoman, seemed to need as much instruction as [she] did in the good works performed by the state" (192). Gallant's satire is already multidirectional. "These people" range from a bank clerk and a bullfighter's impresario to a former university instructor of Spanish literature who "having taken quite the *wrong* stand during the Civil War – he had been *neutral* – now dispensed hand lotion and aspirin in a drugstore on the Calle del Carmen" (192). But there is also "the inevitable Englishwoman" Mavis recognizes in pensions everywhere, who bristles with loathing at the young Canadian's English and removes herself to the far corner of the room with her own assortment of "mineral water digestive pills, Keen's mustard, and English chop sauce" (192).

The freshly expatriate Mavis was so down and out while she was working on this story that she had to pawn her clothes, typewriter, and grandmother's ring, but even in the face of squalor, ideological indoctrination, and ignominy, her cheerful eye for the absurd and her deft control of bathos prevail. Underpinning the authentic events and objects documented by a detached, observant narrator, one always finds an unstated meaning, state, or condition, and the rhythmic lists belong to *a tall-tale dynamic* blending exaggeration, understatement, and precision. Mavis almost starved working on this story because her unscrupulous New York literary agent "forgot" to let her know that *The New Yorker* had accepted two of her stories ("The Picnic" and "One Morning in June") and pocketed the fees himself.

The more retrospective narration of "When We Were Nearly Young" (1960), set in the same space-time, portrays the young Mavis making the rounds of post office, bank, Cook's, and American Express hoping an acceptance letter and money will come. Both plots coincide closely with the lived experience Mavis set down in her diaries as she was taking the pulse of Europe, an extract of which *The New Yorker* published in 2012.[50] I agree that "Señor Pinedo" does not insist on what Besner calls "the shaping force of memory" and is rather at "the transcriptive, documentary edge of Gallant's fictional world" (*Light of Imagination* 17). But I find that "When We Were Nearly Young," in which the narrator insists that the

50 Announced on the cover of *The New Yorker* as "The Hunger Diaries: Mavis Gallant on Starving and Writing in Spain," the extract is part of a first volume of her *Journals*, whose publication date has regrettably been repeatedly delayed and is unknown at this time. (See James Adams.)

city she has merged into is inhabited by a mentality, appearance, sounds, and hopes "as strange as anything [she] might have invented" (*Collected Stories* 214), holds quite a bit of self-reflexive mediation on the relation of time and memory to representation, to which I will return. It performs "the true rediscovery of time" (Woodcock 91),[51] which Besner describes in a later essay as an ongoing and fluent vocation "always subject to and at the same time resistant of memory's categorical interruptions, clarifications, and corrections" ("Reading Muir, Asher, and Frazier" 157–8).

To throw some light on all this borderblur, I want to look at the *gear-shifting between essay and story*, which is particularly manifest in the opening pages of "Varieties of Exile." With the opening sentences ("In the third summer of the war I began to meet refugees. There were large numbers of them in Montreal" [*HT* 299; *VE* 149]), the author sets up a narrative with a specific time, a setting, a protagonist, and a sequence of actions transmitted through a series of verbs in the preterite. The narrative thread of that wartime summer is interrupted by narratorial comments and digressions, then taken up again, but the refugees who appear in the first paragraph disappear until the last. We learn that what the autobiographical nineteen-year-old I-narrator, Linnet, craved was conversation, not romance, but that men in Canada kept their serious talk for other men. We are told that what was expected from the woman "was so limited it was insulting," and that Linnet, who had much to offer, wondered, "Is that all? Is that all you expect?" (*HT* 301; *VE* 150). We are shown a tableau of conventional married life through the eyes of the young commuter: women who have become shrill, discontented Red Queens in housecoats confined behind screen doors through which they yell instructions to children, dogs, and postmen (*HT* 301; *VE* 150–1). From this stative portrait of waste, a waste of female potential, variants of which we encounter in many of Gallant's stories,[52] we veer back in time to a new narrative plane:

> When I was very young, under seven, my plan for the future was to live in every country of the world and have a child in each. I had confided it: With adult adroitness my listener had led me on. How many children? Oh, one to

51 Without naming the device of anamnesis, George Woodcock draws attention to how Gallant's texts are successful records of an age because they are "inhabited by people so carefully drawn and individually realised" in a setting just as "superbly evoked," so that the past "comes alive ... as *experience* more than as history" (91).

52 The ontological discomfort couched in this passage stems from the female protagonist's desire to produce rather than reproduce. The unease is thus different in kind from the discomfort of the frivolous bride Lily in "Let It Pass," which stems from a love of consumption, not production.

> a country. And what would you do with them? Travel in trains. How would they go to school? I hate schools. How will they learn to read and write, then? They'll know already. What will you live on? It will all be free. (*HT* 301–2; *VE* 151)

What occurs is a shift to the self-portrait melded with a sketch in the form of a slice-of-life. The scene with its immediacy effect also revolves round the narrator's stance on relations between the sexes, on marriage, the family, children, from the vantage points which move from that of the older, narrating I ("When I was very young") to that of the child protagonist, the narrated self. Gallant makes this interruption in the narrative lively through the free direct speech – as if the narrator stood aside – of the series of conventional questions and iconoclastic answers. The responses come from a child who believes that babies happen "in the manner of a long card game with mysterious rules" (*HT* 302; *VE* 151), a child who has indignantly rejected the accurate version of the facts of life because she has "never come across it in books" (*HT* 302; *VE* 151). The genre-bending here involves part exposition preparing us for a coming narrative encounter, part exemplum-cum-manifesto making a point: freedom. Just as quickly as the narrator leaped from the age of nineteen to the age of seven does she leap back again into the original narrative. The perception of "plain facts," and fiction's power to reflect them as well as reflect on them, shifts to the plain facts themselves, with a new series of verbs in the preterite, beginning with "The commuters on the Montreal train never spoke much" (*HT* 302; *VE* 152). We readers are now prepared for the story of "one man" who stands out from all the "anonymous others." We expect our two protagonists to meet. They do. We expect them to interact. They begin to. But the particular once more shifts to the general. True to the device of antonomasia, the "one man" (*HT* 302; *VE* 152), Frank Cairns, is "stamped, labelled, ticketed" (*HT* 304; *VE* 153) as a type, a category, the exemplar Gallant wants. Linnet spots him easily as belonging to a "species of British immigrant known as remittance men" (*HT* 304; *VE* 153) – those sons who had offended their parents and were shipped out as "golden deportees" (*HT* 305; *VE* 154) to British territories with an annual stipend so long as they remained in exile.

The highly methodical observation[53] arrests the action and hurls out into another genre, that of the essay, which the author signposts on the

53 A double seriation has unfolded, with one ternary ("stamped, labelled, ticketed") followed by a second taking the form of rhetorical questions which draw in the reader ("by his tie [club? regiment? school?]"), in turn followed by a quaternary series ("by his voice, manner, haircut, suit") to make the conclusion even more ineluctable.

page via blanks which frame beginning and end. Linnet spots Frank Cairns as an "RM" all the more easily "from having had one in the family" (*HT* 304; *VE* 153), her father – modelled on Mavis's own half-Scottish one, as she confirmed during one of our conversations. The first of the "six crimes" entailing the reasons for banishment which the narrator gives is "Conflict over the choice of a profession" (*HT* 304; *VE* 154). Albert Stewart Roy de Trafford Young, the young, disgraced, freshly exiled son of a British landed family, notably wanted to be a painter. Mavis caricatures her father's artistic choice in her fictionalized text as the son wanting to be "a tap-dancer" (*HT* 305; *VE* 154), perhaps not so far off from the banishing parental perception.

This interpolated essay by a keen social observer and commentator, which has often been noted for its metatextual terms,[54] is both analytical and interpretive. From the personal point of view of the older narrator looking back ("the pound was *then* one to five" [*HT* 305; *VE* 154]), and with the father and Frank Cairns as base image and overlay, the essay analyses all aspects of politics, the politics that regulate human society from the smallest units (the family) to the largest geopolitical ones (the empire). All aspects of authoritarianism are ironically displayed and denounced. These range from class and patriarchy to the institution of marriage and gender roles, notably women's relegation to the role of "unpaid servant, social secretary, dog walker, companion, sick nurse" (*HT* 306; *VE* 155). Rather remarkably, all the while the author turns narrative into essay, she careens from essay to drama. Listing the reasons for banishment other than choice of profession, fragments of direct speech in various voices transform statements into instant scenes suffused with immediacy:

> Dud checks – "I won't press a charge, sir, but see that the young rascal is kept out of harm's way." Marriage with a girl from the wrong walk of life – "Young man, you have made your bed!" Fathering an illegitimate child: "... and broken your mother's heart." (*HT* 305; *VE* 154)

---

54 The narrator declares for instance that remittance men "were characters in a plot" which began "with a fixed scene, an immutable first chapter" (*HT* 305; *VE* 154). Although she denounces the scenario as "a load of codswallop" (*HT* 305; *VE* 154) which eschews the issue of free will, Cairns *is* a character in a plot that begins with a fixed scene whose self-reflexive quality is buttressed through embedding. The writer is also writing about a budding writer writing about a remittance man. In a chest of drawers twist, when Cairns comes across the scribbled title of the story, "The Socialist RM," the RM that the story is about becomes the reader of the (framed) story.

The author's special brand of multivocality theatrically connects factual statement to atomized ersatz dialogue to showcase the economic or sexual grounds of the misdemeanours. By ventriloquizing, Gallant moreover individuates the universal.

The Russell Banks who remarks on Gallant's gift for accurate recording[55] is the same Banks who judiciously draws attention to her structures: "they are digressive, regressive, and circular; they leap forward in time one minute and linger in pockets of loss the next; they ruminate and fulminate and explicate (viii). Gallant's imprint is in her cumulative design or Form,[56] which banishes notions of narrative progress by substituting recurrence and pattern for successive sequence. In this, *like the modernist painters drawn to primitive art and the composers drawn to folk music, both related to questions of origins,* Gallant pulls the genre of the short story (and with the dense episodic *Green Water*, even the novel) back to its sources, the spiralling folk tale, anecdote, or sketch.[57]

Mansfield had appropriated Chekhov's Russian method privileging what Woolf called the "cloudy and vague, loosely trailing rather than tightly furled" ("An Essay in Criticism," *Collected Essays* II: 257). In turn, expropriating certain facets of Mansfield's satirical sketch-cum-story, the young, equally Chekhov-mad Mavis began to shape it and make it her own. Recalling Chekhov's curves, and the Eastern aesthetic favouring the serpentine and the arabesque, Gallant's stories are spirals, constructed in her own words "rather like a snail" (Gallant in Hancock 45). They move slowly, as Woolf would describe it, "like clouds in the summer air" ("An Essay in Criticism," *Collected Essays* II: 257), leaving an ungraspable wake of meaning in our minds which gently fades.[58] This is the Russian manner of impressionistic brushstrokes rather than what Woolf called the compact French method, embodied by Maupassant, who ended his

55 Banks declares, "she seems to have remembered everything that occurred in Montreal in the 1930s and 1940s and everyone whom she even so much as glanced at" (xi).

56 I mentioned in chapter 2 the modernists' fascination with the concept of *eidos*, which for the ancient Greeks signified both Form and Essence.

57 Like its cousins the fable, parable, and allegory, the sketch is rather like a puff pastry, the imbricated layers of which portray societal predilections, and often advance an argument or lesson on the right way to live.

58 Typical of the cloud-like non-closure the early modernists admired, part II of Chekhov's "The Bishop" dwindles off rather like Eliot's whimper, then spirals back up to Part III and IV, in which the ill Bishop Peter becomes worse and dies. Reversing classic pathetic fallacy, Chekhov has the sun shine and the birds sing: everything is as "cheerful, gay, and happy" as the year before and the year to come. All forget him except his old mother "in an obscure provincial town" who mentions her son the bishop to those she meets when she "fetche[s] her cow from pasture," and is not believed (*The Kiss* 97).

stories "with a pinch of gunpowder, artfully placed so as to explode when we tread on its tail" (Woolf, "Phases of Fiction," *Collected Essays* II: 61).[59] Mavis told me she disliked the programmed surprise exploding at the end of a Maupassant or O. Henry story, and she acknowledged Chekhov (whose story collections she owned in two complete editions) as the master of the modern short story. The aesthetic of impersonality and indeterminacy along with the Impressionistic method Mavis made her own (complete with complex curves which in the end shoot off from the equation set up by repeated leitmotifs and fade rather than clinch) was of course at odds with the early *New Yorker* style the magazine's founding editor Harold Ross had propagated and handed on to William Shawn (Lehmann-Haupt). Along with writers like Nabokov, Gallant helped to unsettle the editorial board's attachment to realism and its suspicion of elliptical, impressionistic writing. Readers may indeed have found difficult stories like Gallant's which – as Jane Urquhart, one of Mavis's attentive admirers, has observed – are not so much about events, but rather set out to "illuminate the time that falls between the events" (vii).

59 The French method was also the rule with writers ranging from Katherine Anne Porter and Flannery O'Connor to Hemingway, right up to the final sentence that clinches the circumference and significance of the whole story – for which reason Woolf called Hemingway "modern in manner but not in vision" ("An Essay in Criticism," *Collected Essays* II: 258).

6
Who is I & when is here?

To see a World in a grain of sand,
And Heaven in a wild flower,
Hold Infinity in the palm of your hand,
And eternity in an hour.

William Blake, "Auguries of Innocence"

For ever warm and still to be enjoyed,
For ever panting, and for ever young…
For ever wilt thou love and she be fair

John Keats, "Ode on a Grecian Urn"

I have engaged with the aesthetic framework of a fraught realism which adheres to certain conventional elements of the realist tradition particularly strong in societies inhabiting the edges,[1] but which disrupts other features, such as sequentiality, or a continuous linear action producing an illusion of logic and causality. "The Fenton Child" has served to showcase the spiral pattern of motivic recurrence which substitutes loose poetic association for the tighter realist patterns of consecutiveness passing for consequence. I have been suggesting that Gallant can exemplify how realism collided with Impressionism and Cubist modernism and looked both forward and back. Forward to the postmodern era (literally and physically haunted by modernism [Hutcheon, *A Poetics of Postmodernism* 49]), but

1 Matt Cohen claimed as late as the 1980s that realism was still the mainstream narrative mode in English-language fiction generally, and in Canada particularly (68). In a Harvard address Carol Shields contributed to a book I co-edited, the writer referred to her vantage point anchored in the margins of both planet and genre as being on the edge of the edge (Shields, "A View from the Edge of the Edge").

also back to the Romantic Idealists, who were fascinated by the concept of the Form and Essence (*eidos*) beyond matter or visible reality. I have already discussed Gallant's ostensibly modernist contrapuntal play with past and present, memory and experience, mind and world in "Bonaventure," for instance, in which she radically reconstructs distorted apprehensions of time through the standpoints of the young (who telescope an earlier generation's lived experience with a prehistorical or ahistorical space-time) and the old (who overset what *was* onto what *is*). Such play is also grounded in the Romantic concern (manifest in the lyric poetry of the epigraphs above) with perception, subjectivity, and time. Not time as sequence (clocktime), I hasten to add, but time as an eternal moment (Goethe's *Der Augenblick*).

Like the early modernists before her, Gallant plugged into the lyrical impulse which dovetailed with the sublime and rested on privileged moments of breakthrough, apocalyptic spots of time from which surge an access of understanding allowing us to see a totality which our analytical powers fail to apprehend (Kant, *The Critique of Judgment*). Her lyrical impulse, like the Imagists' and the Romantics' before them, is atemporal, similar in the way it collapses time into a moment to the syncretic, intertwining, echoing process of mythmaking.

Technically speaking, Gallant wields the rhetorical tropes of discursive displacement effortlessly, from frame-breaking – that writerly equivalent of Cubist angle-breaking discussed in my previous chapter – to metaphor and irony. The way she disrupts realist space-time and shows disjunctive spaces of both mind and world synchronically is clearly *analogous with the Cubist agenda*: depicting what is concealed from one located and temporal vantage point so as to replace succession by simultaneity in time and space. Their common agenda is rooted in the awareness that the ontological structures of reality are interlocked with a vantage point, which in turn is rooted in the space we are melded to and the time or speed it takes to tear us away to another point. Not so far, actually, from Keats's ekphrastic dialogized meditation in "Ode on a Grecian Urn" on movement and stillness, time and space, through the verbal representation of a graphic representation of "slow time" (*Complete Poems* 344)[2] – a slow time which I will show Gallant enacting textually.

The motivic variations I have discussed thus function like musical counterpoint and reprise, or even the play with instrumental colour and

2 In the ode's intermedial competition, Keats's speaker finds the powers of poetry inferior to those of the visual arts (see *Complete Poems* I.3–4; II.1–2); this contrasts with Hegel, who sees poetry as the highest form of art, and its sister arts its servants (*Aesthetics*).

timbre, but they also cohabit as elements of *collage*. So does the jigsaw contiguity of narrative and non-narrative modes, a form of generic interpenetration related to the disruptive Cubist practice of presenting three-dimensional objects in the middle of represented bidimensional ones. So, too, does the intertextual web of cultural references which we have seen thread through Gallant's work. At times signposted, as in the epigraphs which serve as off-texts informing the reading, but often disguised and displaced, these multivocal intertexts cry out to be recognized or at least sensed to be pre-existing, culturally familiar material. When they are, they bifurcate and refract in a Cubist way the already unstable voice and viewpoint. Ondaatje marvels at her effortless multiview, namely how she "slips into and out of minds and moods so quickly that we often miss the technical craft of that journey" (x). That technical craft is precisely what I set out here to elucidate. Like Ondaatje, I admire the ease with which Gallant's trademark narrators give "the air of being attached, lazily, almost accidentally, like a burr to some character – an Italian servant perhaps, a tax consultant, an art dealer ..." (ix, original suspension points). I find Ondaatje's burr simile judicious, as is his adverbial phrase, "almost accidentally," both of which point at that high degree of virtuosity which allows a performer to erase all visible trace of work or effort. During the joint reading in Paris with Jhumpa Lahiri, who had selected the stories for Mavis's collection then in press, *The Cost of Living* – twenty pieces spanning the first twenty years of writing – Lahiri paid tribute to the way her mentor's brilliant swerves in viewpoint had inspired her own craft. In her introduction to the story collection, Lahiri too stressed the notions of performance and virtuosity. She called these feats of multiview "the narrative equivalent of what acrobats do as they leap from one swinging bar to another," adding that the feat was ambitious enough in a novel, but absolutely "forbidding in the restricted confines of short fiction" ("Introduction" x).

I concur, and have also been arguing that Gallant's use of the metaphor and of double space-time retrospective narration is painterly and cinematic. In her multilayered, multidimensional, multigeneric works, the devices are linguistic equivalents of deconstructed binocular vision and stereoscopic vision, offering distinct but overlapping visual perceptions simultaneously, even of that which is out of frame or invisible. I have argued analogies with the visual techniques of weighting carried out by modernist artists, who emphasized different features of bulk, line, stance, and light over accustomed realistic depictions, and whose reshaping was often perceived as deformed. Gallant's innovation consists in *transmuting strategies from a visual medium devoid of temporal notions to a literary medium in which time has always been the nerve centre*. In this sub-chapter I continue to think more in terms of process than of product, and to read Gallant's work in terms of *how* it is what it is, which I find points to what it means. I zoom in more closely on how, once settled into the seeming-to-be-real of Gallant's texts, readers encounter sudden Cubic swerves in logic or causal connections alongside swerves in viewpoint and voice which at times (albeit differently from Dos Passos's trademark intercutting of simultaneous situations) take on Sonia Delaunay's *simultanéisme* and Marshall McLuhan's "all-at-once-ness" (63).

simultaneism vs clocktime

The textile designer and painter Sonia Delaunay launched what the poet Guillaume Apollinaire dubbed Orphic Cubism. She engineered the simultaneous perception of juxtaposed colours (*simultanéisme*) which Georges Seurat had less radically deployed, investigating the way adjacent areas of analogous hues or intensities, or else of complementary colours opposite on the colour wheel, generate relations or harmonies which – when perceived simultaneously – interact dynamically, pulsate, and appear to morph. One can detect precisely such pulsation and morphing – found in Delaunay's *Bal Bullier* and *Prismes électriques* (1913, 1914) – in "The Fenton Child" when, through Nora, we readers perceive simultaneously the apologue of Marie-Antoinette adjacent to the interwoven stories of Neil, Ninette, and Geraldine. The way Gallant shifts effortlessly from the Fenton, Abbott, and Cochefert narratives to non-narrative asides, inquiries, and meditations is the scribal version of how Sonia Delaunay did away with lines in her paintings and simply let the edge of the paint constitute its own border with the adjacent colour area – which "advanced" or "receded" depending if it was a warm or cool colour. Like Delaunay's pictures (and like the art on this book's cover), Gallant's texts abound in colour echoes or afterimages. Yet while the visual artist limited her agenda to a simultaneity of colours, Gallant also plugged into the simultaneity of space (and therefore of time) that was the concern of the Cubists determined to transform temporal succession into all-at-once-ness. Her pyrotechnic viewpoint swerves are strongly analogous to the deconstructed shapes of a Henry Moore reclining figure or to Picasso's multiple variants of his Portrait of Dora Maar (arguably inspired by Cézanne's rejection of single-point perspective), which *stretch the structure of seeing to provide physically impossible simultaneous views*.

Ondaatje has observed that Gallant has "a brilliant sense of place" and gives us "an underground map of Europe in the twentieth century" (ix). Banks has declared that "Time is the great subject of all Gallant's work" (xi). Both have acknowledged being dazzled by her ability to play with the codes of voice and viewpoint. It is by deploying multiview and multivocality to perfection that Gallant dissolves realists' space-time. She ruptures the modern concept of a chronological time flowing forward which Walter Benjamin has termed a "homogeneous and empty time" (*On the Concept of History*), in favour of a fully immediate *jetztzeit* (a now-time or rather here-and-now), a present which is not merely a transition, but in which "time originates and has come to a standstill (*Stillstellung*)" (*On the Concept of History*). Throughout my discussion, I have drawn attention to the dissolution between outside and inside views as well as between character and narrator, and to the collision or else conflation of restricted view and omniscience, when intradiegetic narrators know more than they should and omniscient narrators know less. I have analysed the writer's use of either free-floating or localized narrators in patterns of involvement or detachment, of disclosure or concealment. I have explored how memory and perception meld and mutually diffract sensory material in the mind, and I have discussed the extreme form of anamnesis, which conjoins two time periods to the extent that the past events are re-experienced rather than remembered. I argue that Mavis is interested in the protean multiforms of the consciousness which dovetail with the God-like simultaneity of messianic time in which, as Benjamin has remarked, God's eye sees past, present, and future all at once, so that the *jetztzeit* or here-and-now is eternal. Time dilating into eternity is a common *topos* in master texts such as Edmund Spenser's *The Faerie Queene*, whose last stanza distances itself from Mutability "soon cut down" by "Short Time" and its "consuming sickle," and aspires to

> that same time when no more change shall be,
> But stedfast rest of all things, firmly stayd
> Upon the pillours of eternity,
> That is contrayr to Mutabilitie (677)

Mavis personally encountered sudden moments of epiphany or pure bliss that took her out of short time, and through such moments of immediacy, her writing blasts the subject's present or past outside of a homogeneous linear sequence. Deeply interested in the mind and the process of thinking, she also seems aware that thinking involves "not only the movement of thoughts but also their zero-hour [*Stillstellung*]" where thought "crystallizes as a monad" (Benjamin, *On the Concept of History*). Salman Rushdie has pointed out in his essay "In God We Trust" that good writers insist on following both roads of simultaneity and linearity, and Gallant naturally is among those who hold on to the importance of "sequence, of narrative, of society as a story" (*Imaginary Homelands* 382).

Her propensity for the condensed *Stillstellung*, akin to the epiphany which gestures to an unknowable numinous world beyond our own, is a textually directed impression-point (Gerlach) which gives articulation to the whole. It is arguably how, like Munro (see Dvořák, "Dailiness"), Gallant harnesses the tension between event or chronotopic experience and the unfurling of symbol – which might explain why Carol Shields in private referred to "the divine Mavis" and "the divine Alice."

In the previous sub-chapter, my discussion of "Varieties of Exile" began to showcase the retrospective first-person narration, favoured by modernist[3] (and postmodern) writers because it confers the same capacity to slide back and forth on the axis of time as does the device of the omniscient narrator. I have suggested how by using the double I technique, Gallant layers time to come to terms with the past in as full a way as the fulgurant picture or film still allows. She draws the (self)-portrait of Linnet by overlaying the perspective (*now*) of the older narrator, who both recalls and anticipates onto the shifting vantage points of the child (who experiences), and the young adult Linnet (who both experiences and remembers). The child's standpoint is grounded in a far-removed *then,* and the young adult's is rooted in a more proximal *then*, which often takes on the immediacy (and the terminology) of a *now*. The author refracts the temporal angle in the manner of an anamorphosis to add the undeniable poignancy, richness, and depth distance can offer. Yet the strategy also serves to blur a past which "*whizzes* by," which can be apprehended only as "a picture, which flashes its farewell in the moment of its recognizability" (Benjamin, *On the Concept of History*, original stress). When Frank Cairns, who through their discussions of shared books has acquired an individuated presence, enlists in the war, it is the narrator who asks the reader, "Did we write to each other?" and confesses, "That's what I can't remember" (*HT* 318; *VE* 166).

To demonstrate this quite anti-Proustian approach, I first need to spotlight how Gallant excels in a Cubist technique of representation by destabilizing how we sense time, and by unsettling the cognitive mapping of the subject-centred perceptual apparatus. *To liberate the text from the linear temporality of clocktime, Gallant syncopatingly plays with narrative rhythm* (alternatively called tempo, speed, or duration) *and aspect*, the relations of frequency grammarians and narratologists have identified between the telling and the action. She pairs tempo and aspect in electrifying combinations in the writing process which always followed the initial surge of ideas, during which the material would flow onto the

3 Joyce's story collection *Dubliners* (1914) – especially "Araby" – spring to mind.

page in longhand as if she were taking dictation. As she pointed out to all in the afterword to her *Paris Stories*, images and whole scenes would appear, like "disconnected parts of a film" ("Afterword," 375), and she likened even her complete first draft to "an unedited film" (376). During this editing process, flashbacks collide with flashforwards and the time scheme leaps years between lines, or brakes to extend seconds indefinitely, achieving the timelessness of the snapshot or film still. For Gallant chooses with care from the tempi which regulate the relations between diegetic or story time and discourse time: the time of telling or narration (which corresponds to our time of reading).

The tempi range from the high speed of ellipsis (when action occurs but discourse is suspended, or rather stops and starts again, leaving a temporal break) to its reversal, the stasis of the pause (in which action is suspended but the discourse is not). These extreme forms on the axis of speed entailing, say, a line per century or a hundred lines per minute frame two moderate canonical forms. These are the dramatically immediate scene (when discourse time is equal to story time), and the even more normative summary (when discourse time is shorter than story time) – a variable covering all ground between the scene and ellipsis or elision. Unerringly selecting her tempi for their modes and functions, Gallant tends to disdain the traditionally dominant summary. Perhaps because it tends to impart an illusion of objectivity she does not choose to cultivate. Or perhaps because the summary traditionally constitutes the background to scenes as well as a connective between them, both of which her fat-free prose treats as "just rice pudding" and does away with.

Gallant favours the scene, which sets up a slice-of-life reality effect conducive to imparting a lesson or moral, and at times dilates it and expands it to the limits of the pause, in a drawing out or stretch in which discourse time is greater than story time.[4] Since it takes longer to tell than it does to happen, *the effect of slow time is analogous to cinematic slow motion*, when the representation proceeds at less than usual speed and takes longer than the action. Gallant also likes to break and brake, namely to oscillate between the extreme forms of acceleration and deceleration. I have shown how her static pauses harbour a metaphysical meditation. It is through what her high-speed ellipses omit that her texts become so poetic,[5] but also so dynamic. As Wolfgang Iser was among

4 What Gerald Prince calls stretch (92–3) Bernard Dupriez dubs dilatation or expansion in narrative rhythm (403).

5 Bresson, too, declares that one finds poetry "in what's left out, in what is suggested. Pornographic film is the art [*sic*] of showing everything. Cinematography is the art of representing nothing" (*Interviews* 240).

the first to argue in *The Act of Reading: A Theory of Aesthetic Response*, whenever the author interrupts the narrative flow, she gives us readers the opportunity to fill in the gaps left by the text and to assemble the meaning towards which the perspectives of the text have guided us (38). Gallant's ellipses and lateral omissions[6] implement a subtle game of hide-and-seek with her ideal or implied reader: a competent informed reader (Stanley Fish in Iser 30–1), even a superreader (Michael Riffaterre in Iser 30) she imagines endowed with the intelligence and cultural baggage needed to detect, decrypt, and connect.

Gallant's Linnet Muir cycle, first published separately in *The New Yorker,* focuses on key moments in the development of the subject and of consciousness, but also (like Emily Carr's *The Book of Small*) on the development of the nation,[7] for "In those days there was almost no such thing as a 'Canadian'" (*HT 253*; *VE* 107). The writer splits the stories temporally both on the diegetic level (the plots are set between the 1920s and 1940s, but asynchronously) and the extratextual level (staggered publication dates in *The New Yorker*). "In Youth Is Pleasure" abounds with leaps between the different temporalities of the older narrating I and an unstable narrated self who is now child, now young adult. We readers thus need to deal with the standpoints of a narrated child-I discovering her cultural environment and the world of words, and of a narrated adult self discovering the world of work and the world of writing, through which criss-cross the appraisals of the self-conscious older narrating I. After having finished her high school education in New York in 1940, Linnet (like Mavis) returns to Montreal, where she heads for her old French-Canadian nurse, who lives in "the east end of the city – the French end, the poor end" (*VE* 111). I reiterate this statement because its full import unfolds through a connecting triple repetition ("end") which sets up an equivalence: the three qualifying terms (*east/French/poor*) are thus synonymous and interchangeable. Yet the double binary or divide English/French and prosperous/poor is to give way to an unprecedented intermixing of ethnicities, languages, traditions, and values.

6 I can once more call up the subtle nod to young Puss's illicit declaration of love to her brother-in-law in "Cost of Living" – unstated but earth-moving when decoded.

7 Carr's story cycle of place overlaps with the cycle of character through a binary structure of identity construction focusing both on the origins of selfhood and on the origins of community and nation. The writer/painter relates having been born the very year British Columbia joined the new Confederation of Canada. She chronicles the growth of an individual alongside that of a colonial outpost into a capital city: "Victoria, on Vancouver Island, British Columbia, was the little town; I was the little girl" (Carr 75).

The author portrays Montreal as a small-scale model of the world, a laboratory of global upheavals and societal mutations. The space-time mutations ensue partly through the massive waves of political and economic refugees, which the younger, idealistic Linnet in "Varieties of Exile" sees as "prophets of a new social order that was to consist of justice, equality, art, personal relations, courage, generosity" (*VE* 149). The amplifying enumeration engineers progressive disbelief in the exalted standpoint, which then collides head-on with the overset older, wiser narrating voice, which admits that her younger self dismissed as "no more than a deplorable accident" the fact that "the refugees tended to hate one another," and acknowledges that she "did not always [*i.e., yet*] recognise [the] symptoms" of "nationalist pigheadedness" (149). What we see at work is the diffraction and friction of two tectonic plates: the different temporalities of the two subjects which are really one: the narrating I which overlays and interlocks with the narrated self. A past recalled by an adult, lucid narrating I is overset by a future placed in suspension, and the older voice criss-crosses and melds with the vantage point of a young, naïve narrated self who projects herself towards a future which has already passed – a future/past in which exotic refugees have turned to changing their names and eating cornflakes, i.e. have integrated and become plain vanilla.

An opening line in "In Youth Is Pleasure" which relates young Linnet's sudden indifference to her mother, "It was much the way I would be *later* with men I fell out of love with, but I was too young to know that *then*" (*HT* 252; *VE* 105) showcases how this temporal axis in which the story future is already the past allows the voice to slide freely between the anterior and the simultaneous. We find straightforward markers such as "at thirteen" or "when I was ten," and we can cope with these sudden zones in which looking ahead is simultaneously looking back, as in "Years after that, he would try to call me 'Lynn'" (*HT* 265; *VE* 118). But we are misled by shifters normally attached to the present moment of speaking such as *today* and *now*. The *now* of "that June morning and the drive through empty, sunlit, wartime streets are even now like a roll of drums in the mind" (*HT* 259; *VE* 112) conventionally refers to the enunciative present, time of the telling. But the *today* of "After today I would never need to hear this" (*HT* 259; *VE* 112) sows confusion by transgressively referring to the diegetic past, namely the day the eighteen-year-old Linnet left New York for her hometown Montreal and found her nurse Olivia. We are misled by the disrupted opposition between *In the old days* and *Now*:

> In the old days [Olivia] had gone home every weekend, taking me with her if my parents felt my company was going to make Sunday a very long day. Now I understood what the weekends were about. (*HT* 268; *VE* 120)

When is this "now," which should be at the opposite end of the axis beginning "In the old days," when Linnet's father was still alive? It turns out to refer to another diegetic past, more recent but still equally divorced from the enunciative present of the utterance grounded in the narratorial presence, which nestles in sentences such as "I had no idea what he meant and I *still don't*" (*HT* 264; *VE* 117). Gallant, like Emily Carr and Margaret Laurence,[8] makes aesthetic use of cinema's stereoscopic technique of representation, to make an analogy with the optical instrument superimposing two images taken at a slight distance from each other so as to produce an effect of solidity or depth. *Operating in the manner of stereoscopic film's base image plus overlay*, her retrospective narration layers the temporalities of subject and object of telling to achieve the effect Mavis admired in Nabokov's work. "*Time shrinks, stretches, separates and overlaps*," she noted in her *New York Times Book Review* appraisal of Nabokov's 1972 novel (Gallant, "*Transparent Things*," rpt in *Paris Notebooks*, 200). Her remarks hold true for her own work, for which "In Youth Is Pleasure" stands as an exemplar. If our eye misses a line we are years "out of kilter" (*Paris Notebooks* 200), such is the stretching and even distortion in this story of homecoming in which the last eight years since Linnet's father died "were like minutes" to his old friends but "several lives" to the now grown-up child, Linnet (*VE* 119). I align myself with Peter Orner, who in his introduction to Gallant's reissued novels, lauds *Green Water, Green Sky* as a precursor to her later stories where "she moves, seemingly without effort, and often with hardly a transition, back and forth across decades and space, capturing, as so few ever have" – here I think of Proust – "the weight of memory on a page" (Orner, "Introduction" xii).

In "When We Were Nearly Young," the older narrating I back in France and her hungry narrated self living in Spain are separated by a mere nine years, but the story is drenched with time. The narrating voice feels distant, as if it were coming from the end of a tunnel. The narrator tells us nothing about herself – neither name, nationality, nor occupation. Even the I is at first absent, absorbed in the opening sentence's enigmatic collective identity: "In Madrid, nine years ago, *we* lived on the thought of money" (*Collected Stories* 209), and collective occupation: "The thing we had in common was that we were all *waiting* for money" (209). The narrator

8 I am thinking here of the double vision produced by the older narrating I's present utterances encroaching into the past time territory of her younger narrated self in Carr's *Book of Small* (see Dvořák, "Cows and Configurations") and in Laurence's *A Bird in the House*.

goes on to stress her own unreliability in conjuring up an accurate representation of this space-time, but she also insists on an immeasurable internal temporal structure – already latent in the waiting, and lurking in the only other occupation professed: "We began keeping diaries" (213). On the one hand, then, she multiplies rhetorical questions (Were they typical Spaniards?/What was the worst that could happen?) and negative occurrences of stative verbs of cognition (I don't know, I don't remember, No one seemed to know) [213–14]). She invalidates the truth of memory by confessing, "I have never been back to Madrid" (213), and by providing contact with the experienced space-time in collaged sensual shards, fulgurant yet viewed as an eternal present, even future:

> I *see* us huddled in coats, gloved and scarfed, fighting the icy wind, pushing along to the ten-peseta [restaurant]. In another memory it *is* so hot that we can scarcely force ourselves to the park, where we *will* sit under elm trees and look at newspapers. (213–14)

On the other hand, the narrator and her friends approach the slow time of Keats's silent marble figures through the "paralysis" of poverty (213), even the "slowing down" of the timorous, stalemated chess games which lead to "immobility of thought" (214). A perceptual apprehending consciousness *stretches an ostensible calendar time into a subjective ontological time*, measured in terms of sound and silence, both bounded and unbounded by a particular space:

> I remember the dim light, the racket in the street, the silence inside the flat, the ticking of the Roman-numbered clock in the hall. Time was like water dropping – Madrid time. (214–15)

The money finally comes for our narrator, and the fact that its source is never identified (as a magazine's regulatory remuneration of a specific artistic labour, say) outrages her Spanish friends, and allows the writer to differentiate between two existential forms of time:

> My existence had been poised on waiting, and I had always said I was waiting for something tangible. But they had thought I was waiting in their sense of the word – waiting for summer and then for winter, for Monday and then for Tuesday, waiting, waiting for time to drop into the pool. (216)

Yet both the narrator who leaves and her friends waiting as it were for Godot have talked of a "longer future," their thirties, which they all envisaged spatially as an inexorable slide into "an icy subterranean water" where they will remain submerged and frozen (216). For the narrator, the friends in the end are caught "not by time but by the freezing of memory" (217). This piece beautifully exemplifies what Urquhart meant about how events are quite secondary in Gallant's stories, which rather set out to "illuminate the time that falls between the events" (vii). Its admirably low-key, almost chromatic, anti-Proustian closure, which once more takes the opposite position of anamnesis, suggests that time past is but a picture "which flashes its farewell in the moment of its recognisability" (Benjamin, *On the Concept of History*). For when the narrator looks in the diary she kept during that period, all she can find is "descriptions of the weather" (217).

One can clearly see here that Gallant's retrospective narrations fluctuate within the mapping of the subject-centred perceptual apparatus.[9] Simple retrospection is replaced by a *spatial* separation of moments in historical or existential time, which Fredric Jameson has termed a sort of "incommensurability-vision" made up of non-synchronous temporalities of local, national, and even global cultures – a vision that "does not pull the eyes back into focus but provisionally entertains the tension of their multiple coordinates" (372). This tension in which differential identities are negotiated and articulated often creates the effect of an anamorphosis. Such anamorphic images are discernible in the Montreal depicted in "In Youth Is Pleasure," in which a sum of viewpoints holds together separate moments of consciousness, synthesized into a residual unity by a process of ideation. The city to which eighteen-year-old Linnet has returned collides with the city of recollection[10] cloaked with the epic splendour of her former child's standpoint, sustained by the dynamic of nostalgia.

> If I say that Cleopatra floated down the Chateauguay River, that the Winter Palace was stormed on Sherbrooke Street, that Trafalgar was fought on Lake Saint Louis, I mean it naturally; they were the natural backgrounds of my exile and fidelity. (*HT* 257; *VE* 110)

The collision in the narrator's consciousness is made manifest in the doubly ternary parallelisms between the local and the global, in which the

9 When I discussed the external narration of "Bonaventure," I showed how through the partial, distorted perspective of the young, Gallant nonetheless radically reconfigured an internally apprehended time.

10 For discussions of Gallant's layered depictions overlaying lived experience with images of memory and imagination, see Besner, "Reading Linnet Muir, Netta Asher, and Carol Frazier: Three Gallant Characters in Postcolonial Time," and Dvořák, "Le Montréal de Mavis Gallant: Les pouvoirs du je/u."

glamorous, legendary sites of victory and death (Egypt/Russia/the high seas), inhabited by larger-than-life heroes, clash with the prosaic places of Chateauguay River, Sherbrooke Street, and Lake Saint Louis (notably reduced to a puddle when equated with Nelson's Atlantic). The older Linnet's quest to retrieve a vanished space-time, rooted as it is in the eternal present of enunciation (*I say/I mean*), creates a third space. It is the hiatus and friction between the distanced image of the represented self and the object of her gaze on the one hand and the enunciative positioning of the narrating subject on the other which produces this space. These are reinforced by the recurrent deployment of counterpoint, the head-on encounter and commingling of distinct discursive universes. This Third Space of enunciation theorized by Bhabha (1–2) is a space into which the receiver is drawn, just as the perceiver is drawn into a Cubist sculpture. It is a space which interrelates with the personal experience shaping the enunciative stance and the contemporary extratextual world of the receiver. A site where cultural, aesthetic, and axiological mutations are articulated and negotiations made possible.

In its desire to provide systematic intelligibility, postcolonial theory has subjected shared and shareable literary forms to a certain principle of reducibility. The principle construes the aesthetic object in a manner indissociable from its moral import or political message. As Besner observes, many postcolonial critics have wished to identify and even equate the formal features of relatively new literatures ("the temporal layerings, disturbances, discontinuities, ruptures, and always incipient hauntings") with their societies' status as "former, emerged, and emergent colonies" as these "reflect *and* suppress, summon up *and* batten down, conjure with *and* consign back to near-oblivion the insistent and troubled traces of their recent, and less recent past" ("Reading Muir" 157, original italics). As Besner remarks playfully, Gallant's works for over half a century performed their distinctive versions of this "powerful and painful operation, often without an anaesthetic" (157).

the subject-centred perceptual apparatus

Gallant's various forms of indeterminacy, the breaking and braking of narrative rhythm, are actually manifestations of a strong authorial presence inscribed in a tradition of manipulative narrators stretching back to Austen, Sterne, and even Chaucer. Gallant as an authorial presence likes to remain invisible, but nonetheless guides the reader towards an interpretive position. The greatest disruption of the authoritative subject positions we readers expect to find within the text lies in how the writer upsets *deixis*, the set of references regulating the production of discourse.

The bottom often drops out from under our feet in our encounters with all three forms of deixis (time, place, and person) for which the reference points are first and foremost the identity of the speaker, then the derivative time and place of speaking: the speaker's now and here. When Gallant flits in and out of multiple minds, showing the inner pictures of a myriad individual subjects, we run head on into the riddles underpinning her oeuvre, especially the variations on the central I-riddle. Where is the story coming from? Where is the concealed "author" located? Who is the speaking self? Whose shoes or even whose "skin" are we in? The deictic shifts in enunciative positioning (often engineered via a use of free indirect style of narration as virtuosic as that of Austen, Woolf, and Mansfield) do amount to changing skins. The mercurial shifts are those of a virtuoso, a writer who herself had often changed skins. As I argued in my discussion of "The Ice Wagon" at the end of chapter 3, the author's multiview – viewing characters from the inside and the outside simultaneously or in quick succession – can be illuminated by a visual equivalent, the cinematic technique of *eyeliner matching*. The cutting from a character's gaze from a certain angle to the focus of his or her gaze (from the same angle: her eyeliner) amounts to the viewer seeing through the eyes of the character. Gallant's literary eyeliner matching is buttressed by three other disruptive deictic techniques which can be better apprehended in that they have also been adopted by cinematic editing. These range from radical *jump cuts,* involving abrupt discontinuity (see "Bonaventure"), and *cross-cutting* between actions in two different locations occurring simultaneously (see "The Fenton Child"), to the equivalent of musical and literary counterpoint: *parallel editing*, which draws parallels or contrasts between two different space-time locations.

Parallel editing, which we have encountered in stories like "Ice Wagon" and "The Cost of Living" is also the staple feature of "Let It Pass" (1987), the opening story of the experimental trilogy published in deliberate chronological disorder. The story is actually a sequel to "The Concert Party," which appeared in *The New Yorker* the year after to provide the before, by writing beyond the beginning.[11] Calling up the remarkably true voices of the male I-narrators in "Baum, Gabriel" and "The Latehomecomer," the first-person narrator of "Let It Pass," the Anglo-Quebec Canadian diplomat Steve Burnet tells us how Carlotta, the fifteen-year-old American daughter of a former wife who left him for another man decades ago, turns up on his doorstep in the south of France. Steven takes

11 The third story of the character cycle, "In a War" (1989), writes even further beyond the beginning.

Carlotta sightseeing, notably to a symbolic space[12] – a Saracen fortress he had first seen with his bride Lily. The contrapuntal structure alternates fragments of the present visit with Carlotta with episodes from the past visit (and past life) with the young Lily, managing to meld present and recent past enmeshed with historical past via the issue of authenticity or "fakery" (*VE* 233): that of an American couple pouring money into rebuilding and refurbishing a ruin to make it look the way they imagine it may have done. The clashing of viewpoints and voices and of their corresponding times dissolves a cluster of indeterminate borderlines. Those between the guides then and now; between the young Carlotta and the young Lily; between the two Stevens, the mature avuncular narrating subject and the history student narrated self – who already had to tell the bride he took to France not to take gossip for history; between even the old, once young, acquaintance Victor de Stentor who kept/keeps as servants clandestine foreigners, once Italians and Yugoslavs, now Tamils and Pakistanis. We wonder: which self is this, where is here, when is now, and even *where is here in time: when is here*?

Gallant plays across the different notions of culture and subjectivity which accompany those of time, pointing out enigmatically in "Let It Pass" that certain distances "could not be measured under any system" (*VE* 236). Arriving at the fortress from ancient times, Carlotta – from the double vantage point of her youth and New World upbringing – declares the Saracens should have paved their driveway. She mistakes the French Revolution for the Russian one and the castle round for a "Soviet walk-about" (238). When told a rich Cuban lived in the castle "Long, long before Fidel Castro," for her "no such time existed" (237) – just as in "Potter" (1977) – Laurie's idea of history "began with the Vietnam War" (*Collected Stories* 451). In one of the author's trademark conceits, Carlotta collapses the whole of past time into "a dollhouse, immeasurable periods crammed under a small roof" (*VE* 233), manifest when she gives her opinion of four ancient tapestries depicting Wisdom, Virtue, Sobriety, and King Solomon greeting the Queen of Sheba: "the colors were like mud, and the whole thing needed to be dry-cleaned" (242). "Put yourself in the other fellow's place," Aunt Elspeth used to tell her nephew narrator (*VE* 287). What we readers encounter by putting ourselves in Carlotta's place is a "flattened present" and an "engorged past" which the author lights up with an analogy to visual art: "a cartoon drawing of a snake that has swallowed history whole" (237).

12 See the ethno-sociologist Henri Lefebvre's distinction in *La Production de l'espace* between representations of space and representational or symbolic space.

Previous texts notorious for their convoluted digressions and narrative suspensions (from *Tristram Shandy* to *Ulysses*) remained nonetheless chronologically linear in global diegetical movement. I argue that Gallant not only resorts to the technique of multiple focalization but also transposes the strategy to the diegesis itself, atomizing and layering the unfolding of event, positioning us readers along with herself "in the zone between thought and possible action" (Ondaatje x). In "Let It Pass" and "The Concert Party," for instance, we are forever before or after the event: Lily (and also her friend Edie) running off with a lover. As I have shown, the transposition onto the axis of retrospective narration (which allows flashbacks and flashforwards) is a major way of liberating the text from clocktime. I shall now examine more closely how the writer shuffles and combines the modes of aspect and tempo the better to unsettle the mapping of the perceptual apparatus.

The mode of predilection of the French *nouveau roman,* unfurling when Mavis arrived in Paris, was that of repetition and variation – analogous to the small, infinitely repeated brushstrokes building up a complex field in an Impressionist painting. The novels resorted to free-floating narrators and a transgressive but mechanical deployment of aspect or frequency. The repetitive aspect, in which a reoccurrence of the telling (with or without variations) does not correspond to any reoccurrence in the story or related event, is a trademark practice for Alain Robbe-Grillet. (And for Faulkner before him, for that matter, for the French *nouveau roman* is actually a late variety of modernist autotelic reflexivity [Wilde 144; Hutcheon, *A Poetics of Postmodernism* 52], such an extreme form of metafiction that Hutcheon likens it to abstract art [52]). Relating *n* times what happens only once amounts to a destabilizing strategy mingling retrospection and anticipation to produce uncertainty, multiplicity, and flux (which we find for instance in *Le Voyeur* and *Projet pour une Révolution à New York* [1955 and 1970 respectively]). I have already discussed how through her image clusters Gallant participates in a process of recursion practised by painters ranging from the Impressionists to the Cubist Realists. She also utilizes the repetitive aspect in painterly, Pointillist touches to displace an event from the realm of clocktime towards a metaphysical threshold. I have addressed her recourse to the aspect in "The Cost of Living," in which the recurrent tellings of one single action (Louise and Sylvie's first meeting) give the event the watershed aura of a mythical event, quasi-analogous to that separating Before and After the Christian Era. Gallant also resorts to the repetitive frequency's reverse gear, the iterative, which relates only once what happened *n* times. I can surmise why she resorts to both. These relations of frequency both bend and twist the normative, familiar singulative (which relates once what happened once), redolent with an automatic truth effect because the telling so comfortably corresponds to the action. She may also deploy both because these aspects allow her to displace an event outside of clocktime. The aim can be to propel it into comedy, as we saw in "Baum, Gabriel," in which a one-time event (a surrender) is incongruously treated as happening over and over), or to nudge it towards a metaphysical threshold.

This is precisely what we find in Gallant's Linnet Muir cycle, in which the author deploys the repetitive and iterative frequencies to impart events (such as the death of the father) with a haunting ontological quality. When Mavis's mouthpiece Linnet depicts her childhood in "Voices Lost in Snow," the death is foretold in multiple, Pointillist touches. In the middle of a reported conversation, the narrator announces proleptically, "He was barely thirty-one and had a full winter to live after this one – little more" (*HT* 336; *VE* 102). In an earlier sequence of the same story, the death surges in a brief but double flashforward colliding with a flashback, when the older narrating I describes the weekly excursions from the countryside where the family was then living to downtown Montreal. She begins, "On Saturdays my father and I came in together by train. I went to the doctor, the dentist, to my German lesson" (*HT* 325; *VE* 92). One can see that Gallant's narrator deploys the iterative aspect, encompassing with one narrative act (*came, went*) several occurrences of the same events. Readers are projected into the time zone of the diegetic past in which the iterative ("had to") soon cohabits with a one-time event drenched with meaning ("gave"): "After that, I *had to* get back to Windsor Station by myself and on time. My father *gave* me a boy's watch so that the dial would be good and large" (*HT* 325; *VE* 92). The intrusion of the present time of utterance ("I remember") then projects readers from story past to the conditional of a near future ("would not be long"):

> I remember the No 83 streetcar trundling downhill and myself, wondering if the watch was slow, asking strangers to tell me the hour. Inevitably – how could it have been otherwise? – *after his death, which would not be long in coming*, I would dream that someone important had taken a train without me. My route to the meeting place – deviated, betrayed by stopped clocks – was always downhill. As soon as I was old enough to understand from my reading of myths and legends that this journey was a pursuit of darkness, its terminal point a sunless underworld, the dream vanished. (*HT* 325; *VE* 92–3)

The near future "would not be long" is close to the story time, shown through the child's standpoint as a projection *forward*. But it is also in proximity with a farther future – a future closer to the present time of utterance (*I remember*), presented through the preterite as a projection *backward* (*as soon as I was*), in which the features of recent, *recurrent* dream (signalled by the frequentative mode of "would dream") – namely the stopped hour-piece, the downward slide – echo the original features of a singular, that is, specific, event. An attentive rereading discloses that the distortion grounded in repetition and the accumulation of micro-perspectives and discrete vantage points is accentuated through a conflation of sundry other devices of temporal and spatial heterogeneity.

By December 2013 Mavis became too ill to leave her bed and too tired to focus on the books I had been reading to her since she lost her sight. I told her one day I was teaching *Varieties of Exile* and had just given my graduate class this passage from "Voices Lost in Snow" for their end of term commentary. She was delighted when I offered to read her the extract. It was a remarkable experience, for my listener was rediscovering the fine writing as I went along as if someone else had authored it. She expressed signs of empathy with the child character-narrator but also, sharp as ever, immediate appreciation of writerly finds underpinning an apparent simplicity. When I arrived at "the dream vanished," Mavis said, "That's wonderful." I shall now examine the paragraph which leads up to the extract just scrutinized, at the end of which Mavis took in her breath, sighed blissfully, and said, "That's extraordinary."

The scene begins with the words "It was my father's *custom* if he took me with him to visit a friend on Saturdays not to say where we were going ... being young, I was the last person to whom anyone owed an explanation" (*HT* 325; *VE* 92). We understand first of all that one narrative act will encompass and unify multiple occurrences, and secondly, that we are in the realm of a coded ritual, made up of representative acts of social cohesion which Northrop Frye, resting on Aristotle, terms "the epiphany of the myth, the manifestation or showing forth of it in action" (*The Secular Scripture* 55). Gallant's narrator effectively presents us not with the human actions or *praxeis* which interest the historian, but with the symbolic actions "representative of human life in a more universal perspective" (55), which interest the poet. Frye's portrayal of ritual as "a conscious waking act" in which there is paradoxically "always something sleep-walking about it" (55), an overlay of conscious act and unconscious meaning, lights up Mavis's scene. Let us look at the writerly cocktail that follows the opening statement exposing the weekly ritual. It involves a stretching from standard tempo into slow time and then into the freeze of the pause, which suspends the action in mid-motion to achieve an effect of timelessness:

> These Saturdays have turned into one whitish afternoon, a windless snowfall, a steep street. Two persons descend the street, stepping carefully. The

child, reminded every day to keep her hands still, gesticulates wildly – there is the flash of a red mitten. I will never overtake this pair. Their voices are lost in snow. (*HT* 325; *VE* 92)

The violent Vlaminckian contrast of colour and gesture, the flash of red on the white snowfall blurring sky with ground combined with the collision of stillness and gesticulation, fuse in turn with a temporal shift to a historical present (*descend*) which conflates the story told with the telling (then/now). It metamorphoses in turn into a synoptic present consubstantial with truth (*is*), and a boundless future (*will never overtake*). This future which announces infinity mingles with a fulgurant irrecuperable past to form a *jetztzeit*, an infinite present (*Their voices are lost in snow*), achieving the almost surreal effect of a painting or snapshot. Like a photograph, it fixes what *was* and induces us to believe that it is both a pseudo-presence and a token of absence. It does not merely reorder time from the linear mode of organization found in the world to the cyclical mode of Gallant's discursive world. This technical equivalent of the pictorial still is suffused with the photograph's conflation of a referential reality and veracity, overset with the haunting quality of a death already occurred but forever looming. This collision which both Roland Barthes and Susan Sontag have investigated respectively (in *La Chambre Claire, Note sur la photographie*, and *On Photography*)[13] is what renders Gallant's mingling of voice, memory, and death moving, in the rhetorical sense of *movere*, which amounts to controlling the receiver through affect, notably by setting up a network of subjective, emotional resonances centred on the narrator. Yet what moves this scene into Mavis's "extraordinary," on top of the combinatory play with the deictics of time and place through tempo, frequency, and tense, is *the transmogrifying shift or even rupture in subject* which occurs in dream. In this sleep-walking dynamic, the personal "I" becomes the impersonal "the child"; the inclusive "we" becomes the non-inclusive "two persons/this pair." Through the thickness of time, the narrating subject has aoristically divorced herself from the picture of her narrated self, become another, rather like the ghostly Other in Henry James's "The Jolly Corner."

13 Sontag addresses photography as a "grammar" and "an ethics of seeing," and remarks that photographed images are not so much "statements about the world" as they are "pieces of it, miniatures of reality" (3). Barthes engages with the individual photograph-referent relation, observing that what a snapshot reproduces to infinity happened only once, and that the image repeats mechanically that which can never repeat itself existentially (15).

The play with tempo and frequency in this passage from "Voices Lost in Snow" is remarkable, and I want to show a different demonstration of mastery in a story from the same cycle I have already discussed, "Varieties of Exile." We encounter my selected passage near the end, as the Second World War is coming to an end. It presents the young woman Linnet learning from a newspaper announcement that Frank Cairns has been killed. To be noted first of all is the use of a hybrid form that Gérard Genette terms the pseudo-iterative, in which the iterative, designed to encompass several occurrences as one, contaminates the singulative frequency (the narrator who tells once how she read once and found out once). The effect – a strong sensation of internal time consciousness – is breathtakingly disorienting:

> In the ever-new present I read one day that Major Francis Cairns had died of wounds in Italy. Who remembers now the shock of the known name? It was like a flat white light. One felt apart from everyone, isolated. The field of vision drew in. Then, before one could lose consciousness, vision expanded, light and shadow moved, voices pierced through. One's heart, which had stopped, beat hard enough to make a room shudder. All this would occupy about a second. The next second was inhabited by disbelief. (*HT* 321; *VE* 168)

Alert readers will note the collisions and mutations which abound. The first-person singular signifying an individuated subject metamorphoses into the third-person pronoun "one" after a lightning projection is effected forward and back on the temporal axis between diegetic past (*one day*) and readerly present (*who remembers now?*). The shift from *I* to the all-englobing *one* depersonalizes and impersonalizes. Yet it simultaneously takes on the function of an inclusive, generic pronoun which embraces the totality of the addressees invoked by the rhetorical question, and not only calls on them to bear witness but sucks them into the scene, transforming onlookers into participants. It also extends the particular (one name, one death, one shock) to the general and universal, to the multiplication of names, of losses, of shocks and their suggested recurrences. To *weight* the process and suggest more heavily the universal dynamic and the amplitude of carnage, we find the frequentative mode signifying habitual action (before one *could*, this *would* occupy) contaminating the preterite of the completive point-action verbs (felt, drew, beat). The perceptual point of view, the physical perception through which the event is apprehended in the story, stretches a subjective span of time into an infinite messianic time, while the slow motion is heightened by the simultaneous stretch in discourse time, before both temporal expansions contract back into the "second" of clocktime. We can see that it is the combination of multiple, simultaneous distortions which nudges the passage *outside of world time* and makes it intensely dramatic. This particular moment, only a minute part of experience, becomes through Gallant's art what Schopenhauer calls "a representative of the whole, an equivalent of the endless multitude in space and time"; the above sequence illustrates beautifully how "art pauses at this particular thing" and "stops the wheel of time" (108).

I want to emphasize that it is on account of the central question – who is I? – that we never know for long the related parameters of an utterance underpinning shifters. If the voice is unlocatable, so is the context of production, and *we cannot know when is now and where is here*. Gallant's most radical manhandling occurs within the deictic category of person, which normally allows distinctions among the three coordinates of textual articulation or dialogue: the speaker, the addressee, and everyone else. To a certain extent, like Rimbaud, Gallant seems to be declaring that "*Je est un Autre*" (Rimbaud 344), or I is Another. To light this up more clearly, I shall back up to the passage of "Voices Lost in Snow" which I read to Mavis, beyond the extract I analysed to the segment which precedes (and which closes the story's opening), where Mavis burst out laughing and said it was "wonderful." A scene has illustrated the writer's opening critique regarding her directive parents and their generation, who ignored a child's need to be enlightened. The little Linnet has been scolded for addressing a neighbour as "old cock"– a term she has overheard:

> "Never say that again," my mother said after he had gone.
> "Why not?"
> "Because I've just told you not to."
> "What does it mean?"
> "Nothing."
>
> It must have been after yet another "Nothing" that one summer's day I ran screaming around a garden, tore the heads off tulips, and – no, let another voice finish it; the only authentic voices I have belong to the dead: "... then she *ate* them." (*HT* 324; *VE* 92, original stress)

Hermione Lee, who provided a fresh view of Virginia Woolf in her 1996 biography, astutely observes in her review of Gallant's newly paperbacked *Selected Stories* that Gallant "is a ventriloquist, brilliant at dialogue." One can feel here how the tight form of pure dialogue which does away with narratorial mediation generates the immediacy and truth effect of a slice-of-life scene we have been eavesdropping on. It then shifts into a summary that briefly blurs the single occurrence temporally by overlaying it with the iterative notion of multiple recurrences of unspecified but frequent rhythm ("after *yet another* 'Nothing'"). The summary returns to the conventional singulative of calendar time ("one summer's day") and triggers an equally standard ternary series of point-action verbs (ran/tore/ate).

Yet a glance at the pronouns reveals what my listener Mavis years later found a wonderful verbal performance, as I did: the seismic deictic shift which changes gears from "I" to "she." The double I has exploded; the I that remains has shed the dynamic agent or experiencer status of the narrated self, has been pared down like an onion to mere addresser of the utterance; no, not even that. She is no longer even an interlocutor, for she has handed the discourse over to other voices, and shows that the present is inhabited by the speech of the dead, which she merely authorizes. The deviant alternation, even equivalence, between first- and third-person pronouns deals a blow to our humanist assumptions of a unified self as well as to the cornerstones of the reading pact, which view the confessional first-person pronoun as offering the truth of subjectivity and the third-person as guaranteeing objectivity. Such writing which erases the speaking self takes on a philosophical dimension in which language seems to regulate ontology and individual identity is dissolved as if it were a mere discursive construct.

When Gallant blurs the distinctions between speaker and other in this way, she shatters our notions of subjectivity and agency *in the mode of magic realists* since Flaubert. A provocative statement, I know, which needs explanation. While Jorge Luis Borges and his experimentation with Surrealism is credited with spearheading the emergence of magic realism in the Americas, his brand, like Faulkner's stream-of-consciousness version, is as stylistically convoluted as the title of his story collection *Labyrinths* (English translation 1962). Flaubert's story "Saint Julien l'Hospitalier" (in *Trois Contes* [*Three Tales*], 1877) is equally mythopoeic and fantastical, but stylistically paratactic and minimalist. Bare, pure, and transparent, it exemplifies what Roland Barthes in *Le Degré zéro de l'écriture* [*Writing Degree Zero*] (1953) found characteristic of French post–Second World War literature and which he termed *l'écriture blanche*.[14] It has much to do with voice: the flat, atonal voice of a neutral consciousness dissociated from a social identity, which we find with writers ranging across the planet from Katherine Mansfield and Gabriel García Márquez to Steven Millhauser and Salman Rushdie (notably in

14 Barthes's neutral "écriture blanche" corresponds to the *voix blanche* (translated as "naked speech" in Bresson, *Interviews* 240) which Bresson requires of his actors, a voice "from behind the mask" which expresses itself through rhythm alone (254). This trademark blank delivery is hugely responsible for the rarified atmosphere of his films.

"The Prophet's Hair," 1981). Wondering moreover who is we and who authorizes the collective speech, one can compare the enigmatic opening sentence of Gallant's "When We Were Nearly Young" – "In Madrid, nine years ago, *we* lived on the thought of money" (*Collected Stories* 209) – with other hybrid collective voices hauntingly combined with passive and impersonal locutions which mask agency. Alistair MacLeod's "The Closing Down of Summer" (1976) comes to mind,[15] as does Rushdie's "At the Auction of the Ruby Slippers" (1992), and Millhauser's "The Dream of the Consortium" (1998).[16] One can also find resonances with the double, even triple shapes of the self which overlap and conflate with the speaking subject in Janet Frame's *The Lagoon and Other Stories* (1951), perhaps most notably in "Jan Godfrey."[17]

A close look at the beginning of Gallant's "The Concert Party" (which occupies the time period of "Let It Pass"'s flashbacks) reveals a fluctuating individual subjectivity. This subjectivity goes well beyond the I-self which veers into the third person in "Voices Lost in Snow":[18] the subject actually speaks and thinks through the speech and thought of others. The I-narrator (who turns out to be Steven, the narrator of the rest of the trilogy) thinks back to when he was a young man in the south of France with Lily and another couple, Harry Lapwing and Edie. Lily has just left him for another man, and he wants to change skins with Lapwing:

> I said to myself, O.K., imagine your name is Harry Lapwing. Harry Lapwing. You are a prairie Socialist, a William Morris scholar. All your life this will make you seem boring and dull. (*VE* 287)

---

15 MacLeod's opening moves from "*It* is August ... and the weather can no longer *be trusted*" to the enigmatic "there are no tourists. Only *ourselves*. *We* have been here for most of the summer" (7–8).

16 Deictic uncertainty (who is we/where is here?) suffuses Millhauser's opening sentence: "The purchase of the department store by the consortium filled *us* with uneasiness and secret hope" (125), as well as Rushdie's opening paragraph, relating that mysterious Auctioneers have announced the sale of "the magic slippers" (equally unidentified despite the fraudulent use of the definite article) in the belief that "this prize would tempt *us* from *our* bunkers" (87).

17 See my analysis in Dvořák, "Frame-breaking: 'Neither separate nor complete nor very important.'"

18 One can note a similar I/she oscillation in Emily Carr's aesthetic stylization of lived experience in *The Book of Small* (1942), in which Carr establishes a fictionalized distancing from her autobiographical self by recurrently shifting from the subjective first person to the objective third person. One can note the same oscillation in Nancy Huston's sensationalist, alienating *Histoire d'Omaya* (1985), respectively in alternating chapters and in mid-sentence, and even in Margaret Atwood's first novel, *The Edible Woman* (1969), which has been labelled as realist.

One can note that Gallant breaks the frames between the confessional first person pronoun (a shifter generally accepted as guaranteeing authentic subjectivity) and the second-person pronoun here inhabited by the first. A slippery deictic, the shifter I, proceeds to shake up norms regarding interpersonal experience and to upset stable modes of subjectivity and meaning-making:

> When you went to England in the late forties and said you were Canadian, and Socialist, and working on aspects of William Morris, people got a stiff, trapped look, as if you were about to read them a poem. You had the same conversation twenty-seven times, once for each year of your life:
>
> "Which part of Canada are you from?"
> "I was born in Manitoba."
> "We have cousins in Victoria."
> "I've never been out there."
> "I believe it's quite pretty."
> "I wouldn't know. Anyway, I haven't much eye." (*VE* 287–8)

The referent, Lapwing, is alternately, or both, the speaking self and an Other. Social assumptions regarding a coherent subjectivity are unsettled through a generic *you* ("as if you [i.e., someone] were about to read them a poem"), which melds with a particularly anamorphic *you*. The protean inclusive second-person pronoun implicates the dummy receiver in a universal dynamic, and even, so to speak, sucks the reader into the text as a co-protagonist of the textual world. The chameleon former I who knows far too much for a non-omniscient narrator is doubly transmogrified: first into you, then through the tight form of pure dialogue into a new I. The I of "I was born in Manitoba" is of course not the I of "I said to myself," but occupies or inhabits the you and takes over its enunciative position. By definition, dialogue engineers a strong feeling of presence and the immediacy of the scene, so the shifts in viewpoint, which here are augmented beyond the realist code, are nonetheless naturalized. Since the author has done away with the mediation of the narrative voice and its implied listener, we readers almost feel as if we are eavesdropping.

It becomes even less clear where the voice is coming from and who is in whose skin when we readers learn that just as Lily has left Steven (or is about to, in this time-shift to which we have spiralled back), Lapwing's wife, Edie, runs off with another man. The other deictics of person (your wife/my wife) become referentially unstable, shapeshifting, even plural. One finds a dynamic of haunting which manhandles the distinctions among the coordinates of textual articulation: speaker, addressee, and other. One unfaithful wife, Lily, overlays the base image of another, Edie, in the following collision of resentment and desire seen from the inside in an expandable way: "you" is double (both the speaker and someone else, notably Lapwing), as is "she," the rose garden of a wife:

> With this man she made a monkey of you ... and vanished into Franco's Spain. You, of course, will not set foot in Franco territory – not even to reclaim your lazy, commonplace, ignorant, Polack, lower-middle-class, gorgeous rose garden of a wife. (*VE* 292)

As with the disruptive hyphenated identities in "Let It Pass," in which Steven imagines that Lily may have subsequently married "an Italian composer-conductor," or a "German novelist-essayist-political thinker," or an "Argentinian playwright-designer-poet-revolutionary" (*VE* 242), the outcome of the double-voiced "Concert Party" extract above is a tentative melding of Self and Other, and a blurring of agency. The multiple angles of refraction and resulting slippage illustrate a self-reflexive writing strategy which presents the I-self not as an authoritative subject-position, but as *an indeterminate discursive construct*, indissociable from language, and constantly in flux. As Edward Said puts it, individual identity is "little more than a constituted subject, *a speaking pronoun*, fixed indecisively in the eternal, ongoing rush of discourse" (287). Gallant's slippery I indicates a concern which is deeply epistemological, even ontological, and in today's context of increased longevity but also dementia, of medical and technological advances and ethical blurring (the stuff of Atwood's fiction), her questions are hugely relevant. Just what is a self? What fine line separates you and not-you? What happens to a personal identity over time, and does it matter? At the same time, Gallant is representative of contemporary metatextual preoccupation with issues of authority and authorship, of control and process, on the page and in the world. Just what is a writer, she also seems to ask, as she engages with the concepts of derivation and creation, of imitation and invention, of affiliation and originality. The issues are quietly there in "Concert Party," when the young would-be pianist-protégé, David, performing a varied program in the same dogged style, makes the authorial mouthpiece think of "an anthology of fragments from world literature translated so as to make it seem that everyone writes in the same way" (*VE* 313).

double vision: from short cut to short circuit

I have repeatedly shown how Gallant excels in the deviant torsion of irony, a trope of doubleness which both conceals and reveals, denotes and connotes. I see the slippery concept as a radical short cut (perhaps even what I shall shortly term a short circuit), since it essentially actualizes two levels of meaning simultaneously. That a figure, or even sign, can intend one thing without ceasing to intend another is precisely "what makes language an instrument of knowing" (Urban 112). I have been using the term trope in the French manner, as a site of displacement, a rhetorical figure that slides and turns. I now want to zoom in more closely on Gallant's mastery of that left-field curve of compression, the metaphor – that violent yoking of unlikes where, according to Aristotle, genius lies. The metaphor, a space where mindscape and discourse interact, is (like irony) a figure of thought with a fertile aptitude for cumulation, which engineers double vision. I argue that Gallant makes use of it abundantly because it is both dense and conjunctive. It encompasses wide, disclosing unsuspected analogies or interconnections in a highly compressed space, and engineers equivalence through a forceful yoking and simultaneous deferral, grounded in the perception of the same in the different. By overlaying one signifier over another occupying the same vertical slot in the distributional relations of discourse (see Culler), Gallant's metaphors produce symbolic relations between the dissimilar signifieds, collocate, and conflate. The metaphor is indeed the most condensed form of imagery, with only one phone or vehicle, unlike the simile with its initial ramifying step outward. Yet it is also the most elaborate and dynamic form in that the marks of analogy have been erased – another short cut, as it were.

In "Varieties of Exile," in which Gallant overlays the images of Frank Cairns and her own father to discuss the phenomenon which died along with empire, the exiled remittance man, Frank Cairns is not *like* a curio cabinet; he *is* a curio cabinet. While his clothes, voice, and manner stamp and label him a remittance man, he has broken the mould with his socialism, which "did not fit anything else about him," and made him something "unique of his kind, and almost as good as a refugee" (*VE* 160) – exotic object of the narrator's curiosity:

> What Frank Cairns was to me was a curio cabinet. I took everything out of the cabinet, piece by piece, examined the objects, set them down. Such situations, riddled with ambiguity, I would blunder about with for a long time until I learned to be careful. (163)

Such an extended metaphor, stretching out like a horizontal metonymy in one associated image after another, is a site of displacement which moves us in other directions and generates new meaning: a "turning point" (Gallant, "Style" 6),[19] which, in Mavis's agenda, fiction

19 In "What Is Style?" Mavis explains, "against the sustained tick of a watch, fiction takes the measure of a life, a season, a look exchanged, *the turning point*, desire as brief as a dream, the grief and terror that after childhood we cease to express" (6).

must apprehend. What is especially valuable in analysing the trope is that the transfer of meaning stems from a personal operation based on the author's individual impression or interpretation. The *epiphora*, the transposition or unifying process, assimilates heteroclitic ideas not through logic but through the writer's subjective insight, the domain of vision, intuition, and imagination, which – as Aristotle points out in *Poetics* – cannot be taught. At the heart of the double vision is a torsion, a new state of things stereoscopically perceived through the thickness of a wrenched former state of things, with its previous word usage, categories, and classifications (in which people and cabinets mutually exclude one another).

Metaphors, as I demonstrated in chapter 5, are the privileged recipients of Gallant's syntactic density (whereby apparently similar symbols actually convey graduated shades of differentiation). They are also inversely the recipients of her semantic density (whereby apparently similar things are provided with finely discrete symbols). I have argued throughout multiple close readings that the stylistic cornerstones of Gallant's texts are reduction, essentializing (Goodman), and exemplifying, and that the metaphorically combinative devices which generate repleteness rest on the use of familiar, humble objects as resonant, exemplifying symbols. So what readers often take to be journalistic accuracy, even documentary realism, is, as Manguel observes, "mere scaffolding" (xii) that props up an epistemological, axiological, and ontological questioning. When Gallant takes a short cut and unites two ordinary but dissimilar things such as Cairns and a cabinet, she propels us towards new filiations, and makes us integrate the dispersed. Yet Gallant's yoking of unlikes never resolves the tension between resemblance and dissemblance, the identical and the different. Cairns the cabinet embodies the contradictions and ambiguities of the period's political, social, and cultural cross-pollinated currents of thought. The concretization conveys all the implications of *synthesis and of tension between the components*, as does a foray into the proportional metaphor, more complex than the metaphor of resemblance. Cairns admires the Fabian Society, whose cautious approach to socialist reform our Russian-minded narrator despises:

> His Webbs and his Fabians were plodding and gray. I saw the men with thick moustaches, wearing heavy boots, sharing lumpy meals with moral women. (*VE* 162)

The analogy between socialism and working-class dress and food habits sets up a multilateral system of relations in which heavy boots are to Fabians what indigestible food is to virtuous women. Again in the manner of a short cut, *the equivalences bypass the common logic of language* in its informational function; by triggering multiple sensory perceptions, they set up emotional resonances which are centred on the narrator but which also affect the way we readers feel about the substance of the message. As the rhetorician Michel Le Guern observes, we can argue with a comparison, reject a simile because we reject the reasoning behind the analogy, or even refuse to acknowledge the correspondence upon which a symbol is founded. But the metaphor escapes rational criticism and prevents the censure of logic from repelling the emotional movement that it seeks to share (74–6). In this particular case, Gallant's complex metaphor is buttressed by the complex irony it carries. The young Linnet, the narrated self, is verbally ironic, distancing herself from such unexciting, "plodding" socialists. But there is an overarching structural irony which targets the association the younger narrator makes between a movement championed by intellectuals, artists, and writers like George Bernard Shaw on the one hand and stodgy, uncouth proletarians on the other. The amused distance the young Linnet places between herself and the plodding socialists finds a parallel in the amused distance the older, more experienced narrating subject places between herself and her fiery, categorical Socialist-literary Russian-loving younger self,[20] romantically interested in refugees only so long as they did not start "eating cornflakes" (*VE* 169). The proportional metaphor reflecting the standpoint of the younger Linnet is deflected from its ironic target, and through the clearly stereotyped notions it carries, lights up the older narrator's confession that at this point of time, she confused books and life, projecting onto the world "the twilit Socialist-literary landscape of [her] reading and [her] desires" (149). The metaphor is literally a short cut between the zones of the visible, animate, and concrete and those of the invisible, inanimate, and abstract – in this particular case containing a meditation on time, on the brief moment that is youth, on its endearing tempestuousness, thoughtlessness, and zeal. The aporia central to Gallant's textual production is palpable in these encounters of tension and fusion. A *forever unresolved friction*

20 In numerous afterthoughts or asides, the older narrating I intervenes to confess the naïveté of her green narrated self. I have already evoked how she idealized refugees and could not imagine they could be infected by the "Nationalist pigheadedness" (149) she had learned to recognize in local terms. Shocked to learn that the Wrens enlisted only whites, young Linnet "believed that Roosevelt, Stalin, Chiang Kai-Shek, and de Gaulle did not know, and that should it ever come to their attention they would be as shocked as [she] was" (168). On a smaller scale, she imagined a friend Cairns deferred to as being "older than anyone – which might have meant forty-two" (*VE* 160).

is precisely what engenders meaning, the substance of the message grounded in the metaphor's poetic function of symbolizing one thing through another.

I called attention to Gallant's "a/mazing" imagery right from the start in my introductory chapter, referring specifically to a breathtaking mixture of homely metaphor and simile redolent with metalinguistic and societal irony. In one of Linnet Muir's first jobs, depicted in "Between Zero and One," the employees are "handed a folded thought." This startling conceit compressing the abstract ("thought") and the concrete ("handed/folded") metonymically triggers a clothing simile: "a folded thought *like* a shapeless school uniform." The simile in turn modulates into an extended metaphor: "handed ... and told, 'There, wear that.' Everyone had it on, regardless of fit" (*VE* 145; *HT* 296). This site of conformity and ready-made, literally tailored thought turns out to be a government agency called Dominion Film Center, which the narrator ironically dubs her "first brush with the creative life" (145). The folded thought conceit is as remarkable in its naturalness and simplicity as it is in the way it makes the intangible visible and palpable. It proves to be part of a speculative discourse opening out onto the vista of a dystopian society regulating inner as well as outer environment. It arrests, but does not fix, exemplifying as it does Ricoeur's *métaphore vive*. Unlike stock metaphors and dead metaphors which have become integrated into the organized language system (Saussure's *langue*), an original or live metaphor such as Gallant's here, which results from a leap of her imagination, is an individual, innovative language act (Saussure's *parole*). The philosopher Maurice Merleau-Ponty, who also distinguishes between *parole parlante* (creation in its nascent state) and *parole parlée* (which benefits from already available meanings like a fortune already acquired) (229), gives the live metaphor a maieutic role. He argues that the metaphor is the locus of the gestation of meaning and even of the genesis of the world (241–5). I align myself with this notion, and want to show how Gallant's semantic innovations, an effort of *parole* over *langue*, do not describe the world but create overlapping visions, new worlds in the Proustian sense of my epigraph.

Gallant also likes to begin her worldmaking with a simile – which is enclosed in the logical sphere of communication and serves to provide clarification – and then move on to a metaphor, which she frequently extends to arrive at a fuller vision. In "Varieties of Exile," still under scrutiny, she observes in a tight chiasmus that few remittance men were fit to do much of anything, being "well schooled but half educated, in that specifically English way" (*VE* 156), as well as being too uncompetitive to survive in the New World without a fixed income. She provides additional clarification through a simile which she then transforms into one of her hallmark extended metaphors:

> They were like children waiting for the school vacation so that they could go home, except that at home nobody wanted them: The nursery had been turned into a billiards room and Nanny dismissed. (*VE* 156)

The simile's comparison between remittance men and children packed off to boarding school, both groups unwanted by their families, functions within the sphere of communication. We readers are free to admit or to contest the reasoning behind the analogy. But the metaphor it crystallizes into contains the dynamics of a subjective, emotional standpoint which cannot be refuted, but only felt. Operating here is the emotive function, centred on the speaker, and the conative function, oriented towards the addressee or projected reader who is drawn into the mood. This particular image materializes in space and time the abstract concept of banishment, and, by building a psychophysiological connection of sorts between the addresser and us addressees, produces a fraught mood melding head and heart: both disdain for these immature, irresponsible members of society, and pathos for those who will never grow up and can never go home. After a quite factual essay-like presentation of the customary remittance contract conditions, Gallant spirals back to her analogy, adding the metaphor of a "cosmic headmaster" meting out cruel punishment to these "naughty children" (156):

> Yes, they were like children, perpetually on their way to a harsh school; they were eight years of age and sent "home" from India to childhoods of secret grieving among strangers. (*VE* 156)

The recursion of the same analogy (reinforced by the interjection "yes" providing the reader with a complicitous role in a pseudo-dialogue) interestingly entails inversion along with a weighty intertext. The children banished to boarding schools, yearning to return to the parental home, have morphed into colonial children of Empire, ripped out of peripheral dominions where they have put down roots to be reformatted in the metropolis still called "home," in the violent manner Rudyard Kipling depicts in the autobiographical story "Baa Baa, Black Sheep" (1888), hauntingly related by an omniscient narrator ventriloquizing his small exiled focalizer, Punch, also grieving among strangers. As does the base image of this canonical pre-text, in which God is "a Creature that stood in the background and counted the strokes of the cane" (Kipling 179), Gallant's discourse conditions readerly responses to the normative attitudes and value-references of origins which the writer presents and undermines. In her case those of the expatriate colonials in the dominion of Canada (such as her father), who, traumatized by their exile, nonetheless continued to reproduce (or impose on their descendants) the belief system of the European metropolis. For

> this wound, this amputation, they would mercilessly inflict on their own children [notably four-year-old Mavis] when the time came – on sons always, on daughters sometimes – persuaded that early heartbreak was right because it was British, hampered only by the financial limit set for banishment: It costs money to get rid of your young. (*VE* 157)

Gallant's curious conceit, a compressed metaphor grounded in antithesis, implies that heartbreak has a passport, and the torsion of the syllogistic parallelism (British/right) sets up an equivalence between nationality and ethics. These join up with a transferred epithet or hypallage – that "black angry day" (156) the first father originally decreed the first banishment. It is naturally not the day that was angry. Obeying an aesthetic agenda of indirection, the hypallage, a figure known as the changeling, unexpectedly shifts or even *short circuits the relations in the proposition.* The displaced lexeme resonates dissonantly and deflects the meaning. Or rather it sets up a twinning of meaning, an arrangement and rearrangement which calls attention to both elements separately and entails a double vision, a double meaning: an angry father *and* an angry day, in the classic buttressing manner of pathetic fallacy. All of the figures I have just discussed present forcible deviations in the utterance which are equivalent to the wrenching in the story. All demonstrate a higher order of the aesthetic through one of its prerequisites, which Jerrold Levinson identifies as a homologous relation between content and form, "between what a work represents or expresses or suggests, and the means it uses to do so" (*The Pleasures of Aesthetics* 10). All also covertly express a value judgment which only once raises its head overtly (in the adverb "mercilessly"). The covert textual activity adds emotional charges one after the other to make the addressee adhere to information of a higher order. It bears witness to a higher truth, carrying out an existential function which Ricoeur declares consubstantial with the metaphorical process (*La Métaphore vive* 313). Just as I find it is with the metonymical process.

Metonymy, like metaphor, implies a transfer, but this trope is based not so much on analogy or vertical substitution as on a discursive, horizontal logical link, implying a relation of belonging. Gallant's way of thinking, of perceiving the world, is indeed metaphorical, but also highly metonymical, concerned as she is with the true in word and thing: the harmonious conjunction between outer, visible form and the interiority of the thing. Mavis's aesthetic world view was actually close to the Aristotelian ontology promoted from Scholasticism to the early modernists,[21] trying to apprehend the beautiful and the good, and ready to equate inner moral beauty with *honestum*.[22] The true, the good, and the beautiful are convertible and indissociable. As Umberto Eco encapsulates it, truth consists in the disposition of the form with respect to the interiority of the object, while beauty is the disposition of the form with respect to its exteriority (*Art et beauté* 48). Beyond the notions of factual exactness and textured reality effect, then, as I stated in my introduction, "true" for Mavis also signifies "right" and "genuine."

Her texts trace the links between object and place, exterior and interior, cause and effect, the general and the particular, the material and the moral, juggling them to produce relations of inclusion. Her writings bring together and fill with significance apparent trifles, actually glints of reality that illuminate unseen correspondences. I have repeatedly shown how Gallant employs figures that are dominantly synthetic and conjunctive, associating disparate elements towards a common denominator. I have also drawn attention to the fraught dynamics of her writing which entail creating a web of ramifications that produce an expanding cross-network of analogies. *This centrifugal, outward moving, disjunctive web paradoxically cohabits with an inverse, centripetal, conjunctive movement towards synthetic resolution or unity.*

The devices I have investigated function precisely in this double manner. Chiasmus reproduces on the page, with its criss-cross syntactic order, the correspondences or similarities in the world. Enumeration serves to accumulate and connect; even chaotic enumeration with that odd man out invites us to apprehend a unity of perspective. Still on the scale of augmentation, counterpoint commingles spatially or temporally distinct isotopies or worlds of discourse. Metonymy conjoins two semantic fields just as anamnesis conjoins two periods in time, and the metaphor discloses the same in the different.

A stroll through various stories can light up further how Gallant submits such junctions to realist restitution, but also diverts them towards a higher order, whether political, ethical, or phenomenological. In my second chapter I analysed the poetics of rhythm in "A Painful Affair," related

21 Joyce's mouthpiece Stephen Dedalus reminds us of Plato's definition of beauty as "the splendour of truth," but adheres to the equation Keats made famous and asserts more tamely that "the true and the beautiful are akin" (Joyce, *A Portrait of the Artist* 188).

22 Manguel ultimately found reductive his own term "scaffolding" for Gallant's realist details. After her death, he told David Macfarlane that what mattered to Mavis "was an accuracy that was synonymous with truth and honesty and that therefore became an aesthetic quality" (Manguel qtd in Macfarlane).

through the outraged viewpoint of Henri Grippes. The story opens with a long, convoluted sentence as pompous as the focalizer, studded with semaphores signalling the genre of satire to which it belongs:

> Grippes's opinion remains unchanged: He was the last author to receive a stipend from the Mary Margaret Pugh Arts Foundation, and so it should have fallen to him – Henri Grippes, Parisian novelist, diarist, essayist, polemical journalist, and critic – to preside at the commemoration of the late Miss Pugh's centenary. (*Collected Stories* 893)

Deflation erupts straight away through the sonority and onomastics. The onomastics of the name "Pugh" debunks the ceremony as well as the arts foundation, which we soon learn Grippes – like his rival Victor Prism – has milked for all it is worth. Inversely to onomatopoeia, which turns noises into words, the name operates as a phonic intensive counter-onomatopoeia, whose sound effect suggests its (quite ungenteel) meaning. Gallant uses the signifying wavelengths of onomastics to mock her main protagonist as well. Grippes's name evokes a contagious infection (*la grippe* is French for influenza). To be "*grippé*" is to be down with the flu, then, but the term also has other meanings – all pejorative. It evokes grippage, machines that have jammed, and also calls up the notion of taking a dislike to someone (*prendre quelqu'un en grippe*). By choosing names that signify, the author signals that her characters are structuring figures or types, marked as exempla. They participate in a subcategory of synecdoche recurrent in Gallant's oeuvre, *antonomasia*, which functions metonymically, providing a short cut from the particular to the general, using an individual subject to point to a group or category – in Miss Pugh's case to the Investment Trusts and Arts Foundations, which, it is suggested, churn out mediocre publications by subsidized moochers.

I wish to call attention here to the lengthy parenthetical afterthought which casually follows the opening sentence quoted above:

> (This celebration, widely reported in Paris, particularly in publications that seemed to have it in for Grippes, took place in a room lent by the firm of Fronce & Baril, formerly drapers and upholsterers, now purveyors of blue jeans from Madras. The firm's books reveal that Miss Pugh was the first person ever to have opened a charge account – a habit she had brought from her native America and is thought to have introduced into France.) (*Collected Stories* 893).

One can note further debunking via the firm which hosts the venue, a company which exemplifies entropy. The economic (and thus moral) decline is not denoted, but simply resonates in the wares, which originally evoked solidity and respectability, and which have shifted to the sphere of mass consumer goods and cheap labour. Implied in the amused distance of the undertext is the notion that the economic decline is experienced as an existential depreciation. Yet a closer look at the form of the message provides additional enlightenment. I have repeatedly evoked Gallant's systematic recourse to parenthesis. It is such a trademark feature of Gallant's style that Michel Fabre has astutely observed that "An entire critical study should be devoted" to it, and posits that this type of *a parte* offers "a key for 'decoding'" the text (155). Parenthesis is one of the figures of augmentation perceived as a crescendo, which include metaphor and enumeration. The technique of adding adjacent assertions within parentheses, as in this case, or simply introduced by dashes or even commas, allows a statement to invade another syntactically independent unit, often ironically. The parenthesis here separates the initial premise (Grippes should have been invited to preside) with the outcome: "But the honor did not fall to M. Grippes" (893).

Yet all the while it breaks up the syntactic development of the exposition, it not only encloses but includes and opens out. The present of narrative is layered over in the manner of in-camera double exposure. Overlaid onto the base image of the Mary Margaret Pugh Arts Foundation is Miss Pugh's charge account with Fronce & Baril, a fraught fusion which anticipates the subsequently listed components of the Pugh Memorial Committee: "the American Embassy, the Chase Manhattan Bank (Paris),[23] the French Ministry for Culture, and other intellectual oatcakes" (893) – with the bank innocently sandwiched in the middle. Roiling within the long and the short parentheses is the author's ironic voice saying what she means at a slant, or to borrow W.H. New's terms,

> oversetting, so that a reader might hear (through the *performance* of a given set of words) not only their split levels of *implication* but also the divergent *relation* between an apparent surface intent and an often political undertow. (*Grandchild of Empire* 13, original stresses)

Antonomasia has the quasi-allegorical function of concretizing an underlying truth. It generates what the rhetorician Henri Morier calls the "*noema*," the theme or moral, coterminous with New's undertow, which

23 One can note the resonances which roil in this yet another casual parenthesis.

in this case moves through a new series of parentheses from political in the broad sense to moral and ethical:

> Think of Grippes, Miss Pugh's youthful protégé, fresh from his father's hog farm in Auvergne, dozing on a bed in her house (a bed that had belonged to Prism a scant six months before), with Rosalia, the maid, sent along every half hour to see how he was getting on with chapter 2. Think of Grippes at the end, when Miss Pugh's long-lost baby brother, now seventy-something – snappy Hong Kong forty-eight-hour tailoring, silk shirt from Bangkok, arrogant suntan – turned up at her bedside, saying, "Well, Maggie, long time no see." (*Collected Stories* 893–4)

Although none of the terms taken individually is a symbol in itself, the passage taken globally functions structurally like a simile or extended comparison. The comically grotesque specimens of humanity feed off one another like vultures, an appraisal the omniscient narrator confirms obliquely through things (and through parentheses). Grippes declares that he managed to be by Miss Pugh's bedside at the end, and "distinctly heard her say something coherent about the disposal of her furniture" (896). He also gets Miss Pugh's Legion of Honour after her brother learns "it would not fetch one franc, his floor price, at auction" (894). Some of Miss Pugh's furniture, which he and Rosalia have previously removed "for safety," turns up in the parlour of Rosalia's son, "permanent mayor and Mafia delegate of a town in Sicily" (897). Finally, through a disorderly but scrupulously detailed enumeration, Prism lays claim to

> Miss Pugh's library, her collection of autograph letters (Apollinaire to Zola), her matching ormulu-mounted opaline urns, her Meissen coffee service, her father's cuff links, her Louis XVI-period writing table, and the key to a safe-deposit vault containing two Caillebottes and a Morisot. (894)

Gallant's narrator is detached and lightly amused, but her irony carries a moral charge, grounded as it is in the pragmatic evaluative function of the trope which I evoked in my introductory chapter: it interrogates and "it judges" (Hutcheon, *A Theory of Parody* 53).

In a much earlier story, "The Other Paris" (1953), we encounter a similarly amused but benevolent narratorial instance which mocks the way its young expatriate American protagonist naively conflates two distinct spheres of human existence. Carol has accepted the marriage proposal of the government agency department head she has known less than three weeks. Not being in love is not an issue:

> From a series of helpful college lectures on marriage she had learned that a common interest, such as a liking for Irish setters, was the true basis for happiness, and that the illusion of love was a blight imposed by the film industry, and almost entirely responsible for the high rate of divorce. Similar economic backgrounds, financial security, belonging to the same church – these were the pillars of the married union. (*Collected Stories* 120–1; *OP* 4)

One discerns a stratification of voices: the narrator's overset by the college lecturer's in turn interpreted by Carol's, visible in the delightfully jejune and absurdly precise Irish setter parenthesis. One is not always quite sure where the voice comes from: is for instance the out-of-place value judgment "helpful" to be imputed to the focalizer Carol or to the ironic edge of the utterance or both? The multivocality (intensified throughout by parenthesis) parodically reproduces the speech of current opinion disseminated by our institutions: stock phrases which conceal a sclerosis of thought as well as language. Carol has integrated the going point of view of the college-educated (if we can consider lectures on marriage to constitute an education), but she prudently also wants to conform to the common view which the film industry both absorbs and propagates. So "Carol, with great *efficiency*, nearly at once set about the *business* of falling in *love*" (121). The incongruence of perceiving the act of falling in love as a business venture which can be carried out successfully through will and hard work is foregrounded through a conceit startling in its simplicity. The free indirect discourse giving us access to Carol's mind contends that "Love required only the right conditions, like a geranium" (121). The homely organic simile calling up standardized suburban window boxes which yokes the abstract with the incongruous concrete, is extended to ramify in turn into different forms of human experience. Like a geranium in dismal weather or surroundings, love would wither in a cottage or a furnished room, but "Given a good climate, enough money, and a pair of good-natured, *intelligent* (her college lectures had stressed this) people, one had only to sit back and watch it grow" (121, original italics). The equation of love and geraniums needing only sun or watering cans demonstrates the hallmark gesture of synthetic reduction I have been discussing. One can also note how the writer *combines the reduction with exaggerated weighting, a cocktail of distortion which characterizes the ironist and caricaturist*, whether verbal or visual. Having simplified, Gallant gives to the required ingredient of "intelligent people" a double weighting. First, the reinforcement provided by the italics captures the readerly gaze, and second, the disruptive parenthesis with its unsyntactic positioning slows down the meaning-making.

Mavis had a predilection for the stylistic depictions of graphic art, from the selective deformation of eighteenth-century political and social caricatures to those of Sem, George Grosz, and Saul Steinberg (who has produced a number of *The New Yorker*'s caricatures and cover art). Her skills of distortion – visible here in the simultaneous reduction and supplementation –are precisely what make Gallant such a remarkable ironist. I will devote my next book exclusively to the writer's ironic vision and satirical agenda, to her incursions into caricature, parody, and pastiche, and to the techniques she shares with visual caricaturists. I have repeatedly demonstrated throughout my discussion the author's standpoint in front of the spectacle of the human comedy, ranging from benevolent amusement to sympathy and even outrage, superimposing a high-altitude detachment onto pragmatic engagement and appraisal.

Before moving on to my concept of the rhetorical short circuit, I shall conclude this discussion on double vision and the short cut by giving one final example of Gallant's deployment of certain writerly procedures which we find easier to identify when they are pictorial. In this instance it will serve to clarify her multiple and complex reference system. The story "The Four Seasons" depicts a community of English expatriates in northern Italy during the unfurling of fascism and the Second World War, focusing in particular on the Unwins and a young Italian woman they employ but conveniently forget to remunerate. The story is replete with structural, dramatic, and cosmic ironies investigating unbalanced power relations in general and targeting in particular a diasporic community sensitive to only its own interests and blindly bent on perceiving Mussolini as a peacemaker. Our attention is directed to Carmela, the little Italian servant, as an exemplifying symbol of subservience. The writer's figuring, comprising once more a homely analogy, performs several integrated and interacting functions. The narrating voice states that "As for the Unwins, they were as used to Carmela as to the carpet, whose tears must have seemed part of the original pattern now" (*Collected Stories* 73). The equivalence of Carmela and carpet is weighted through the anacoluthon or syntactic break "whose tears," apparently belonging to both. The equivalence is further buttressed through the sonorous link of full alliteration and assonance which overlays a pseudo-identity on highly disparate things. Equating Carmela with a familiar object which receivers are accustomed to treading on is a short cut which sets up a multilateral system of intuitive interconnections of subordination striving to make sense of the world. These are compressed relations, both culture-specific and time-locked and cross-cultural and timeless, in which Carmela is to the

Unwins what the Italians are to the English, or what the Jews are to the Nazi Germans, but also what the traditional rural community is to the urban middle class, and what the female is to the male.

Carmela does not actually become a carpet, however. People (and animals) elsewhere in Gallant's texts do turn into other things. To take just a couple of examples from stories analysed in chapter 4, "Saturday" and "Bonaventure," readers run into "Russian bundles" that cross themselves (*HT* 35) and, more covertly, a piggy and a praying mantis that Ramsey leaves with "the cat and the cannibals" (194). The troubling magical transformations call up Gregor Samsa, the insect/human creature in Kafka's *The Metamorphosis* (1915), and Seth Brundle, the insect/human hybrid in George Langelaan's arguably derivative short story "The Fly" (1957), in turn adapted by David Cronenberg to the screen in 1986 (and in 2008 to the opera, which premiered in Paris). Brundle's mutation is technologically explicable: a simple glitch which occurs during an experiment in transmitting matter through space, when a clandestine fly climbs on board. Gregor's transformation into the Samsabeetle is inexplicable. The new reality he wakes up to is fantastical; yet, as Cronenberg himself observes in his introduction to Susan Bernofsky's new translation of *The Metamorphosis*, it is "played out on the level of the resolutely mundane and the functional." Like Kafka's, the transformations we stumble across on Gallant's pages are also played out on the level of the mundane. They too perform transformations in consciousness and being which – albeit not fantastical – can be sensed and gestured to more than explicated. They do so through a contagious transmutation of perception, played out in and through language. This I propose to explicate, under my concept of the rhetorical short circuit.

Gallant's mechanism resides in manipulating her vintage feature, simile or comparison. She namely reiterates it all the while compressing it into a conceit. To take the simplest example from "Saturday" mentioned above, Gérard, lost, found himself on a Montreal curb swept by a spring tempest of snow, while "A few people, bundled as Russians, scuffled by" (*HT* 34). On the following page, when a funeral procession passed by, "The Russian bundles crossed themselves" (*HT* 35). The textual short cut from simile to compressed metaphor radically changes the nature of the human beings under scrutiny, unlike the Frank Cairns/curio cabinet metaphor. In "What Frank Cairns was to me was a curio cabinet" (*VE* 163), Cairns is a cabinet in the narrator's mind, but does not cease to be Cairns. But in "Saturday," local "people" become objects imported from elsewhere, like Russian cars. *Since this short cut triggers a radical transmutation in perception and Being, I liken the estrangement effect to the mechanism of an electrical short circuit*, resulting from an unorthodox contact of components which causes a diversion of the current. In Gallant's case, the contact is not unintended but programmed, and the diversion is not accidental but deliberate.[24] In "Bonaventure," with "the cat and the cannibals" (*HT* 194) Gallant sets up an even more striking bypass between points on a circuit. The author expects her readers to pay attention. Those who do are stunned only momentarily by the company the cat keeps. They miss a beat, but then remember that a couple of pages before, Ramsey had evoked the savage cat and "the cannibal magpies, the cannibal jays" (192). The unusual group of cat and cannibals is united by sound but different in kind. Birds normally belong to the category of prey, but these – predators which devour their own – defy the notion of typological classification. The term cannibals actually triggers a double "sea change / Into something rich and strange" (Shakespeare, *The Tempest* I.ii.404–5). It morphs into birds and back again into its most common acceptation: human predators, among which, following Ramsey's lead, we have confusedly identified the ostensibly nurturing Katharine Moser, who has undergone an ontological transformation into a praying/preying mantis.

The linked story cycle narrated by Steve Burnet ("Let It Pass," "In a War," and "The Concert Party") discussed above is rife with grating instances of fluctuating selves, evocative of the frame-breaking in "Baum, Gabriel" analysed in chapter 4, yet more radical. Two distinct diegetic levels collide in "In a War," unsettling and fusing their respective subjectivities into a version of Cronenberg's hybrid Brundlefly. What is the reader to make of a statement such as, "Her soldiers, pronounced dead, got up to receive a decoration" (*VE* 286)? The passage echoes a previous episode depicting the young Lily Quale playing soldiers with a group of little girls. In a pattern of frame-breaking, the army that was not under Lily's command got shot on sight. "The victims lay down and" – here the expected "died" is diverted to – "got their coats wet" (278). The current is deviated from the sublime (death) to the mundane, which is sustained when "The soldiers started to pick lumps of snow from each other's coats" (279). The mechanism seems to follow the same procedure in the story's concluding episode. Still playing at war, Lily gave out silver paper

24 Chekhov, too, was adept at what I term the short circuit, albeit in a manner less dense, closer to my short cut. At the end of the ball in "Anna Round the Neck" the tired ladies of charity hand over their takings "to the old lady with a stone in her mouth" (*The Kiss* 215). The wrong-footed reader needs to think back to the Emperor dancing with Anna, then leading her to meet his wife, an old lady "whose enormous chin was so out of proportion to the rest of her face it looked as if she had a large stone in her mouth" (*The Kiss* 214).

medals to her resuscitated soldiers, who declared unheroically, "I've got mud on my coat. I'm going to catch it at home" (286). But the next sentence deviates, operates a spatial, temporal, and existential short circuit, and in spite of apparently petty components, careens back into the sublime:

> In that war, *or one like it*, Vince Whitton *begins* to whine: "Beryl, my feet are getting cold. I'm hungry. I have to go to the bathroom."... He stops snivelling for a minute, and moves closer to Leo. (286)

Alongside the parallel of that pretend war and "one like it" – namely the "real" one in which Leo has enlisted – the switch from the classic tense for storytelling to which Gallant has been conforming (the preterite) to a present tense resonates synoptically, especially for a flash*back*, a fulgurant past in which Leo, already gone off to fight, is still there. He is doubly there, in an infinite *jetztzeit* of overlapping worlds. The scene showing humans playing at war stretches to planetary and cosmic proportions. "In that war, or one like it," Vince Whitton, or one like him – such as Leo – is cold, and hungry, and tired, and frightened. The invisible narrator makes no spoken point, expands no profound reflection. Only another short circuit follows. When the little players are exposed to the feared Mr. Quale's displeasure, they "freeze ... hardly breathing, small creatures in an open field, hoping they have become the white of the snow around them and the hawk will leave them alone" (286). Yet there are other small creatures in open fields, and other hawks, which do strike. The sentence which follows, visually foregrounded by a paragraph break, simply states, "Leo's death made two of the English newspapers in Montreal" (286). And we are left holding our breaths. The characters in Gallant's world often have "bone-barren lives," W.H. New remarked in his review of *From the Fifteenth District,* which he read at the same time as Atwood's *Life Before Man.* Yet Atwood's characters, "chocolate rabbits without centres," somehow "don't matter," he finds, while (as Leo here demonstrates) Gallant's characters "*do* matter," perhaps because, New posits, "The texture of Gallant's stories ... work to expose the fabric of consequence rather than the tissue of appearance" ("Haunting" 154, original stress).

I wish to complete my investigation of Gallant's short circuits by returning to the novel which has been "overlooked for nearly half a century" (Orner, "Introduction" xi), *A Fairly Good Time,* which begins with gardens turned into parlours and statues sprouting leaves. On his first visit to Paris, the young Bartók marvelled in a letter to a friend back home at the "divine godless city" which was "the centre of the world" (*Levelek*

56), built with an art he felt surpassed all others.[25] He marvelled not only at the architecture, but also at the French art of the city garden. What amazed the Hungarian in 1905 was exactly what was to amaze Mavis in 1950, and what she would turn into story in *A Fairly Good Time* – namely stumbling across Maupassant or Gounod in a bush. Bartók was enchanted with French fantasy, with the "unique" way the French used art to sublimate nature, scattering vases and statues of poets and musicians among the flower beds, groves, and shrubbery. In the epistolary opening section of *A Fairly Good Time*, the no-nonsense Canadian mother writing to her Paris-based daughter, Shirley, presents things from a different perspective than spellbound Bartók on the other side of the looking glass. Both agent and object of Gallant's characteristic double-edged irony, she mocks her target, but simultaneously discloses that indigence of the imagination which Shirley (often a Mavis avatar) had fled:

> I know the French know nothing about Nature and do their best to turn gardens into parlors. It was your father's opinion that they do not distinguish between trees and statues, and are completely taken aback every Spring to see all these statues putting out leaves. (5)

Radically shortening the process by which humans can change nature into art and art into nature entails compressing or deleting elements, bypassing them by taking an incongruously direct route. The sculpted shrubs of classic French landscaping take on the bizarre contours of fantasy or magical realism, and the resulting hybrid plant-statue is comically close to our Samsabeetle.

The mother's letter to Shirley, in which she alludes to her own wedding trip to England the year George V died, triggers another rhetorical short circuit. Shirley thinks back and remembers, "Once she found George the Fifth on a beach" (*FGT* 10). This surreal statement bypasses the common logic of language as communication, charged as it is with tension between the components brought forcibly into contact (George V/beach). *The short circuit involves both compression and expansion*, and requires us to read to the left and to the right of the startling statement.

> Who was he? He was crown, beard and profile on twenty-five Canadian cents – at one time, Shirley's allowance. Once she found George the Fifth on a beach and brushed the sand away, saying, "What can I buy with this? (10)

---

25 The quotes in English from this Hungarian volume of Bartók's correspondence are my translations.

Substituting the person for the effigy intensifies an already powerful metonymy which conjoins the small and the grand, object and concept: crown/king; coin/purchasing and political power. The conjunction is in addition vexed by the contact of Canadian coin and British king, a by-pass incongruous to both the politicized and the historically unaware. Extending the metonymy on the level of the mundane and functional (stumbling across the king covered in sand) triggers one of *the eruptions of the bizarre which* – along with time-shifts, labyrinthine plots, and use of dream – *the writer shares with the surrealists and magic realists*, out to fuse speech with unbridled thought.

A leopard in the dark is another instance of a short circuit redolent of surrealist surprise. Meant to derail, the process entails adding a phonic trope to the already identified mechanism: repetition with a difference conjoined with compression. My example shows how *the short circuiting via phonic play partakes in the rhythmic practice of syncopation* I have engaged with, also involving off-beat displacements. Shirley dreads opening her mother's letters, and leaves them unopened for days, as though fearing that "some form of unsatisfied justice might leap out of them and claw her to death" (41). For "that was the way she envisioned justice – a leopard in the dark" (41). The startling conceit is interestingly cliché-based: it self-reflexively wrenches the ready-made formula for the unknown out of other people's mouths and, by diverting it, brings it to life. The simultaneous resurrection and mutation lie in the shift from leap to leopard, a startling transformation of image (the eye) brought about by sound (the ear). With this rather Joyce-like altered configuration or metaplasm (involving substitution and supplementation of sounds or letters), *Gallant performs with sound the torsion her metaphors achieve with imagery*. When "leap" mutates into "leopard," the writer draws the attention of readers accustomed to silent reading back to the sound itself. Unlike Joyce, however, she does not stress the sound at the expense of the sense, but rather to give the sense a strange thickness that makes it new, even to our eyes: what better leap than a leopard's?

Gallant does occasionally play with cliché and metaplasm to disrupt the sense. Displaying a Joycean fascination with the plastic versatility of the English language's building blocks, she demonstrates that a rabbi is just one letter away from a rabbit. Shirley leafs through one of Renata's novels one night as she waits for her friend to sleep off the effects of an illegal[26] abortion–related suicide attempt. Relating the whole episode later in a letter to the husband who left her the night she stayed away,

26 The main story is set in 1963, and abortion in France remained illegal until 1975.

Shirley describes the stereotyped plot entailing a plane emergency landing, an Austrian ski lodge, a large black dog, a neo-Nazi, and an intertextual touch of the fantastic involving Mephistopheles, Margareta, and Faust:

> The poodle assumes a sinister attitude on page 102 and tells the neo-Nazi that his wife is secretly the daughter of a famous rabbi and magician. A misprint in the book made it "rabbit" but the next page had it right. (191)

We are naturally in the multivocal realm of pastiche – Shirley telling it straight in the confessional first person, but the omniscient narrator making sure the reader wonders how on earth a poodle could be sinister. A metatextual swerve then derails the series of already unsettled narrative stereotypes; the metaplasm rabbi/rabbit produces a mental image that is both vivid and absurd. The disruptive rhetorical figure posits an interchangeability encountered only in Alice's Wonderland, and it even compresses ontologically dissimilar beings onto the same ontological plane, creating a Brundlebunny via a single letter.

Such *ontological crunches* are rife in the novel, often resting on animal imagery (which could be the subject of a whole book). Shirley "heard a rat at the door" and sprang up to "let the rat in" (191) – the rat turning out to be Renata's lover, who then morphed at the foot of the bed into a "kneeling gnat" (196). One can detect a trademark modernist, even surrealist, process dictated by the free association of thought devoid of that straitjacket: reason. In Gallant's statement, the form, through both the ear [*n*] and the eye (which takes in that the *g* and *k* are silent parasites), takes precedence over the sense, but in taking control, it performs an existential twist. In a more radical instance, Madame Roux, Shirley's landlady, came out of her shop one day as our protagonist walked by. Shirley "turned, stopped, smiled, ever willing to be a spider's friend" (103). The normal circuit is set up through the ternary sequence of ordinary verbs, then diverted into contact with an unorthodox element, resulting in a shock. Careful readers go back to *Go* and beyond, and find the component which triggers the Samsaspider short circuit. Ever since Philippe picked up and left Shirley, his things kept disappearing surreptitiously. Shirley suspected Madame Roux had been commissioned to smuggle his important belongings away, saw her in her mind's eye opening drawers, unfolding letters, "looking, peeping," and imagined her transformed, "shrunken, with six spider legs and a spider's eyes" (103). Unnatural, surreal Samsabeetles and Brundleflies abound in Gallant's oeuvre, then, but so do Arcimboldo-style monstrous mergers of human and vegetable. As dawn comes, Shirley makes out her artist-friend Renata's portraits stacked around the room. Renata's sitters want the likeness kept simple, which to them "means unwinding one's chignon and letting it trail along the birch tree they know Renata will provide as a throat" (197). The arresting birch tree throat makes us pay attention. As with a visual anamorphosis, we step to the left of the sequence and re-encounter Renata's trademark stylistic features: small ears, an empty expression, and a long neck. We realize that we have once again been brought to grapple with the perceiving subject. The amused nod to Modigliani also metacritically encourages us to reflect on artistic creation, its share of derivation and invention, and to smile at the formulaic mannerisms of imitation.

7

"How can you tell what somebody's worth? What's the measure?"

Remaining with *A Fairly Good Time* as my object of scrutiny, I shall conclude with the novel's arguably most elaborate instance of the short circuit: when Shirley meets Proust. The motif of meeting is one of literature's most universal motifs, often combined with other motifs, such as recognition or the epiphany (Bakhtin 98). This particular meeting engineered by Gallant is chronologically impossible, of course, as is the epistolary exchange in the quirky story, "Mau to Lew: The Maurice Ravel-Lewis Carroll Friendship," in which historical subjects from different nation-states and temporal planes[1] communicate and even switch identities. In both cases, the way the author doubles and folds over her chronotope or time space to short circuit the hiatus and make the intersection fictionally possible calls attention to the historical thickness of time, as well as to its connection with the cognitive process. The process of Gallant's own "concrete artistic cognition (artistic visualisation)" (Bakhtin 85) diverts the Shirley/Proust contact into folk-mythological time. By having Claudie Maurel introduce Shirley to the iconic Proust in a Parisian café's everyday time and red leather decor, the author derails the novel from adjacent moments of real-life sequences and plunges it into *the mode of marvellous metamorphosis*. In this neither historical nor quotidian encounter in which scale clashes with background, one can find traces of the Greek epic's condensed mythological event which unfolds into a scene or tableau, in which historical time is interwoven into mythological time.

In a brasserie, then, Shirley's young friend, Claudie, has presented a delicate-looking young man as someone with an important but undefined literary heritage: "'*Proust*,' said Claudie carelessly" (*FGT* 174). The appellation moves from an impersonal formality to a first-name-basis

1 Carroll had published his Alice books before Ravel was even born.

informality (which I show through my italics), just as in "Mau to Lew" Ravel progressively signs on with "Dear Dodge," then "Dear Lew," and finally signs off with "Keep in touch, Mau." In a process of graduated repetition and variation, Shirley learned that "*Young Proust* worked only for the sake of dignity and to pay for his own cigarettes" doing "consumer research," since his father, "a nose-and-throat specialist, made him an adequate allowance" (174). Anachronistic terms showcase a cumulative, fraught temporal juncture, in which the contemporary socio-economic lexical field of work collides with romantic notions of the artist as solitary demiurge. Along with Shirley, we readers learn that Claudie and her young man planned to go to Lebanon as volunteers in refugee camps, and "should the refugees turn out to be ungrateful and unrewarding," to "one of the Israeli kibbutzim reserved for zealous foreigners" (175). These grand geographic, sociopolitical, and ideological considerations intrude not so much to be interpreted,[2] as to light up the pettiness of the private lives seeking spectacle and self-aggrandizement. Shirley advised Claudie not to leave behind Alain (her illegitimate incest-derived Brundlefly son-brother). "'Yes, do take him,' said *Marcel Proust* in a thin voice" (177), and then completely abandoned himself to Gallant's art of sinking. When they finally stood up to leave, Shirley "thought she noticed *Marcel* pocketing the change she had left for the waiter" (178). With a modernist suspicion of certainty, the author at intervals triggers these unorthodox bypasses[3] to short circuit the alethic modality governed by operators of possibility and impossibility, as well as the epistemic modality governing affairs of knowledge.

Gallant's performance paves the way for postmodern writers like Rushdie who observe that "the conventions of what we call realism are quite inadequate" (*Imaginary Homelands* 376). Rushdie proclaimed in his 1985 essay "'In God We Trust" that "A form must be created which allows the miraculous and the mundane to coexist at the same level – as the same order of event" (376). He may have overlooked Canadian among other writers, and Gallant in particular. Her work ostensibly embodies, among the opposed pairs of ideas which according to Rushdie humans have sought to understand themselves, the "eternally warring myths of stasis and of metamorphosis" (291). Her taste for transfiguration, which

---

2 Gallant does indulge in an ironic under-text which questions the authenticity of certain kibbutzim oriented to Westerners starved for exoticism.

3 Shirley challenges Claudie's sister Marie-Thérèse in a later free indirect discourse segment, "Why shouldn't Claudie be married to Marcel Proust and go and live with him in the Middle East? Did it sound less intelligent than anything Marie-Thérèse, or her mother, or Shirley herself had ever done?" (*FGT* 225).

I have investigated above, ostensibly aligns Mavis with Rushdie's claim that

> Stasis, the dream of eternity, of a fixed order in human affairs, is the favoured myth of tyrants; metamorphosis, the knowledge that nothing holds its form, is the driving force of art. (291)

Metamorphosis is indeed Gallant's magical vehicle for conceptualizing and portraying kismet – that personal, individual fate isolated from a cosmic or historical whole. It is charged with enough energy to apprehend the entire life of a subject through what Mavis termed its determining turning points ("Style" 6). These are the exceptional moments which shape the definitive image or essence of the individual and the course of his or her subsequent life, during which the subject may become other, or at least take on a different image. Yet, unlike Rushdie, Mavis does not forget that throughout history societies have valued stability over mutability, as show the final stanzas of Spenser's *Faerie Queene* discussed in the first part of this chapter.

In *A Fairly Good Time*, things occur by chance, one of the forms of the principle of necessity. In this it aligns itself with both Greek romance and the Baroque novel, in which events are determined by random contingency (Bakhtin 100–6). Likewise, Gallant's female protagonist moves through space, seeking or fleeing, but she exercises little agency. Shirley is the patient, in the linguistic sense of the one on whom an action is performed, the one to whom things happen. She runs up against injunctions and deontic modals from sundry sources, beginning with the first chapter, in which the speaking subject, her mother, tells her,

> *Don't* cry whilst writing letters. The person receiving the letter is apt to take it as a reproach. Undefined misery is no use to anyone. *Be* clear, or, better still, *be* silent. If you *must* tell the world about your personal affairs, *give* examples. *Don't* sob in the pillow hoping someone will overhear. (*FGT* 8)

Deontic logic comes from all fronts, asserting that certain actions or states of affair are compulsory, reprehensible, or permissible. Shirley is put to trial and endures the directives imposing the standards of desirable conduct, the norms and expectations of her habitat.[4] Yet she always emerges *unchanged*. It is in a complex way that the author engages with

4 Philippe, for instance, "taught her not to serve spaghetti because it was messy to eat and made it seem as if they could not afford to pay a butcher" (*FGT* 28).

the factors of human identity, the question of human transformation, the correspondence between identity and self and between transformation and identity, and the very concept of selfhood or essence.

I have repeatedly shown how Gallant employs figures that are dominantly synthetic and conjunctive, associating disparate elements towards a common denominator. I have also drawn attention to the fraught dynamics of her writing which also creates a web of ramifications that produce an expanding, outward moving cross-network of analogies. As I have demonstrated in my analyses of her favourite devices (from enumeration, chiasmus, and counterpoint to metonymy and metaphor), Gallant's centrifugal, outward moving, disjunctive web paradoxically coexists with an inverse, centripetal, conjoining movement towards synthetic resolution or unity. The fraught coexistence, *symptomatic of the writer's period and whole cultural habitat*, gains in being contextualized.

Broadly speaking, the deliberate disruption of wholeness, of balance and order which prevailed in the first half of the twentieth century in the denotational and nondenotational aesthetic fields deployed dynamics of representation which were undeniably centrifugal. I use centrifugal in the double sense of the term, both efferent and separatist, implying the separation of elements or parts as well as their dispersion away from a centre or norm. Yet paradoxically, underlying the centrifugal disparities and disciplinary particularities one finds a surprising centripetal force straining back towards a certain unity, discernible in areas from theosophy to Husserl's eidetic reduction. Floating in the air are the two currents of Cubism, analytic (disjunctive) and synthetic (conjunctive in its all-at-once-ness), both of which are transfigured in literary works such as *The Waste Land* and *Ulysses*. Eliot both draws on and dynamites the master narratives of Western culture, yet he corrects and controls the centrifugal dispersal of unidentified flying objects by famously providing readers with explanatory notes which make the furiously disparate references cohere with respect to a fundamental core or canon. *Ulysses* too is structured like an exploding fragmentation bomb, but its author's search for connectedness is also manifest in the subtitles-cum-signposts (analogous to Eliot's adjunct note apparatus) with which Joyce too collapses the tension between ancient Greece and contemporary Dublin in preference of a certain simultaneity with the past.

At the same time, Russian formalists such as Vladimir Propp set out to uncover the general characteristics of language (a metalanguage) and the transcultural, transhistorical, invariant, and universal patterns in storytelling. Saussure's heuristic distinction between parole (speech) and langue (the underlying organized symbolic system which actual utterances plug into) entailed separating the cultural from the individual, and also the essential from the accessory.[5] Roman Jakobson's structural analysis of the distinctive features of language (in the process of development or disintegration) set out to explain the universal laws underlying the phonological structure of the world's languages. Lévi-Strauss identified patterns of thought common to all humans, operating in the cross-cultural units of myth combinable in endless variants. Ur-myth can be envisaged in terms of either the high (one overarching transcultural language) or the low (the deep grammar of society) – as can Propp's ur-story and Bartók's ur-music. Bartók, a passionate musical ethnographer, tracked down and recorded ancient melodies from Central Europe to North Africa. These melodies' divergences from the European tonic system and their convergences with one another (notably a structure based on one magnetic tonal centre around which motifs revolve in an expanding spiral, astonishingly similar to Gallant's structural spiralling) made him suspect a common origin (Citron 70–1), which in turn took on anthropological and philosophical resonances, and also pointed to the general monist yearning for Unity part of *l'air du temps*.[6] Stravinsky concluded his *Sacre* with a change in beat in every bar, and the Bartók pursuing an ur-music still had one foot on the brake and the other on the accelerator (Citron 90). His experiments with polytonality (even before Stravinsky), which disrupted the binary of major *or* minor, especially offered the luxury of "both/and," by simultaneously using multiple scale systems: tonal, modal, and pentatonic. Similarly, the visual arts' permanent revolution entailed renewing with figuration and reinventing classic realism (see for instance the Cubist Realists, the older Derain, and his disciple Balthus).

As I have demonstrated throughout (but especially in my chapter on dissonance and syncopation), *the sensual symbol systems of music and the visual arts showcase most clearly this unending tension-resolution dynamic*, which Gallant makes her own. I have grappled with how she achieves her agenda of regularity and cognitive dissonance or disturbance. Her dissonance in *A Fairly Good Time* takes on *both* of the harmonic functions musical dissonance can exercise, usually consisting of *either* preparing a resolution *or* maintaining an unresolved grating effect. On the one hand, then, flux in the novel under scrutiny is rampant in the context and in the writing itself, characterized by its Chekhovian use of incongruity and farce, its digressive, cumulative design, its ellipsoidal

5 Terry Eagleton has noted that Husserl and Saussure produced work roughly at the same time as Joyce and Eliot (Eagleton 110), who also situated themselves within the recombinable but closed symbolic systems I addressed in my introductory chapter.

6 The dialectic Eco identifies between the Renaissance and the modernist world views in *The Aesthetics of Chaosmos* (evoked in my first chapter) can thus equally be found within the modernist world view itself.

structural convolutions spiralling ahead and back, even beyond the beginning. Maintaining the dissonant roughness along with syncopating displacements, Gallant's time-shifts are subtle and fluid and the multi-view effortless, buttressed by life writing's devices of staging the self, the journal and the letter, which transfigure external observation into interior monologue. Particularly remarkable is her morphing from third person to confessional first person, made possible by the blend of letter and diary which Shirley ostensibly writes for Philippe, with no guarantee the intratextual addressee will ever read it as we do. We are never sure when is now, where is here, and who is I or you.

As I suggested above in the sub-chapter, "the subject-centred perceptual apparatus," in which I aligned myself with Said, Gallant's slippages present the I-self as an indeterminate discursive construct, constantly in flux. Yet the writer pauses before a quandary: if individual identity is little more than a speaking pronoun in the ongoing rush of discourse (Said 287), what happens to our epistemological and ontological notions of subjectivity and agency? The dissonant chords seem to cry out for a resolution into consonance. *A Fairly Good Time* seems to embody a both/and stance regarding the "eternally warring myths of stasis and of metamorphosis" (Rushdie, *Imaginary Homelands* 291) with which humans have tried to understand themselves. On the one hand, I have shown, transformation is rife in the writing itself. Yet while the structural convolutions in turn house ethical convolutions and interrogate existential issues, sea-changes on the other hand are curiously absent in the self. A whole gallery of portraits so vivid and alive they could walk off the page *displaces the focus aporetically from the construction of the self as process towards a consideration of the self as product.*

Forgetful, untidy Shirley is "comfortable in chaos" (13), her watch is forever "somewhere or other, perhaps in a pocket of her raincoat" (19), but like her creator, she is endearing, imaginative, and book-loving, and can always be counted on to stand by her friends in need, even to care for strangers. In the backstory beyond the beginning, she has lost her father, then a young husband, Pete Higgins, in a freak accident, while in the main story she has had a miscarriage, her second husband deserts her and arranges to put her out of her own apartment (now his, through French law), and she loses her job (at which she tends to forget to show up). Significantly, she keeps on being the same person, even if a shifting perceiving subject causes Cubist refraction.

"*We have all been abandoned* was all she knew about the universe" (*FGT* 44), the narrator tells us. The day Shirley miscarried Philippe summed her up differently. Because she "could speak without weeping about her dead father," never mentioned her dead young husband, and "was not crying now, he believed that she cast sorrow off easily and that grief was a temporary arrangement of her feelings. He thought this to be an American fact which made for a comfortable existence, without memory and without remorse" (44–5). The signs of mediation ("he believed, he thought") invalidate the propositions, as do the resonances with the title, *A Fairly Good Time*, a partial quote which omits but nods to the dark first segment of its pre-text, Edith Wharton's *The Last Asset*,[7] disclosed in Gallant's epigraph to guide our interpretation:

> There are lots of ways of being miserable, but there's only one way of being comfortable, and that is to stop running round after happiness. If you *make up your mind not to be happy* there's no reason why you shouldn't have a fairly good time. (Edith Wharton, qtd in *FGT*)

Our protagonist Shirley has indeed resigned herself to replacing happiness with being comfortable and having a fairly good time, including with the young man who lives upstairs, but unlike Philippe, who "*still* believed people to be as they seemed" (45), alert readers are encouraged not to consider attitudes of the heart to be "easily defined" (45).

Yet in a simultaneous centripetal dynamic, many of the novel's other characters are quite easily defined – much like the "Goya people" (27) the painter conjures up on canvas. There are Shirley's French counterparts (her priggish journalist husband Philippe Perrigny and his mother and sister, Colette), and even her own mother, Mrs. Norrington, and her mother's oldest friend, Mrs. Castle. Lapidary concision melded with repleteness and distortion abound. A few observations regarding Mrs. Norrington gleaned from multiview's different angles perform an effect as big as life all the while reducing the subject to her essential attribute. Shirley's militant, dogmatic mother, we learn, gave everything she owned "to a sect that did not believe in blood transfusions." She expected "the end of the world and would not eat an egg unless she had first met the hen" (213).

Philippe had "a tranquil belief that because he was French he was logical" (19). Yet his assigned articles on issues from the Norman practice of spiking infants' bottles to the Berlin Wall and the declining Hungarian birthrate are all subtitled "A Silent Cry" or "The Soundless Cry" in a heavy-handed borrowing from Edvard Munch's expressionist pictures known in France as "Le Cri." Philippe's sociopolitical outlook actually belongs to "the domain of magic" (17) rather than Cartesian reason. He took Shirley along

7 Hermione Lee interestingly remarks that "Gallant has something of Wharton's fine, cool eye for social shifts and conflicts" and that both writers have left behind cultures they often return to in their work (Lee).

with him to a meeting at which "the language probably spoken by the aristocracy on lost Atlantis had been discussed, and during which someone tried to prove a link between the name Mao and the noise made by a cat" (17). Shirley thought Philippe invulnerable and "because he was accurate, superior to herself" (45). She expected him to intellectually and sentimentally build a figurative house for her and "invite her inside," but he married her for a literal house – her apartment, which the housing shortage in Paris made invaluable – before deciding that her generous mode of life was "like a house without doors," and that her "easy sympathy, her quick good faith and ready remorse were going to be of no use to him" (45).

As for the Perrigny women, Gallant brings them to life through their habitat and habits. She continues to use familiar, domestic objects made strange, and deploys the distance and double vision of irony allowed by an earnest focalizer presenting facts overset by an amused external narrator. The Perrigny windows were always shut and their curtains drawn tight "lest someone flying low in a helicopter try to peer in and see what the Perrignys were having for lunch" (29). In Madame Perrigny's "anxious universe" – the effective hypallage simplicity itself – meat "created cancer," and four-course meals remained for days in her stomach, "undigested, turning over and over like clothes forgotten in a tumble dryer" (26): a simile redolent of the tall tale's combination of understatement and hyperbole. Colette's character can be grasped through her very French obsession with her liver, rendered masterfully through the arms *visual* caricaturists use to depict and even essentialize their targets: simplifying and exaggerating. *Calling up the situation cartoons* by George Grosz, Karl Arnold, and Thomas Theodor Heine (notably his trademark bulldogs), which Mavis enjoyed for the way they both condensed and emphasized, the writer posits any rich food makes the young woman's liver double in size and try to "force its way out through her skin" (26). Colette can "snap it back in place" (26) or else shrink it with a two-day diet of boiled water (that has vaguely encountered carrots and parsley). When, shortly after meeting Philippe, Shirley invited them to dinner for the first time and served a Scandinavian meal of pickled herring, pork, and Danish beer, the women were "not shocked or offended [*protasis*]; they were simply appalled, distressed and terrified of being poisoned [*dissonant apodosis*]" (28).

What Gallant has sketched out for us in a few quick strokes are bold outlines which – *like the stylized Toulouse-Lautrec portraits which define and deform* – house the very essence of these characters. Well after the wedding, transformation is ruled out on both sides. Whenever the Perrigny women came to visit, "they accepted nothing but china tea" (28). Crotchety Mrs. Castle, touring Europe "to show her children back in Canada she did not need them" (29), meets Shirley for a breakfast of pastries – her third, and we view her life entire in one compassionate observation filtered through our focalizer: "Shirley, drinking black coffee as if it were black poison, saw the panic of old age and the need to eat everything soon" (30). When Mrs Castle learns Shirley has helped Renata get an illegal abortion, which Philippe would disapprove of and could get into trouble just knowing about, she in turn sketches another graphic cameo portrait when she evokes the grandparents she thinks Shirley takes after, revealing as much about herself as she does about those she mocks:

> Honest to God, any old bum your grandfather could pick up off the street he'd bring home. There was always some deadbeat eating fried eggs in your grandmother's kitchen. And your grandmother used to read the Word of God *at* them till there wasn't a Christian left among the unemployed. (32–3)

The grandmother thus made the poor pay a price for fried eggs, but Philippe accuses Shirley of wasting her life and her time over people who "aren't worth a thought" (32). This is the moment Shirley asks the weighty question which subtends Gallant's whole oeuvre: "*But how can you tell what somebody's worth? What's the measure?*" (32).

Dismissing the concept of reincarnation Shirley's mother flirted with, Mrs. Castle declares, "I'm darned if I want my soul to come back in any form but me. *Me*, Shirl – me all the way." (37) This "me" is the subject that refuses to lend a bus ticket to Shirley without a penny in her pocket, while Shirley is the subject who pays with borrowed money for a penniless stranger's meal (how she met Claudie) rather than seeing her get into trouble. Can this be a measure of the self and its worth? As is her custom, Gallant displays an agenda of satire in her novel, but hers is not a militant satire bent on changing us for the better. Like ironists from Chaucer and Flaubert to Nabokov and Beckett, she reveals little corrective intent; by distorting external features and revealing inner truth through laughter, she shows instead the spectacle of the human comedy.

Unlike William Godwin and his optimistic ideology of human perfectibility, so widely embraced by modernity, Gallant's "people"[8] undergo

---

8 From the age of four Mavis was "half in life and half in books" (Hancock 28). When working on a story, her characters were realer to her than the people she met on the street. "No one is as real to me as people in the novel," she wrote in her diary about the early novel in progress in Spain. "When I realise they do not exist except in my mind I have a feeling of sadness, looking around for them, as if the half-empty café were a place I had once come to with friends who had all moved away" (Gallant, "The Hunger Diaries" 51).

experiences, even ordeals, which tend not to change them but to establish their identity, affirm what they *are*. The writer's skills in deleting, distorting, and exemplifying are the very ones we encounter in the *pictorial symbol systems*. One thinks of the drawn-out gag on urbanscape based on simplification, repetition, and accumulation, condensed in Tati's choreographed pile-up in *Trafic*, or the scene in *Playtime* in which a loudspeaker's garbled unintelligible announcements repeatedly send the crowd rushing from one end of the airport to the other. In the world of painting one can evoke Fauvists like André Derain, Henri Matisse, and Maurice de Vlaminck, who simplify form but exaggerate colour. One can call up the even more radical symbol system of caricaturists like Hogarth and Honoré Daumier, who display most clearly – because visually – *the agenda of satire in every medium: to inform, deform, reform*. Gallant, however, renounces reforming, and stands not so much on the side of outrageous exaggeration (with gleeful exceptions such as Colette's liver) as in the line of Tati's comic misrule via accumulated minor dissonances. Yet she tentatively suggests a humanity which can be crystallized into two sorts, analogous to the Maurel household's pets: "cats and doves, killers and victims" (*FGT* 151). Or as in the aphorism evoked in my introductory chapter, which states: "There are two races, those who tread on people's lives, and the others" – "the trodden-on" (*HT* 280, 282). Or yet again, less radically, into those who are button matchers and those who aren't.

This consideration, one of Gallant's tours de force, is what I wish to end with. I have already called attention to the serious resonances of Shirley's initial clash with Philippe over the unserious issue of laundry, in the manner of a White Clown–Auguste confrontation. I now want to underline the laundry episode's corresponding sleight-of-hand near the end of the novel. It consists of oversetting the author's existential questioning over that of her mouthpiece, Shirley, through the equally unserious, humble sphere of buttons, in the manner of the first production of *En Attendant Godot*, which the French playwright Jean Anouilh described as "Pascal's *Pensées* as played by the Fratellini clowns" (qtd in McManus 74). Shirley contemplates a heap of clothing on her bed which includes unmatched stockings knotted together (a modest attempt to reorder disorder) and coats she cannot wear because the buttons have been removed at the cleaner's. As she collects her thoughts for her confessional letter to Philippe (which Gallant will blend with speech, thought, and narration), she encounters a modern version of ancient Greek *anagnorisis*, in which an inventory of her belongings leads to an access of knowledge, of the self and the world:

> More than half the garments she owned were useless because some part of them had gone astray. Here was a green silk dress with seven tiny buttonholes

> at the back of the neck, and five of the buttons issuing. Somewhere in Paris existed a shop where they would match the silk – perhaps take a sliver from the hem. Would it not be simpler to give the dress away to Renata, thus transferring the problem? No, she remembered; the errand is everything. If I conquer the errand I subdue life. (*FGT* 183–84)

One pauses at the sweeping statement, "the errand is everything," which raises the petty to the grand. One glance to the left of the statement ("remembered") enlightens us: this is a lesson Shirley has been taught by her White Clown and endeavours to apply. The heroic verbs which follow (conquer/subdue) form a tight chiasmus (with errand/life) in a double collision in which the incongruous match "conquer/errand" interlaces with the incongruous equation and interchangeability of "errand" with "life." The chiasmatic wrenching houses the structural irony, in which the implicit authorial voice invites us to distance ourselves from the unreliable focalizer, the "I" of the free direct speech-thought, so eager to please the going point of view. The plan of action Shirley then sets up for herself gestures once more to Beckett's *Waiting for Godot* (also evoked in my analysis of "When We Were Nearly Young"), namely its caricature of life reduced to its essential banality.

> I shall take a bus or a taxi to this shop after finding out where it is, if such a shop exists. In the meantime, the dress will be hanging in a non-season, between the summer and the winter clothes. One day the shop will ring me and say the buttons are ready. I shall cross Paris once again and collect the buttons and sew them on, providing I have found thread the same shade of green. That is what growing older is all about; that is what the movement of time means. (*FGT* 184)

The copious list of future tenses enacts a fullness on the page overset by an ontological emptiness. *Is that all there is*, Shirley seems to ask, as does Beckett's Gogo or Estragon (French for Tarragon) in both acts I and II of *Godot*. In our material-minded world, is there a point to it all?

Like Beckett (and Eliot), Gallant does not presume to know all about destiny, but she can tell us a great deal about buttons. Shirley's buttons are Beckett's carrots, turnips, and radishes, which actualize making do as well as doing. Eating is one of the acts which help to pass the time as we wait (for Godot, for the shop to call, for the right shade of thread), just as rebelling against or resigning oneself to the root vegetable which happens to be available interrogates free will and what it can achieve (if, like Shirley's shop, it exists), as well as the issue of character, temperament, or nature. This brings us back to the question of two kinds of people, those who match buttons and "tread on people's lives, and the others" (*HT* 280). Shirley draws up an exhaustive list of button-matchers, which includes her mother and Mrs. Castle, her husband Philippe and the husband who died, her mother-in-law and sister-in-law, as well as Renata, M. and Mme Maurel, and yes, Marcel Proust. Everybody except Claudie and herself – with Claudie thinking Shirley is a button-matcher, too, and wanting to be like her, while Shirley wants to "be like Philippe" (184). Shirley determines to conform and start a new life, to "*become* thrifty and careful," to make herself plain and plausible, and to keep her confession short (184). She naturally does not, and the story spirals back to her mother's and Mrs. Castle's earlier advice to be and do just such things, and also ahead in multiple, lengthy, interlacing digressions.

Like Peter in "Ice Wagon" (which also distances itself from the Sartrean existential positioning that plays down how one's historically conditioned habitat limits the self's space of possibilities), Shirley *does not become; she is*. And what is she; what does she stand for, if anything? If something, it is difficult to define. Perhaps a celebration of individualism. Perhaps – also floating in "Ice Wagon" and "The Fenton Child" – a belief in serendipity rather than discipline and authority as the means to negotiate our place in the world, in a universe in which "*we have been abandoned*" (*FGT* 44, original stress). For there is no reason why we "shouldn't have a fairly good time" provided we make up our minds "not to be happy" (Wharton qtd in *FGT* epigraph).

This final series of close readings (in a left-field conclusion which complements the left-field introduction) demonstrate the aerial view and moral vision of *the ironist drawing on a sublime clowning tradition* reaching both back to Shakespeare's Fool and out to the visual arts (notably the contemporary clown caricatures of Gen Paul, Georges Rouault, and Bernard Buffet, some comic, some grimacing). The analyses also point to the place Gallant holds on the international scene, via that historical sense which Eliot argued makes a writer acutely conscious of her place in time, of her contemporaneity (Eliot, *The Sacred Wood*). Grappling with a dialectic between metamorphosis and continuity, Gallant chews up or spits out (Gallant, "Style" 37), evaluating both monuments and novelty, constantly readjusting the relations of her works with the whole. She engages with the permanent and the transient unexplainable by historical circumstances, displaying Eliot's lauded "sense of the timeless as well as of the temporal and of the timeless and of the temporal together" (Eliot, *The Sacred Wood* 72). Mavis even goes beyond the early modernist's wish for authors to write as if "the whole of the literature of Europe from Homer and within it the whole of the literature of his country has a simultaneous existence and composes a simultaneous order"

(Eliot, *The Sacred Wood* 72). She notably breaks out of the strictures of "literature" and of "country," to occupy as I have shown the roomier territories of culture and of language.[9] Gallant provides us with an anatomy of human existence which engages with entomological motifs central to works ranging from Shakespeare's *King Lear* with its chiasmatic equivalence of wanton boys and gods (the treaders) vs flies and humans (the others) and Mansfield's equally fierce "The Fly," to Kafka's tragicomic *Metamorphosis* and Beckett's absurd *Waiting for Godot,* whose clowns have absorbed Samsabeetle's lesson. As Estragon and Vladimir repeatedly remark in a quasi-refrain which houses a philosophical manifesto in sync with Gallant's: "no use struggling;" "no use wriggling." In affinity with her modernist contemporaries, Gallant's stance leans to a comic abstraction which encompasses the dark, as she grapples with who is right or wrong regarding what matters, in what amounts to a painterly, poignant *vanitas.*

---

9 I have notably drawn attention to her statement that she considered herself "a writer in the English language" (Gallant in Hancock 61).

Works Cited

The following print and non-print categories have porous borders, and any attempted classifications reveal themselves to be slippery. Certain cases of borderblur are designated by asterisks.

Film & Stage

Allen, Woody, dir. *Annie Hall*, 1977. Screenplay: Woody Allen, Marshall Brickman. Cinematography: Gordon Willis. Music: Artie Butler. Film.

Bergman, Ingmar, dir. *The Seventh Seal*, 1957 (premiered at the Cannes Film Festival). Screenplay: Ingmar Bergman. Cinematography: Gunnar Fischer. Music: Erik Nordgren. Film.

– *Through a Glass Darkly*, 1961. Cinematography: Sven Nykqvist. Music: Erik Nordgren. Film.

– *Wild Strawberries*, 1957. Cinematography: Gunnar Fischer. Music: Erik Nordgren. Film.

Bresson, Robert, dir. *Launcelot du Lac* [*Lancelot of the Lake*], 1974 (premiered at the Cannes Film Festival). Screenplay: Robert Bresson. Cinematography: Pasqualino De Santis. Music: Philippe Sarde. Film.

– *Les Dames du bois de Boulogne* [*Ladies of the Park*], 1945. Screenplay: Robert Bresson, Jean Cocteau. Cinematography: Philippe Agostini. Music: Jean-Jacques Grünenwald. Film.

Clouzot, Henri-Georges, dir. *Le Mystère Picasso* [*The Picasso Mystery*],* 1955. Cinematography: Claude Renoir. Music: Georges Auric. Sound: Joseph de Bretagne. Documentary film.

Coen, Joel, dir. *Barton Fink*, 1991 (released in France). Screenplay: Ethan Coen, Joel Coen. Cinematography: Roger Deakins. Music: Carter Burwell. Producer: Ethan Coen. Film.

CRONENBERG, DAVID, dir. *The Fly,** 1986. Based on the short story "The Fly" (1957) by George Langelaan. Screenplay: Charles Edward Pogue, David Cronenberg. Cinematographer: Marc Irwin. Special effects designer: Chris Walas. Music: Howard Shore (who subsequently composed the score for the 2008 opera). Film.

DIETERLE, WILLIAM, dir. *The Hunchback of Notre Dame*, 1939. Based on the novel *Notre Dame de Paris* [*The Hunchback of Notre Dame*] (1831) by Victor Hugo. Adaptation: Bruno Frank. Cinematography: Joseph H. August. Music: Alfred Newman. Sound: John Aalberg. Film.

DVONCH, FREDERICK, dir. *The Sound of Music*, 1956.* Broadway musical comedy. Story: Maria von Trapp. Music: Richard Rodgers. Lyrics: Oscar Hammerstein. Set design: Oliver Smith. Stage.

FELLINI, FEDERICO, dir. *Roma*, 1972. Story: Federico Fellini, Bernardino Zapponi. Cinematotography: Giuseppe Rotunno. Music: Nino Rota, Carlo Savina. Film.

FESCOURT, HENRI, dir. *Les Misérables*, 1925. Based on the novel *Les Misérables* (1862) by Victor Hugo. Screenplay: Henri Fescourt. Silent film.

JULIAN, RUPERT, dir. (with Lon Chaney and Edward Sedgwick, uncredited). *The Phantom of the Opera*, 1925. Based on the novel *Le Fantôme de l'Opéra* [*The Phantom of the Opera*] (1910) by Gaston Leroux. Cinematography: Milton Bridenbecker, Virgil Miller, Charles Van Enger. Accompanying musical score: Gustav Hinrichs. Silent film.

KELLY, GENE, and STANLEY DONEN, dir. *Singin' in the Rain.** 1952. Musical comedy. Choreography: Gene Kelly and Stanley Donen. Music: Lennie Hayton, Nacio Herb Brown. Lyrics: Arthur Freed. Film.

LÉGER, FERNAND, dir. (with Dudley Murphy). *Ballet mécanique* [*The Mechanical Ballet*], 1924. Written by Fernand Léger. Cinematography: Man Ray, Dudley Murphy. Original accompanying musical score: George Antheil. Short silent film.

MANKIEWITZ, JOSEPH, dir. *Guys and Dolls,** 1950. Broadway musical comedy; 1955 screen adaptation. Choreography: Michael Kidd. Music and lyrics: Frank Loesser. Set design: Oliver Smith. 1955. Film.

MAYAKOVSKY, VLADIMIR. *The Bedbug*. First performed and published 1929. *The Bedbug and Selected Poetry*. Editing and introduction: Patricia Blake. Trans: Max Hayward and George Reavey. Bloomington, IN: Indiana UP/ First Midland Book edition, 1975. Play.

MURNAU, F.W., dir. *Faust — A German Folktale*, 1926. Written by Hans Kyser, based on Johann Wolfgang von Goethe's play *Faust, Part One* (1808). Cinematography: Carl Hoffmann. Accompanying musical score (in the premiere): Werner Richard Heymann. Silent film.

– *Nosferatu*, 1922 (in France). Unauthorized adaptation of the novel *Dracula* (1897) by Bram Stoker. Screenplay: Henrik Galeen. Cinematography: F.W.

Murnau, Günther Krampf (uncredited). Musical score: Hans Erdmann. Silent film.

Parade, a collaborative Cubist ballet.* First performed 1917. Story: Jean Cocteau. Musical score: Erik Satie. Set and costume design: Pablo Picasso. Choreography: Leonid Massine.

Pinter, Harold. *The Caretaker*. First performed and published 1960. London: Encore Publishing Co. Play.

Preminger, Otto, dir. *Porgy and Bess*, 1959. Operetta/folk opera. Screen adaptation from the 1935 Broadway musical staged by Rouben Mamoulian. Music: George Gershwin. Lyrics: Ira Gershwin and DuBose Heyward. Cinematography: Leon Shamroy. Set design: Oliver Smith. Story: Dorothy and DuBose Heyward, based on their 1927 play *Porgy*.

Reed, Carol, dir. *The Third Man*,* 1949. Novella and screenplay by Graham Greene. Musical score and performance: Anton Karas. Cinematography: Robert Krasker. Starring Orson Welles, Joseph Cotten. Film.

Robbins, Jerome, and Robert Wise, dir. *West Side Story*,* 1957. Broadway musical comedy; 1962 screen adaptation. Choreography: Jerome Robbins. Music: Leonard Bernstein, Irwin Kostal. Lyrics: Stephen Sondheim. Set design: Oliver Smith. Film.

Sjöström, Victor, dir. *The Phantom Carriage* [*Körkarlen*]. 1921. Story: Selma Lagerlöf, based on her 1912 novel *Körkarlen*. Cinematographer: Julius Jaenzon. Silent film.

Tati, Jacques, dir. *Jour de fête* [*The Big Day*],* 1949. Story: Jacques Tati, Henri Marquet, René Wheeler. Screenplay: Jacques Tati, Henri Marquet. Cinematography: Jacques Mercanton. Music: Jean Yatove. Film.

– *Mon Oncle* [*My Uncle*], 1958. Story: Jacques Tati. Cinematography: Jean Bourgoin. Music: Alain Romans, Franck Barcellini. Film.

– *Parade*, 1973. Story: Jacques Tati. Cinematography: Jean Badal, Gunnar Fischer. Music: Charles Dumont. Film.

– *Playtime*, 1967. Story: Jacques Tati, Jacques Lagrange. English dialogue: Art Buchwald. Cinematography: Jean Badal. Music: Francis Lemarque. Film.

– *Trafic*, 1971. Story: Jacques Tati, Jacques Lagrange. Cinematography: Edouard van den Enden, Marcel Weiss. Music: Charles Dumont. Film.

– *Les Vacances de M. Hulot* [*Mr. Hulot's Holiday*],* 1953. Story: Jacques Tati, Henri Marquet. Cinematography: Jacques Mercanton, Jean Mousselle. Music: Alain Romans. Film.

Tornatore, Giuseppe, dir. *Cinema Paradiso*, 1988. Story and screenplay: Giuseppe Tornatore. Music: Ennio Morricone. Cinematography: Blasco Giurato. Film.

Webber, Andrew Lloyd. *Cats*,* musical comedy, stage premiere 1981 (London West End). Story based on T.S. Eliot's *Old Possum's Book of Practical Cats*, adapted by Andrew Lloyd Webber. Dir. Trevor Nunn. Music composed by A.L. Webber. Lyrics: T.S. Eliot, Trevor Nunn. 1998 film (direct-to-video).

WORSLEY, WALLACE, dir., *The Hunchback of Notre Dame,* 1923. Based on the novel *Notre Dame de Paris* [*The Hunchback of Notre Dame*] (1831) by Victor Hugo. Adaptation: Perley Poore Sheehan. Cinematography: Robert Newhard. Silent film.

Music

ANTHEIL, GEORGE. *Mechanical Ballet for Pianos, Percussion, and Airplane Engine.* Composed in 1924 (to accompany Fernand Léger's short film, *Ballet mécanique,* but overlong). Premiered in Paris in 1926.

ARMSTRONG, LOUIS and His Hot Five. *West End Blues.* Composed by Joe "King" Oliver and Earl "Fatha" Hines. 78 RPM released 28 June 1928.

BACH, JOHANN SEBASTIAN. *The Well-Tempered Clavier*, BMW 846–93. Twenty-four preludes paired with 24 fugues in all major and minor keys, composed for solo keyboard. Published in two volumes: 1722, 1744.

BARTÓK, BÉLA. *Allegro barbaro,* solo piano piece. Composed in 1911. Score published in Vienna in 1918. Premiered in Budapest by the composer in 1921 (but allegedly first performed in Kecskemét, Hungary, in 1913).

– *String Quartet No. 2 in A Minor*, Sz. 67/BB 75 (op. 17). Composed 1916–17. Premiered in Budapest in 1918. Published 1920.

BEETHOVEN, LUDWIG VAN. *Grand (Great) Fugue* in B-flat, op. 133, single movement composition for string quartet, 1827.

GERSHWIN, GEORGE. *Rhapsody in Blue.** Symphonic jazz for solo piano and jazz band, banjo, and strings. Composed and first performed in New York in 1924. Published 1924.

HENRY, PIERRE. *Le Microphone bien tempéré* [*The Well-Tempered Microphone*], 1951. A set of electroacoustic pieces for mechanical instruments composed 1950–51. Broadcast in an RTF Paris IV radio series April–May 1951.

MILHAUD, DARIUS. *La Bien-Aimée* [*The Beloved*], op. 101.* One-act ballet score for orchestra and player piano. Composed and first performed in 1928 in Paris.

PURCELL, HENRY. *Ode to St. Cecilia*, Z 328, 1692. Composition for mixed choir, soloists, and orchestra. Composed, first performed, and published the same year.

STRAVINSKY, IGOR. *Le Sacre du printemps* [*The Rite of Spring*], 1913.* Musical score for ballet. Composed and first performed in Paris, 1913. Choreography: Vaslav Nijinsky.

– *The Rake's Progress*, 1951 (premiered in Venice).* Opera with a libretto by W.H. Auden and Chester Kallman, inhabited by William Hogarth's set of paintings of the same name (1732–4).

VARÈSE, EDGARD. *Ionisation.* Composition for percussion ensemble. Composed in France 1929–31; world premiere in New York 1933. Published 1934.

Visual Art

AERTSEN, PIETER. *A Meat Stall with the Holy Family Giving Alms*, 1551. Oil on panel. North Carolina Museum of Art, Amsterdam.

BACON, FRANCIS. *Crucifixion,* 1965. Oil on canvas triptych. Bayerische Staatsgemäldesammlungen Pinakothek der Moderne, Munich.

BUECKELAER, JOACHIM. *The Butcher Shop*, 1568. Oil on wood. Museo Nazionale di Capodimente, Naples.

COURBET, GUSTAVE. *Les Demoiselles des bords de la Seine,* 1857. Oil on canvas. Musée du Petit Palais, Paris.

– *Un enterrement à Ornan*. 1849–1850. Oil on canvas. Musée d'Orsay, Paris.

DELACROIX, EUGÈNE. *Les Femmes d'Alger dans leur appartement,* 1834. Oil on canvas. Musée du Louvre, Paris.

DELAUNAY, SONIA. *Le Bal Bullier,* 1913. Oil on canvas. Musée National d'Art Moderne. Centre Georges Pompidou, Paris.

– *Prismes électriques*, 1914. Oil on canvas. Centre Georges Pompidou, Paris.

DUCHAMP, MARCEL. *Nu descendant un escalier*, 1912. Oil on canvas. Philadelphia Museum of Art.

FILDES, LUKE. *The Doctor,* 1887. Oil on canvas. Tate Britain, London.

HOLBEIN, HANS the Younger. *The Ambassadors*. 1533. Oil on oak. National Gallery, London.

MONET, CLAUDE. *Impression: Soleil levant*, 1872. Oil on canvas. Musée Marmottan Monet, Paris.

MUNCH, EDVARD. *The Scream*. 1893. In four versions and lithograph stone. Oil, tempera, pastel and crayon on cardboard. National Gallery and Munch Museum, Oslo.

PICASSO, PABLO. *Les Demoiselles d'Avignon,* 1907. Oil on canvas. Museum of Modern Art, New York.

– *Les Demoiselles au bord de la Seine, d'après Courbet*, 1950. Oil on plywood. Kunstmuseum, Basel.

– *Portrait of Dora Maar*, 1937. Oil on canvas. Musée Picasso, Paris.

REMBRANDT, *Flayed Ox*, 1657. Oil on wood panel. Musée du Louvre, Paris.

– *The Supper at Emmaus*, 1628. Oil on wood panel. Musée Jacquemart-André, Paris.

– *Pilgrims at Emmaus* or *The Supper at Emmaus*, 1648. Oil on mahogany. Musée du Louvre, Paris.

SANYU. *Pot de fleurs,* 1930. Oil on canvas. Private collection.

SHEELER, CHARLES. *Wheels,* 1939. Gelatin silver print. J. Paul Getty Museum, Los Angeles.

SOUTINE, CHAÏM. *Le Boeuf écorché*, 1924. Oil on canvas. Musée de Grenoble.

STELLA, JOSEPH. *Old Brooklyn Bridge,* 1941. Oil on canvas. Museum of Fine Arts, Boston.

TURNER, J.M.W. *The Fighting Temeraire,* 1839. Oil on canvas. National Gallery, London.

Text (Print/Digital)[1]

Works by Mavis Gallant

"Afterword." *Paris Stories*. New York: NYRB, 2002. 365–78.

The Collected Stories. 1996. (Simultaneously published in Canada as *The Selected Stories of Mavis Gallant* by McClelland & Stewart, Toronto, and in Great Britain in 1997 as *The Selected Stories* by Bloomsbury, London.) Introduction by Francine Prose. New York: Alfred A. Knopf/Penguin Random House and London: Everyman's Library, 2016.

The Cost of Living: Early and Uncollected Stories. Introduction by Jhumpa Lahiri. London: Bloomsbury, 2009.

The End of the World and Other Stories. Introduction by Robert Weaver. Toronto: McClelland & Stewart/NCL, 1974.

A Fairly Good Time. 1970. New York: NYRB, 2016. 1–273.

From the Fifteenth District. 1979. Toronto: McClelland & Stewart/Emblem Editions, 2001.

Going Ashore. Introduction by Alberto Manguel. Toronto: McClelland & Stewart, 2009.

Green Water, Green Sky. 1959. In *A Fairly Good Time*. New York: NYRB, 2016. 275–376.

Home Truths. 1981. Toronto: McClelland & Stewart, Emblem Editions, 2001.

"The Hunger Diaries: Mavis Gallant on Starving and Writing in Spain." *The New Yorker*, 9 July 2012: 48–53. http://www.newyorker.com/magazine/2012/07/09/the-hunger-diaries).

"An Introduction." *Home Truths*. 1981. Toronto: Stoddart, 1992. xi–xxii.

Interview with Daphne Kalotay. *Mavis Gallant, The Art of Fiction* no. 160. *The Paris Review* 153 (Winter 1999). https://www.theparisreview.org/interviews/838/mavis-gallant-the-art-of-fiction-no-160-mavis-gallant.

Interviews also listed under Dvořák, "When Language"; Hancock, "An Interview"; and Lahiri, "Useless Chaos."

Its Image on the Mirror – A Short Novel. In Gallant, *My Heart Is Broken*. 57–155.

Letter to Marta Dvořák, 11 October 1994.

Letter to Dvořák, 1 September 2002.

Letter to Dvořák, 3 May 2008.

Letter to Dvořák, 9 May 2009.

Letter to Dvořák, 19 May 2009.

"Mau to Lew: The Maurice Ravel–Lewis Carroll Friendship." *15 Years in Exile*. Toronto: Exile Editions, 1992. 15–19.

---

1 Writers of fiction mingle with critics, philosophers, and writers who double as theorists. Editions cited are often those in my own library, so more recent publications are available in many cases.

The Moslem Wife and Other Stories. Selected and with an afterword by Mordecai Richler. Toronto: McClelland & Stewart, 1994.

My Heart Is Broken: Eight Stories and a Novel. New York: Random House, 1964.

The Other Paris. Boston: Houghton Mifflin Company, 1956.

Overhead in a Balloon: Twelve Stories of Paris. New York: Random House, 1985.

"Paris Diary (1992)." *The New Yorker*, 24, 31 December, 2001: 102–3.

Paris Notebooks. Toronto: Macmillan of Canada, 1988.

Paris Stories. Introduced and compiled by Michael Ondaatje. New York: NYRB, 2002.

"Paris When It Shimmers." *New York Times*. 4 October 1987. http://www.nytimes.com/1987/10/04/magazine/paris-when-it-shimmers.html.

The Pegnitz Junction: A Novella and Five Short Stories. 1973. Toronto: Macmillan, 1988.

"Preface." *The Collected Stories of Mavis Gallant*. New York: Random House. ix–xix. New York: Alfred A. Knopf/London: Everyman's Library, 2016. 3–16.

"A Prix-view." *New York Times*, 20 October 1974: 46.

"The Pursuit of Pleasure." Rev. of *Secrets of the Flesh: A Life of Colette*, by Judith Thurman. *New York Times*, 17 October 1999. http://www.nytimes.com/1999/10/17/books/the-pursuit-of-pleasure.html.

"*Transparent Things* by Vladimir Nabokov." *New York Times Book Review*, 19 November 1972; repr. in Gallant, *Paris Notebooks*. 200–3.

Varieties of Exile. Ed. Russell Banks. New York: NYRB, 2003.

"What Is Style?" *Canadian Forum*, September 1982: 6, 37. Rpt in Gallant, *Paris Notebooks*. 176–9.

Other Works

Adams, James. "Gallant's Private Journals to Be Published in Canada, US." *The Globe and Mail*. 27 June 2012. https://www.theglobeandmail.com/arts/books-and-media/gallants-private-journals-to-be-published-in-canada-us/article4375337/. Updated 30 April 2018.

Adderson, Caroline. "Mavis Gallant, Amen." *Canadian Notes & Queries* 79 (Spring/Summer 2010): 78–80.

Adiga, Aravind. Interview with/Propos recueillis par Frédéric Joignot, "L'Inde démocratique, derrière les clichés." *Le Monde* 2, 16 May 2009. 40–7.

– *The White Tiger*. Noida, Uttar Pradesh: HarperCollins India, 2008.

Alcott, Louisa May. *Little Women*. 1868. New York: Barnes & Noble Classics Series, 2004.

Aristotle. *Poetics*. Trans. and introduction by Anthony Kenny. Oxford World's Classics. Oxford: Oxford UP, 2013.

Arnold, Matthew. "The Forsaken Merman." 1849. *Victorian Poetry and Poetics*, Ed. Walter E. Houghton and G. Robert Stange. 2nd ed. Boston: Houghton Mifflin, 1968. 420–1.

Atwood, Margaret. *The Edible Woman*. Toronto: McClelland & Stewart, 1969.

– *The Handmaid's Tale*. Toronto: McClelland & Stewart, 1985.

– *Life Before Man*. Toronto: McClelland & Stewart, 1979.

– "*What's So Funny? Notes on Canadian Humour.*" 1974. *This Magazine* 8.3: 24–7. Rpt in *Second Words: Selected Critical Prose*. Toronto: Anansi, 1982. 175–89.

Axmaker, Sean. "Playtime." www.tcm.com/tcmdb/title/813134/playtime/articles.html.

Ballantyne, Emily, Marta Dvořák, and Dean Irvine. *Translocated Modernisms: Paris and Other Lost Generations*. Ottawa: U of Ottawa P, 2016.

Bakhtin, Mikhaïl. *The Dialogic Imagination*. Ed. M. Holquist. Trans. C. Emerson and M. Holquist. Austin: U of Texas P, 1981.

Balzac, Honoré de. *Le Père Goriot*. 1832. Paris: Livre de poche, 2004.

Banks, Russell. "Introduction." *Varieties of Exile*, by Mavis Gallant. New York: NYRB, 2003. vii–xiii. Also titled *Montreal Stories*. Toronto: McClelland & Stewart, 2004. "Introduction," vii–xiii.

Barbour, Douglas. "Transformations of (the Language of) the Ordinary: Innovation in Recent Canadian Poetry." *Essays on Canadian Writing* 37 (Spring 1989): 30–64.

Barr, H.A., Jr. *Picasso, Fifty Years of His Art*. New York: Museum of Modern Art, 1946.

Barrie, J.M. *Peter Pan*. 1911. Oxford: Oxford UP, 2007.

Barthes, Roland. *La Chambre Claire, Note sur la photographie*. Paris: Collection Cahiers du Cinéma/ Gallimard, 1980.

– *Le Degré zéro de l'écriture*. 1953. Paris: Editions Points, 1972.

– *Essais critiques*. Paris: Seuil, 1964.

Bartók, Béla. *Levelek, Fényképek, Kéziratok, Kották*. Ed. János Demény. Budapest: Magyar Müvészeti Tanács, 1948.

Baudelaire, Charles. *Le Spleen de Paris: Petits poèmes en prose*. Paris: Flammarion, 1997.

Beckett, Samuel. *En Attendant Godot*. 1952 (first published in French); 1953 (premiered in Paris). *Waiting for Godot*. New York: Grove Press, 1954, 2011.

– *How It Is*. 1961 [originally *Comment C'est*]; 1963 [English self-translation]. New York: Grove Press, 1994.

– *More Pricks Than Kicks*. 1934. Richmond, London: Calder Publications, 1995.

– *Watt*. 1953. New York: Grove Press, 1959.

Benjamin, Walter. *On the Concept of History*. 1940. Trans. Dennis Redmond. http://www.marxists.org/reference/archive/benjamin/1940/history.htm.

– "The Storyteller." *Theory of the Novel: A Historical Approach*. Ed. Michael McKeon. Baltimore: Johns Hopkins UP, 2000. 77–93.

BERENDT, JOACHIM-ERNST. *Le grand livre du jazz*. Paris: Editions du rocher, 1994.

BESNER, NEIL. *The Light of Imagination: Mavis Gallant's Fiction*. Vancouver: U of British Columbia P, 1988.

– "Reading Muir, Asher, and Frazier: Three Gallant Characters in Postcolonial Time." *Tropes and Territories: Short Fiction, Postcolonial Readings, Canadian Writing in Context*. Ed. M. Dvořák and W.H. New. Montreal/Kingston: McGill-Queen's UP, 2007. 155–63.

BHABHA, HOMI. *The Location of Culture*. London and New York: Routledge, 1994.

Bhagavad Gita (part of *The Mahabharata*). Trans. Shanta Tumkur and Vrindar Nabar. Wordsworth Classics, 1997.

BLAKE, WILLIAM. *Blake's Poetry and Designs*. Selected and edited by Mary Lynn Johnson and John E. Grant. New York: Norton, 2008.

BLOM, ERIC, ed. *Mozart's Letters*. Selected from *The Letters of Mozart and His Family*. Introduction by Eric Blom; trans. and annotated by Emily Anderson, 1938. Harmondworth: Penguin Books, 1956.

BOETHIUS. *The Consolation of Philosophy*. Trans. Victor Watts. London: Penguin, 1999.

BORCHERT, TILL-HOLGER, and Julien Chapuis. *Van Eyck to Dürer: The Influence of Early Netherlandish Painting on European Art, 1430–1530*. London: Thames & Hudson, 2011.

BOYAGODA, RANDY. "In Paris with Mavis Gallant, Writer." *The Walrus*, 12 July 2007. https://thewalrus.ca/in-paris-with-mavis-gallant-writer/.

BRESSON, ROBERT. *Bresson on Bresson: Interviews 1943–1983*. Ed. Mylène Bresson. New York: NYRB, 2016. Trans. by Anna Moschovakis from *Bresson par Bresson: Entretiens 1943–1983*, rassemblés par Mylène Bresson. Paris: Flammarion, 2013.

– *Notes on the Cinematograph*. Trans. Jonathan Griffin. New York: NYRB, 2016.

BRETON, ANDRÉ. *Manifestes du surréalisme* (containing *Manifeste du surréalisme*, 1924, and *Second manifeste du surréalisme*, 1930, and *Prolégomènes à un troisième manifeste du surréalisme ou non*, 1942). Paris: Gallimard nrf, Collection Idées, 1972.

BRYDON, DIANA, and Marta Dvořák. "Introduction: Negotiating Meaning in Changing Times." *Crosstalk: Canadian and Global Imaginaries in Dialogue*. Ed. D. Brydon and M. Dvořák. Waterloo: Wilfrid Laurier UP, 2012. 1–19.

BUCKNELL, BRAD. *Literary Modernism and Musical Aesthetics: Pater, Pound, Joyce, and Stein*. Cambridge: Cambridge UP, 2001.

BURNETT, FRANCES HODGSON. *The Secret Garden*. New York: Frederick A. Stokes Co., 1911.

CARR, EMILY. *The Book of Small*, 1942. Toronto: Irwin, 1986.

CAUGHIE, PAMELA, ed. *Disciplining Modernism*. London: Palgrave Macmillan, 2010.

CHAUCER, GEOFFREY. *The Canterbury Tales*. 1387–1400. In *The Works of Geoffrey Chaucer*. Ed. F.N. Robinson. 2nd ed. Boston: Houghton Mifflin, 1961. 17–265.

– *Troilus and Criseyde*. Circa 1380–1385. Trans. into modern English by Nevill Coghill. Harmondsworth: Penguin, 1971.

CHEKHOV, ANTON. *The Kiss and Other Stories*. Trans. and introduced by Ronald Wilks. London: Penguin, 1982.

CHION, MICHEL. *Jacques Tati*. Cahiers du Cinéma. Collection "Auteurs." Paris: Seuil, 1987.

CHRISTIE, AGATHA. *The Murder of Roger Ackroyd*. 1926. London: HarperCollins, 2013.

CITRON, PIERRE. *Bartók*. Paris: Seuil, 1994.

CLEMENT, LESLEY D. *Learning to Look: A Visual Response to Mavis Gallant's Fiction*. Montreal/Kingston: McGill-Queen's UP, 2000.

COCTEAU, JEAN. Jean Cocteau. Interview by William Fifield. *The Art of Fiction* No. 34. *The Paris Review* (Summer–Fall 1964). http://www.theparisreview.org/interviews/4485/jean-cocteau-the-art-of-fiction-no-34-jean-cocteau.

COETZEE, J.M. "Emperor of Nostalgia." Rev. of *The Collected Stories of Joseph Roth*. *New York Review of Books*, 28 February 2002. http://www.nybooks.com/articles/2002/02/28/emperor-of-nostalgia/.

– *Waiting for the Barbarians*. 1980. London: Penguin Books, 1999.

COHEN, MATT. "Notes on Realism in Modern English-Canadian Fiction." *Canadian Literature* 100 (1984): 65–71.

COLE, OLIVIA. "To thaw and feel: Frozen emotions and lost souls in a near-perfect collection of stories." *Financial Times*, 12 December 2009: 19.

COLERIDGE, SAMUEL TAYLOR. *The Rime of the Ancient Mariner*. 1798. https://rpo.library.utoronto.ca/poems/rime-ancient-mariner-text-1834.

CONRAD, JOSEPH. *The Heart of Darkness*. 1899. London: Penguin Classics, 2007.

CRAFT, ROBERT. Robert Craft's *Stravinsky: Chronicle of a Friendship*. New York: Alfred A. Knopf, 1972.

CRONENBERG, DAVID. "The Beetle and the Fly." *The Paris Review*. 17 January 2014. Blog. https://www.theparisreview.org/blog/2014/01/17/the-beetle-and-the-fly/.

CULLER, JONATHAN. *Structuralist Poetics: Structuralism, Linguistics, and the Study of Literature*. London: Routledge, 1975.

DANTE ALIGHIERI. *The Inferno* (*The Divine Comedy* 1). 1320. Trans. Anthony M. Esolen. New York: Modern Library, 2003.

DANTO, ARTHUR C. *Beyond the Brillo Box: The Visual Arts in Post-historical Perspective*. Berkeley: U of California P, 1992.

DAVEY, FRANK. "Thinking on Poetics." *Open Letter* Twelfth Series, No. 8, *Poetics and Public Culture* (Spring 2006): 174–8.

DAVIES, ROBERTSON. "The Novels of Mavis Gallant." Mavis Gallant special issue, *Canadian Fiction Magazine* 28 (1978): 69–73.

DELESALLE, CATHERINE. "Dwelling In-Between: Rituals and Jazz as Reconcilable Opposites in "The Forest Path to the Spring." *Malcolm Lowry's Poetics of Space*. Ed. Richard J. Lane and Miguel Mota. Ottawa: U of Ottawa P, 2016. 129–4.

DERRIDA, JACQUES. "La structure, le signe et le jeu dans le discours des sciences humaines." *L'Ecriture et la différence*. Paris: Seuil, 1967. 409–28.

DESAI, ANITA. *In Custody*. 1984. London: Vintage, 1999.

DOBOZY, TAMAS. "'Designed Anarchy' in Mavis Gallant's *The Moslem Wife and Other Stories*." *Canadian Literature* 158 (Autumn 1998): 65–88.

DORRIS, MICHAEL. "A Gallant Storyteller: *The Collected Stories of Mavis Gallant*, by Mavis Gallant." *The Los Angeles Times*, 6 October 1996. articles .latimes.com/1996-10-06/books/bk-52256_1_mavis-gallant.

DOS PASSOS, JOHN. *Manhattan Transfer*. 1925. London: Penguin Classics, 2000.

DUPRIEZ, BERNARD. *A Dictionary of Literary Devices: Gradus, A–Z*. Trans. and adapted by Albert W. Halsall (from *Gradus: Les procédés liitéraires* [Paris: Christian Bourgois, 1984]), Toronto: U of Toronto P, 1991.

DVOŘÁK, MARTA. "Alice Munro's 'Lovely Tricks' from *Dance of the Happy Shades* to *Hateship, Friendship, Courtship, Loveship, Marriage*." Alice Munro special issue, *Open Letter* 11.9 (Fall 2003)/12.1 (Winter 2004): 55–77.

– "Cows and Configurations in Carr's *The Book of Small*." *Tropes and Territories: Short Fiction, Postcolonial Readings, Canadian Writing in Context*. Ed. M. Dvořák and W.H. New. Montreal/Kingston: McGill-Queen's UP, 2007. 134–154.

– "Disappearance and 'the Vision Multiplied': Writing as Performance." *Carol Shields and the Extra-Ordinary*. Ed. M. Dvořák and Manina Jones. Montreal/ Kingston: McGill-Queen's UP, 2007. 223–37.

– "Frame-breaking: 'Neither separate nor complete nor very important.'" Janet Frame special issue, *Commonwealth Essays and Studies* 33.2 (Spring 2011): 137–49.

– "Like a Spoonful of Water in a River: An Appreciation of Mavis Gallant." *Translocated Modernisms*. Ed. E. Ballantyne, M. Dvořák, and D. Irvine. Ottawa: U of Ottawa P, 2016. 23–41.

– "Mavis Gallant's Fiction: Taking the (Rhetorical) Measure of the Turning Point." *Varieties of Exile: New Essays on Mavis Gallant*. Ed. Nicole Côté and Peter Sabor. New York: Peter Lang, 2002. 63–74.

– "Le Montréal de Mavis Gallant: Les pouvoirs du je/u." *Etudes Canadiennes* 64 (2008): 187–94.

– "The Other Side of Dailiness: Alice Munro's Melding of Realism and Romance in *Dance of the Happy Shades*." *Etudes anglaises* 67.3 (July–Sept. 2014): 302–17.

– "When Language Is a Delicate Timepiece: Mavis Gallant in Conversation with Marta Dvořák." *The Journal of Commonwealth Literature* 44.3 (2009): 3–22.

DVOŘÁK, MARTA, and W.H. NEW, eds. *Tropes and Territories: Short Fiction, Postcolonial Readings, Canadian Writing in Context.* Montreal/Kingston: McGill-Queen's UP, 2007.

EAGLETON, TERRY. 1983. *Literary Theory: An Introduction.* Oxford: Blackwell, 2nd ed., 2004.

ECO, UMBERTO. *The Aesthetics of Chaosmos. The Middle Ages of James Joyce.* Trans. Ellen Esrock. Cambridge, MA: Harvard UP, 1989.

– *Art et beauté dans l'esthétique médiévale.* Trans. Maurice Javion. Paris: Grasset, 1997.

– *The Role of the Reader: Explorations in the Semiotics of Texts. Bloomington*: Indiana UP, 1984.

ELIOT, T.S. *Collected Poems, 1909–1962.* London: Faber & Faber, 1975.

– *Old Possum's Book of Practical Cats.* 1939. London/Boston: Faber & Faber, 1987.

– *The Sacred Wood: Essays on Poetry and Criticism.* 1921. New York: Macmillan, 1972.

– *The Use of Poetry and the Use of Criticism.* London: Faber & Faber, 1964.

– *The Waste Land.* 1922. *Collected Poems, 1909–1962.* London: Faber & Faber, 1975. 63–105.

"T.S. Eliot, the Poet, Is Dead in London at 76." *New York Times*, 5 January 1965, n.pag. http://www.nytimes.com/books/97/04/20/reviews/eliot-obit.html.

ENRIGHT, D. J. *The Alluring Problem: An Essay on Irony*, Oxford: Oxford UP, 1986.

Everyman and Medieval Miracle Plays. Ed. A.C. Cawley. London: Dent/New York: Dutton, Everyman's Library, 1967.

FABRE, MICHEL. "'Orphans' Progress,' Reader's Progress: Voice and Understatement in Mavis Gallant's Stories." *Gaining Ground: European Critics on Canadian Literature.* Ed. Robert Kroetsch and Reingard M. Nischik. Vol. 6. Shirley Neuman, gen ed. Edmonton: NeWest Press, 1985. 150–60.

FAULKNER, WILLIAM. "Faulkner at Virginia." Tape T-145a, length 33:02. Rouss Hall, 12 May 1958. http://faulkner.lib.virginia.edu/display/wfaudio30_1.

FISCHER-DIESKAU, DIETRICH. *The Fischer-Dieskau Book of Lieder.** Chosen and introduced by D. Fischer-Dieskau with English trans. by George Bird and Richard Stokes. New York: Alfred A. Knopf, 1977.

FLANNER, JANET (Genêt). *Paris Journal, 1944–1955.* 1965. Ed. William Shawn. Vol. 1. New York: Harcourt Brace Jovanovich, 1988.

– *Paris Journal, 1965–1970.* 1971. Ed. William Shawn.Vol. 3. New York: Harcourt Brace Jovanovich, 1988.

FLAUBERT, GUSTAVE. *Le gueuloir, perles de correspondances de Gustave Flaubert.* Selected by Thierry Gillyboeuf. Illustrator Daniel Maja. Paris: Le Castor Astral, 2016.

– *Oeuvres complètes et Annexes*. Paris: Arvensa, 2014.

Frame, Janet. *Faces in the Water*. 1961. London: The Women's Press. 1980.

– *Janet Frame Stories and Poems: The Lagoon and Other Stories; The Pocket Mirror.* 1951. Auckland: Random House New Zealand, 2004.

Francastel, Pierre. *Histoire de la peinture*. Paris: Gonthier, 1983.

Fried, Michael. *Flaubert's "Gueuloir": On "Madame Bovary" and "Salammbô."* New Haven and London: Yale UP, 2012.

Frye, Northrop. *The Secular Scripture: A Study of the Structure of Romance*. Cambridge, MA: Harvard UP, 1976.

Fürst, Lilian R. *Fictions of Romantic Irony*. Cambridge, MA: Harvard UP, 1984.

Gavron, Jeremy. "The Highest Form of Flattery? In Praise of Plagiarism." *The Guardian*, 24 February 2018. https:://www.theguardian.com/books/2018/feb/24/straightjacket-originality-homage-plagiarism.

Genette, Gérard. *Palimpsestes: La littérature au second degré*. Paris: Seuil, 1982.

– *Seuils*. Paris: Seuil, 1987.

Gerlach, John. *Toward the End: Closure and Structure in the American Short Story*. Tuscaloosa: U of Alabama P, 1985.

Gide, André. *Les Faux-Monnayeurs*. 1925. Paris: Gallimard, 1972.

Godard, Barbara. "Modalities of the Edge, Towards a Semiotics of Irony: The Case of Mavis Gallant." Special Gallant issue, *Essays on Canadian Writing* 42 (Winter 1990): 72–101.

Godin, Christian. *La Totalité réalisée: Les Arts et la littérature*. Vol. 4 of *La Totalité*. Seyssel: Editions Champ Vallon, 1997.

Gold, Herbert. "Surrounded by Small Hearts." Rev. of *Hotel Savoy*, "Fallmerayer the Stationmaster" and "The Bust of the Emperor." *New York Times Book Review*, 8 February 1987. http://www.nytimes.com/books/99/10/31/specials/roth-savoy.html?_r=1.

Goodman, Nelson. *Languages of Art*. Indianapolis: Hackett Publishing, 1976.

– *Ways of Worldmaking*. Indianapolis: Hackett Publishing, 1978.

Grant, Judith Skelton. "Mavis Gallant (1922–)." *Canadian Writers and Their Works*. Ed. Robert Lecker, Jack David, Ellen Quigley. Intro. George Woodcock. Toronto: ECW, 1989. 22–80.

Greimas, Algirdas Julien. *Sémantique structurale*. Paris: Larousse, 1966.

Grice, Herbert Paul. *Studies in the Way of Words*. Cambridge, MA: Harvard UP, 1991.

Halloran, Dennis Hugh. *The Classical Landscape Paintings of J.M.W. Turner*. Madison: U of Wisconsin P, 1970.

Hamon, Philippe. "Clausules," *Poétique* 24 (November 1975): 495–526.

Hancock, Geoffrey. "An Interview with Mavis Gallant." Special Gallant issue, *Canadian Fiction Magazine* 28 (1978): 18–67.

Hegel, G.W.F. *Aesthetics: Lectures on Fine Art*. 1835. Trans. T.M. Knox. Vol. 1. Oxford: Oxford UP, 2010.

HEIDEGGER, MARTIN. *Being and Time*. 1927 (German edition); 1962 (first English edition). Trans. John Macquarrie and Edward Robinson. Oxford: Blackwell Publishing, 2005.

HELM, MICHAEL. "For Mavis Gallant." *Brick* 93 (Summer 2014). http://brickmag.com/mavis-gallant.

HEMINGWAY, ERNEST *Death in the Afternoon*. 1932. London: Vintage, 2000.

– *Fiesta: The Sun Also Rises*. 1926. London: Arrow Books/Random House, 2004.

– *A Moveable Feast* (Restored Edition). London: Arrow Books/Random House, 2011.

HEMINGWAY, SEAN. "Introduction." *A Moveable Feast* (Restored Edition), by Ernest Hemingway. London: Arrow Books/Random House, 2011. 1–13.

HENIGHAN, STEPHEN. "Remembering Mavis Gallant: Why Her Urban Stories Have Never Felt More Relevant." *Globe and Mail*, 21 February 2014. http://www.theglobeandmail.com/arts/books-and-media/remembering-mavis-gallant-why-her-urban-stories-have-never-felt-so-relevant/article17037124/.

HODGINS, JACK. *A Passion for Narrative: A Guide for Writing Fiction*. Toronto: McClelland & Stewart, 1993.

HOFMANNSTHAL, HUGO VON. *Der Rosenkavalier. Komödie für Musik in Drei Aufzügen. Musik von Richard Strauss, Op. 59*. 1911. London: Boosey & Hawkes, 1943.

HOTCHNER, A.E. "Don't Touch 'A Moveable Feast'." *New York Times*, 19 July 2009: A19. http://www.nytimes.com/2009/07/20/opinion/20hotchner.html.

HUSTON, NANCY. *Histoire d'Omaya*. 1985. Paris: Actes Sud, 1998.

HUTCHEON, LINDA. *Irony's Edge: The Theory and Politics of Irony*. London and New York: Routledge, 1994.

– *Narcissistic Narrative: The Metafictional Paradox*. 1980. Waterloo, ON: Wilfrid Laurier UP, 2006.

– *A Poetics of Postmodernism: History, Theory, Fiction*. 1988. New York and London: Routledge, 1999.

– *Splitting Images: Contemporary Canadian Ironies*. Toronto: Oxford UP, 1991.

– *A Theory of Parody: The Teachings of Twentieth-Century Art Forms*. Urbana and Chicago: University of Illinois Press, 2000.

HUTCHEON, LINDA, and Michael Hutcheon. *Opera: Desire, Disease, Death*. Lincoln and London: University of Nebraska Press, 1996.

"In Transit: Twenty Stories by Mavis Gallant." *Fiction Book Review*, 4 January 1989. https://www.publishersweekly.com/978-0-394-57575-9.

ISER, WOLFGANG. *The Act of Reading: A Theory of Aesthetic Response*. London and Henley: Routledge and Kegan Paul, 1978.

ISHIGURO, KAZUO. *The Unconsoled*. London: Faber & Faber, 1995.

JAMES, HENRY. "The Jolly Corner." *Short Fiction: An Introductory Anthology*. Ed. Gerald Lynch and David Rampton. Toronto: Harcourt Brace Jovanovich, 1992. 210–237.

– "Preface." *The Portrait of a Lady*. 1881, 1908. Harmondsworth: Penguin, 1977. v–xviii.

JAMESON, FREDRIC. *Postmodernism or, the Cultural Logic of Late Capitalism*. Durham: Duke UP, 1991.

JANEWAY, ELIZABETH. "Everything was wrong about Shirley, including her name. *A Fairly Good Time*, by Mavis Gallant." *New York Times*, 7 June 1970: 5, 34.

JARVIS, SIMON. "Prosody as Cognition." *Critical Quarterly* 40 (1998): 3–15.

JOFFROY, PIERRE. "Inventeur de 'l'essentialisme': San-Yu, peintre chinois de Montparnasse. *Le Parisien Libéré*, 25 December 1946: 25.

JONES, ADAM MARS. "The Cost of Living by Mavis Gallant." *The Guardian*, 6 December 2009. https://www.theguardian.com/books/2009/dec/06/cost-of-living-mavis-gallant.

JOYCE, JAMES. *Dubliners*. 1914. Harmondsworth: Penguin, 1970.

– *Finnegans Wake*. 1939. Centennial edition. New York: Viking Press/Penguin, 1982.

– *A Portrait of the Artist as a Young Man*. 1916. London/Toronto: Granada, 1982.

– *Ulysses*. 1922. Harmondsworth: Penguin, 1968.

KAFKA, FRANZ. *The Castle*. 1926 (first German edition); 1951 (complete, definitive German edition); 1930 (first English translation). Trans. Willa and Edwin Muir (first edition), Eithne Wilkins and Ernst Kaiser (added material). Harmondsworth: Penguin, 1957.

– *The Metamorphosis*. 1915. With an introduction by David Cronenberg, translation and afterword by Susan Bernofsky. New York: W.W. Norton & Co., 2014.

KAKUTANI, MICHIKO. "Books of the Times; Spiritual Orphans." Rev. of *Home Truths*, by Mavis Gallant. *New York Times*, 20 April 1985. http://www.nytimes.com/1985/04/20/books/books-of-the-times-spiritual-orphans.html.

KANT, IMMANUEL. *The Critique of Judgment*. 1790. Trans. Werner S. Pluhar. Indianapolis: Hackett Publishing Company, 1987.

KAPLAN, SYDNEY Janet. *Katherine Mansfield and the Origins of Modernist Fiction*. Ithaca: Cornell UP, 1991.

KARPELES, ERIC. *Almost Nothing: The 20th-Century Art and Life of Józef Czapski*. New York: New York Review Books, 2018.

– *Paintings in Proust: A Visual Companion to* In Search of Lost Time. London: Thames & Hudson, 2008.

KAVENEY, ROZ. "T.S. Eliot's *The Waste Land*: The Radical Text of a Wounded Culture." *The Guardian*, 17 April 2014. http://www.theguardian.com/commentisfree/belief/2014/apr/17/ts-eliot-waste-land-radical-text-wounded-culture.

KEATS, JOHN. *The Complete Poems*. Ed. John Barnard. Harmondsworth: Penguin, 1977.

KEEFER, JANICE KULYK. "Strange Fashions of Forsaking: Criticism and the Fiction of Mavis Gallant." *Dalhousie Review* 64.4 (Autumn 1984): 721–35.

KINGSLEY, CHARLES. *The Water Babies, A Fairy Tale for a Land Baby.* 1863. Oxford: Oxford's World Classics, 2014.

KIPLING, RUDYARD. "Baa Baa, Black Sheep." 1888. *The Man Who Would Be King and Other Stories*. Oxford: Oxford UP/Oxford World Classics, 1999. 170–97.

KRISTEVA, JULIA. *Desire in Language: A Semiotic Approach to Literature and Art.* Trans. T. Gora, A. Jardine, L.S. Roudiez. New York: Columbia UP, 1980.

LAGERLÖF, SELMA. *Thy Soul Shall Bear Witness!* [*Körkarlen*]. 1912. English trans. 1921. Reissued: *The Phantom Carriage*. Trans. Peter Graves. Chester Springs, PA: Dufour Editions, 2011.

LAHIRI, JHUMPA. "Introduction." *The Cost of Living,* by Mavis Gallant. London: Bloomsbury, 2009. vii–xxii.

– "'Useless Chaos Is What Fiction Is About': Jhumpa Lahiri interviews Mavis Gallant." *Granta* 106 (2009): 102–55.

– "Mavis Gallant's Choice." *The New Yorker*, 20 February 2014. http://www.newyorker.com/online/blogs/books/2014/02/mavis-gallants-choice.html.

LANE, RICHARD J., and MIGUEL MOTA, eds. *Malcolm Lowry's Poetics of Space.* Ottawa: U of Ottawa P, 2016.

LANGELAAN, GEORGE. "The Fly." 1957. https://alancook.wordpress.com/tag/the-fly-by-george-langelaan/.

LEE, DENNIS. "Cadence, Country, Silence: Writing in a Colonial Space." *Open Letter* 2.6, *Refinding the Language* (Fall 1973): 34–53.

LEE, HERMIONE. "Lost in Transit." Rev. of *The Selected Stories of Mavis Gallant. The Guardian*, 6 March 2004. https://www.theguardian.com/books/2004/mar/06/featuresreviews.guardianreview23.

LEFEBVRE, HENRI. *La Production de l'espace*. 1974. Paris: Editions Anthropos, 2000.

LE GUERN, MICHEL. *Sémantique de la métaphore et de la métonymie*. Paris: Larousse, 1973.

LEHMANN-HAUPT, CHRISTOPHER. "Books of the Times: Harold Ross Biography Disputes the Earlier Ones," *New York Times*, 24 April 1995. http://www.nytimes.com/1995/04/24/books/books-of-the-times-harold-ross-biography-disputes-the-earlier-ones.html.

LÉVI-STRAUSS, CLAUDE. *La Pensée sauvage*. 1962. Paris: Plon, Pocket, Coll. Agora, 1990.

LEVINSON, JERROLD. *Music, Art, & Metaphysics: Essays in Philosophical Aesthetics*. Ithaca: Cornell UP, 1990.

– *The Pleasures of Aesthetics: Philosophical Essays*. Ithaca: Cornell UP, 1996.

LEVINSON, Stephen C. *Pragmatics*. 1983. Cambridge: Cambridge UP. Online since 2018. https://doi.org/10.1017/CBO9780511813313.

– *Presumptive Meanings: The Theory of Generalized Conversational Implicature*. Cambridge, MA: MIT Press, 2000.

LINDSAY, MAUD, and Emilie Poulsson. *The Joyous Travellers*. Boston: Lothrop, Lee, and Shepard Co., 1919; London: Harrap, 1921.

LOCKE, JOHN. *An Essay Concerning Human Understanding*. 1690. Ed. Roger Woolhouse. Harmondsworth: Penguin Classics, 1997.

LOHAFER, SUSAN. *Reading for Storyness: Preclosure Theory, Empirical Poetics, and Culture in the Short Story*. Baltimore: Johns Hopkins UP, 2003.

LOWRY, MALCOLM. 1961. *Hear Us O Lord from Heaven Thy Dwelling Place*. New York: Carroll & Graf, 1986.

MACCULLOCH, DONALD B. *The Wondrous Isle of Staffa*. Glasgow: Alex MacLaren & Sons, 1934.

MACFARLANE, DAVID. "Traces of Mavis: How a Great Canadian Writer Died Penniless in Paris." *The Walrus*. 18 March 2015. https://thewalrus.ca/traces-of-mavis/.

MACLEOD, ALISTAIR. "The Closing Down of Summer." 1976. *As Birds Bring Forth the Sun and Other Stories*. Toronto: McClelland & Stewart (NCL), 1992. 7–31.

MANGUEL, ALBERTO. "Introduction." *Going Ashore,* by Mavis Gallant. Ed. Alberto Manguel. Toronto: McClelland & Stewart, 2009. xi–xiii.

MANSFIELD, KATHERINE. *Selected Stories*. Oxford: Oxford UP, 1981.

MARTIN, SANDRA. "Writer Mavis Gallant Dies at Age 91." *Globe and Mail*. 18 February 2014. https://www.theglobeandmail.com/arts/books-and-media/writer-mavis-gallant-dies-at-age-91/article16930775/ Updated 17 April 2018.

MAY, THOMAS. *Ionisation*, Edgard Varèse. https://articulatesilences.wordpress.com/2012/07/12/ionisation-edgard-varese.

MCLUHAN, MARSHALL. *The Medium Is the Massage: An Inventory of Effects*. Harmondsworth: Penguin, 1967.

MCMANUS, DONALD. *No Kidding!: Clown as Protagonist in Twentieth-Century Theatre*. London/Mississauga: Associated University Presses, 2003.

MERLEAU-PONTY, MAURICE. *Phénoménologie de la perception*. Paris: Gallimard, 1945.

MESCHONNIC, HENRI. *Critique du rythme: Anthropologie historique du langage*. Lagrasse: Verdier, 1982.

MICHAELIDES, SOLON. *The Music of Ancient Greece: An Encyclopaedia*. London: Faber, 1978.

MILLHAUSER, STEVEN. "The Dream of the Consortium." *The Knife Thrower and Other Stories*. New York: Vintage, 1999. 125–43.

MOORE, LISA. "Mavis Gallant in Malibu." *Brick* 89 (Summer 2012). http://brickmag.com/mavis-gallant-malibu.

Morier, Henri. *Dictionnaire de poétique et de rhétorique*. Paris: Presses Universitaires de France, 1961.

Muhlstein, Anka. *Monsieur Proust's Library*. New York: Other Press, 2012.

– *The Pen and the Brush: How the Passion for Art Shaped Nineteenth-Century French Literature*. New York: Other Press, 2017.

Mukherjee, Neel. "Journey into the Interior: A Master of the Short Story Dissects the Material and Emotional Lives of Cosmopolitans." *The Times*, 12 December 2009: 11.

Munro, Alice. *Dance of the Happy Shades*. Toronto: Ryerson Press, 1968.

Nabokov, Vladimir. Interview with Jane Howard. *Life Magazine*, 20 November 1964. http://www.libros.am/book/read/id/346977/slug/strong-opinions (also accessible at https://spad1.wordpress.com/tag/interview/).

– *Pnin*. 1957. Harmondsworth: Penguin, 1983.

– *The Real Life of Sebastian Knight*. 1941. Harmondsworth: Penguin Classics, 2012.

– *Transparent Things*. 1972. New York: Vintage/Random House, 1989.

New, W.H. "The Art of Haunting Ghosts." Rev. of *From the Fifteenth District*, by Mavis Gallant. *Canadian Literature* 85 (Summer 1980): 153–5.

– *Grandchild of Empire: About Irony, Mainly in the Commonwealth*. Vancouver: Ronsdale Press, 2003.

Ondaatje, Michael. "Introduction: A Handful of Small Shipwrecks." *Paris Stories*, by Mavis Gallant. New York: NYRB, 2002. vii–xii.

Orner, Peter. "Introduction." *A Fairly Good Time*, by Mavis Gallant. New York: NYRB, 2016. vii–xix.

– "The Way Vivid, Way Underappreciated Short Stories of Mavis Gallant." Interview with Joe Fassler. *The Atlantic*, 4 June 2013. http://www.theatlantic.com/entertainment/archive/2013/06/the-way-vivid-way-underappreciated-short-stories-of-mavis-gallant/276528/.

O'rourke, David. "Exiles in Time: Gallant's 'My Heart Is Broken.'" *Canadian Literature* 93 (Summer 1982): 98–107.

Plaskett, Joseph. *A Speaking Likeness*. Foreword by George Woodcock. Vancouver: Ronsdale Press, 1999.

Plato. *Republic*. Trans. and introduction by Robin Waterfield. Oxford World's Classics. Oxford UP, 1993.

Plesch, Véronique. *Painter and Priest: Giovanni Canavesio's Visual Rhetoric and the Passion Cycle at La Brigue*. Notre Dame, IN: University of Notre Dame Press, 2006.

Pope, Alexander. *The Rape of the Lock*. 1712. *Eighteenth-Century English Literature*. Ed. Geoffrey Tillotson, Paul Fussell Jr., Marshall Waingrow. New York: Harcourt, Brace & World, 1969. 567–78. https://www.gutenberg.org/files/9800/9800-h/9800-h.htm.

– *Peri Bathous: Or, Martin Scriblerus, His Treatise of the Art of Sinking in Poetry.* 1727. *Eighteenth-Century English Literature.* Ed. Geoffrey Tillotson, Paul Fussell Jr., Marshall Waingrow. New York: Harcourt, Brace & World, 1969. 611–34.

PRINCE, GERALD. *A Dictionary of Narratology.* Lincoln: University of Nebraska Press, 1989.

PROSE, FRANCINE. "The Ice Wagon Going down the Street by Mavis Gallant." *Brick* 91 (Summer 2013). https://brickmag.com/the-ice-wagon-going-down-the-street-by-mavis-gallant/.

– "Introduction." *The Collected Stories*, by Mavis Gallant. New York: Alfred. A. Knopf, Emblem Editions, 2016. xi–xx. Also published as "Mavis Gallant's Magic Tricks." Page-Turner. *The New Yorker*, 3 August 2016. http://www.newyorker.com/books/page-turner/mavis-gallants-magic-tricks.

PROUST, MARCEL. *Contre Sainte-Beuve.* 1913. Paris: Gallimard, 1954.

– *Du côté de chez Swann.* 1913. Paris: Gallimard, Livre de Poche, 1954.

– *Le Temps retrouvé.* 1927. Paris: Pléiade, 1989.

REYNOLDS, SUSAN SALTER. Rev. of *The Cost of Living*, by Mavis Gallant. *Los Angeles Times*, 8 January 2010. http://articles.latimes.com/2010/jan/08/entertainment/la-et-book8–2010jan08.

RICHIE, DONALD. *Japanese Portraits: Pictures of Different People.* 1987. Tokyo: Tuttle Publishing, 2006.

RICOEUR, PAUL. *La Mémoire, l'Histoire, l'Oubli.* Paris: Seuil, 2000.

– *La Métaphore vive.* Paris: Seuil, 1975.

– *Temps et récit I.* Paris: Seuil, "Points," 1991.

– *Temps et récit III: Le Temps raconté.* Paris: Seuil, "Points," 1985.

RIFFATERRE, MICHAEL. "Intertextual Representations: On Mimesis as Interpretive Discourse." *Critical Inquiry* 11 (1984): 141–62.

RILEY, CHARLES A. *Free as Gods: How the Jazz Age Reinvented Modernism.* Lebanon, NH: ForeEdge/University Press of New England, 2017.

RIMBAUD, ARTHUR. "Lettre à Georges Izambard." *Oeuvres de Rimbaud.* Ed. Suzanne Bernard. Paris: Garnier, 1960.

ROBBE-GRILLET, ALAIN. *Projet pour une révolution à New York.* Paris: Editions de Minuit, 1970.

– *Le Voyeur.* Paris: Editions de Minuit, 1955.

ROMNEY, JONATHAN. "Jacques Tati's *Playtime*: Life-Affirming Comedy." *The Guardian*, 24 October 2014. https://www.theguardian.com/film/2014/oct/24/jacques-tati-playtime-intensely-complex-life-affirming-comedy.

ROSS, STEPHEN, and A.C. LINDGREN, eds. "Introduction." *The Modernist World.* New York: Routledge, 2015.

ROTH, JOSEPH. *Hotel Savoy.* 1956 (German). 1986 (English trans.). Trans. John Hoare. London: Granta Books, 2000.

– *The Radetzky March*. 1932 (German). 1933 (English trans.). Revised trans. Eva Tucker. London: Allen Lane/Penguin Books, 1974.

Rothman, Joshua. "Mavis Gallant in *The New Yorker*." 18 February 2014. http://www.newyorker.com/books/double-take/mavis-gallant-in-the-new-yorker.

Roy, Gabrielle. *Bonheur d'occasion* [*The Tin Flute*]. 1945 [English translation 1947]. Montreal: Boréal, 2009.

Rushdie, Salman. "At the Auction of the Ruby Slippers." *East, West*. London: Vintage, 1995. 85–103.

– *Imaginary Homelands*. London: Granta, 1992.

– "Introduction." *Midnight's Children*, by Salman Rushdie. London: Vintage, 2006. ix–xvii.

– "The Prophet's Hair." *East, West*. London: Vintage, 1995. 33–58.

Russolo, Luigi. *The Art of Noise*. 1913. Trans. Robert Filliou. www.artype.de/Sammlung/pdf/russolo_noise.pdf.

Sacks, Harvey. *Lectures on Conversation*. Vol. 1. Oxford: Blackwell, 1992.

Said, Edward. *Beginnings: Intention and Method*. New York: Basic, 1975.

Saussure, Ferdinand de. *Cours de linguistique générale*. 1916. Paris: Payot, 1969.

Savigneau, Josyane. "Mavis Gallant, nouvelles intimes." *Le Monde/Le Monde des Poches Littératures*, 7 February 1997: 3.

– "Nouvelliste Mavis Gallant." *Le Monde,* 21 February 2014: 14. http://www.lemonde.fr/disparitions/article/2014/02/19/mort-de-la-nouvelliste-canadienne-mavis-gallant_4369419_3382.html.

Schaeffer, Pierre. *In Search of a Concrete Music*. Trans. Christine North and John Dack. Berkeley/Los Angeles: U of California P, 2012. Originally published as Schaeffer, *A la recherché d'une musique concrète*. Paris: Seuil, 1952.

Schopenhauer, Arthur. *The World as Will and Idea*. 1818. Ed. David Berman. Trans. Jill Berman. London: J.M. Dent, Everyman, 1997.

Scofield, Martin. *The Cambridge Companion to the Short Story.* Cambridge: Cambridge UP, 2006.

Sewell, Anna. *Black Beauty, The Autobiography of a Horse*. 1877. Scotts Valley, CA: Createspace Independent Publishing Platform, 2017.

Shakespeare, William. *The Complete Works of William Shakespeare*. Cambridge Text established by John Dover Wilson. Cambridge: Cambridge UP, 1984.

Shanes, Eric. *The Life and Masterworks of J.M.W. Turner*. 1990. New York: Parkstone Press, 2008.

Shelley, Percy Bysshe. *A Defence of Poetry. English Romantic Writers*. 1821. Ed. David Perkins. New York/Chicago: Harcourt, Brace & World, 1967. 1072–87.

Shields, Carol. E mail to Marta Dvořák. 3 December 2001.

– "A View from the Edge of the Edge." *Carol Shields and the Extra-Ordinary*. Ed. Marta Dvořák and Manina Jones. Montreal/Kingston: McGill-Queens UP, 2007. 17–29.

SHKLOVSKY, VIKTOR. "Art as Technique." *Literary Theory: An Anthology*. 1916. Ed. Julie Rivkin and Michael Ryan. Malden, MA/Oxford UK: Blackwell, 2004.

SIEMERLING, WINFRIED. "Perception, Memory, Irony: Mavis Gallant Greets Proust and Flaubert." Special Gallant issue, *Essays on Canadian Writing* 42 (Winter 1990): 131–53.

SOLNIT, REBECCA. *River of Shadows: Eadweard Muybridge and the Technological Wild West*. New York: Viking, 2003.

SONTAG, SUSAN. *On Photography*. London: Penguin Books, 1978.

SPENSER, EDMUND. *The Faerie Queene. The Complete Poetical Works of Spenser*. Ed. R.E. Neil Dodge. Cambridge Edition reprint. Boston: Houghton Mifflin, 1936. 138–677.

STAFF, ROVI. "Edgard Varèse. *Ionisation*, for 13 percussionists." http://www.allmusic.com/composition/ionisation-for-13-percussionists-mc0002360393.

STEIN, GERTRUDE. 1933. *The Autobiography of Alice B. Toklas*. Harmondworth: Penguin Classics, 2001.

– "If I Told Him: A Completed Portrait of Picasso." *Vanity Fair* (1924). https://www.poetryfoundation.org/poems/55215/if-i-told-him-a-completed-portrait-of-picasso; https://www.youtube.com/watch?v=FJEIAGULmPQ.

STERNE, LAURENCE. *The Life and Opinions of Tristram Shandy, Gentleman*. 1760. New York: Signet Classic/ New American Library, 1960.

STRATTON-PORTER, GENE. *Freckles*. New York: Grosset & Dunlap. 1904.

– *A Girl of the Limberlost*. New York City: Grosset & Dunlap, 1909.

STRAVINSKY, IGOR, and Robert Craft. *Dialogues and a Diary*. New York: Doubleday, 1963.

SWIFT, JONATHAN. "Verses on the Death of Dr Swift, D.S.P.D." *Eighteenth-Century English Literature*. 1731. Ed. Geoffrey Tillotson, Paul Fussell, J., Marshall Waingrow. New York: Harcourt, Brace & World, 1969. 381–9.

SZYMBORSKA, WISLAWA. *Miracle Fair: Selected Poems of Wislawa Szymborska*. Trans. Joanna Trzeciak. New York/London: W.W. Norton & Company, 2001.

TAHOURDIN, ADRIAN. "Anatole France and Proust." *The Times Literary Supplement* blog, 19 September 2013. http://timescolumns.typepad.com/stothard/2013/09/anatole-france-and-proust.html.

TEFFI. *Subtly Worded*. Trans. Anne-Marie Jackson, Robert and Elizabeth Chandler. London: Pushkin Press, 2014.

THACKER, "Short Fiction." *The Cambridge Companion to Canadian Literature*. Ed. Eva-Marie Kröller. Cambridge: Cambridge UP, 2004. 177–93. 2nd ed. 2017, 197–216.

THIEME, JOHN. *Postcolonial Con-Texts: Writing Back to the Canon*. London/New York: Continuum, 2001.

THOMAS, KEITH. "Cleanliness and Godliness in Early Modern England." *Religion, Culture, and Society in Early Modern Britain*. Ed. A. Fletcher and P. Roberts. New York: Cambridge UP, 1994. 56–83.

Tolstoy, Leo. *Hadji Murád. The Kreutzer Sonata and Other Stories.* Trans. Louise and Aylmer Maude and J.D. Duff. Ed. Richard Gustafson. Oxford: Oxford UP, Oxford World Classics, 1998. 344–467.

Urban, W.M. *Language and Reality: The Philosophy of Language and the Principles of Symbolism.* New York: Macmillan, 1961.

Urquhart Jane. "Introduction." *In Transit*, by Mavis Gallant. Toronto: Penguin Canada, 2006. vii–xiii.

Wagner, Cosima. *Journal.** Vol. I: 1869–1872. Vol. II: 1873–1877. Ed. Martin Gregor-Dellin and Dietrich Mach. Trans. from German (*Die Tagebücher,* 1976) to French by Michel-François Demet. Paris: Gallimard, 1977.

Walcott, Derek. "What the Twilight Says: An Overture." *Dream on Monkey Mountain and Other Plays.* 1971. New York: Farrar, Strauss & Giroux, 1998. 3–40.

Walker, Alan. *Franz Liszt.** Vol. 1: *The Virtuoso Years, 1811–1847.* Vol. 2: *The Weimar Years, 1848–1861.* New York: Alfred A. Knopf, 1983, 1989.

Weintraub, William. *City Unique: Montreal Days and Nights in the 1940s and '50s.* Toronto: McClelland & Stewart, 1996.

– *Getting Started: A Memoir of the Fifties.* Toronto: McClelland & Stewart, 2001.

Weiskott, Eric. "Early English Meter as a Way of Thinking." *Studia Metrica et Poetica* 4.1 (2017): 41–65.

Weschler, Lawrence. "The Art World." *The New Yorker*, 9 July 1984: 60–71.

Wharton, Edith. "The Last Asset." *The Collected Short Stories of Edith Wharton.* 1904. Ed. R.W.B. Lewis. Vol 1. New York: Charles Scribner's Sons, 1968. 590–615.

Wilde, Alan. *Horizons of Assent: Modernism, Postmodernism, and the Ironic Imagination.* Baltimore: Johns Hopkins UP, 1981.

Wilkshire, Claire. "'Voice Is Everything': Reading Mavis Gallant's 'The Pegnitz Junction'." *University of Toronto Quarterly* 69.4 (Fall 2000): 891–916.

Wimsatt, W.K. *The Verbal Icon.* Lexington: U of Kentucky P, 1954.

Woodcock, George. "Memory, Imagination, Artifice: The Late Short Fiction of Mavis Gallant." Special issue, *Canadian Fiction Magazine* 28 (1978): 74–91.

Woolf, Virginia. *Collected Essays.* Ed. Leonard Woolf. Vol. II. London: Chatto & Windus, 1972.

– *A Voyage Out.* 1915. New York: Modern Library/Random House, 2001.

Yourcenar, Marguerite. *Mémoires d'Hadrien.* Paris: Plon, 1951.

Zervos, Christian. "Conversation avec Picasso." *Cahiers d'Art* 10.10 (1935): 173–8.

Index

I Index of Mavis Gallant's Writings

Correspondence

Novels/novellas and story collections*

Stories and essays

II Name Index

III Subject Index

Note: The connections between Gallant and the rubric arts are foregrounded under the heading of philosophical aesthetics, habitually applied to visual and sound studies. An equally strong emphasis on the specificities of discourse inhabits the informed headings of language, narratology, rhetoric, and rhythm.

www.ingramcontent.com/pod-product-compliance
Lightning Source LLC
LaVergne TN
LVHW041114090826
844660LV00062B/913/J

* 9 7 8 1 4 8 7 5 0 5 3 0 1 *